Laptop & Tablet Basics for the Over 50s

Windows 8 edition

PEARSON

Harlow, England • London • New York … Hong Kong
Tokyo • Seoul • Taipei • New Delhi • Ca… …aris • Milan

Pearson Education Limited

Edinburgh Gate
Harlow CM20 2JE
Tel: +44 (0)1279 623623
Website: www.pearson.com/uk

First published 2013 (print and electronic)

ISBN: 978-1-292-00263-7 (print)

British Library Cataloguing-in-Publication Data
A catalogue record for the print edition is available from the British Library

Library of Congress Cataloging-in-Publication Data
A catalog record for the print edition is available from the Library of Congress

10 9 8 7 6 5 4 3 2 1
17 16 15 14 13

Cover image © Khoeva Svetlana/Fotolia.com
Print edition typeset in 11/14pt ITC Stone Sans by 3
Printed and bound in Malaysia, (CTP-VVP)

NOTE THAT ANY PAGE CROSS-REFERENCES REFER TO THE PRINT EDITION

Laptop & Tablet Basics for the Over 50s

Windows 8 edition

Joli Ballew

Use your laptop or tablet with confidence

Get to grips with practical tasks with minimal time, fuss and bother.

In Simple Steps guides guarantee immediate results. They tell you everything you need to know on a specific application; from the most essential tasks to master, to every activity you'll want to accomplish, through to solving the most common problems you'll encounter.

Helpful features

To build your confidence and help you to get the most out of your laptop or tablet, practical hints, tips and shortcuts feature on every page:

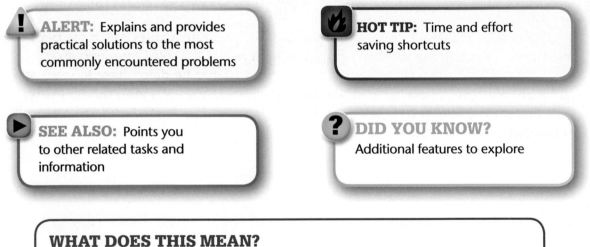

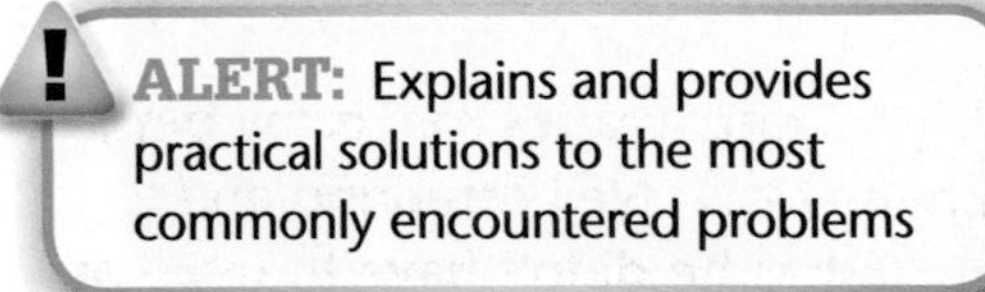

ALERT: Explains and provides practical solutions to the most commonly encountered problems

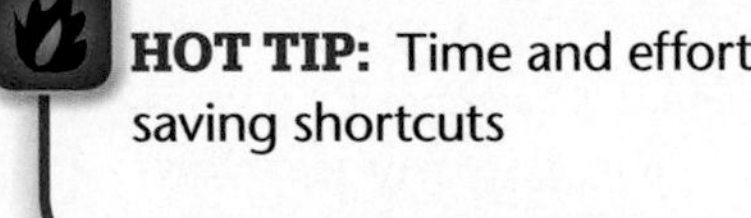

HOT TIP: Time and effort saving shortcuts

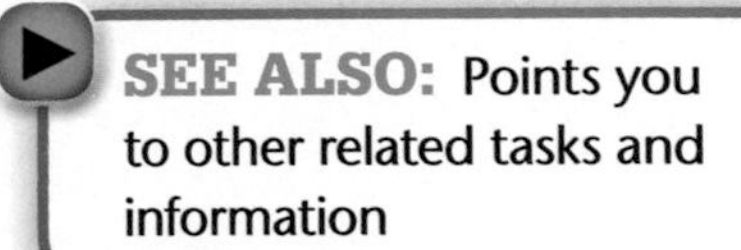

SEE ALSO: Points you to other related tasks and information

DID YOU KNOW?
Additional features to explore

WHAT DOES THIS MEAN?
Jargon and technical terms explained in plain English

Practical. Simple. Fast.

in Simple steps

Dedication:

To Neil Salkind, my friend, agent and mentor; I wish you well in your retirement. I will miss you.

Author acknowledgements:

I am never charged with creating a book; I only write the words. There is an entire team dedicated to the rest of the process that includes acquisitions editors, typesetters, proofreaders, technical editors, and more, all needing special thanks and acknowledgement. For this book specifically, that includes Steve Temblett, Robert Cottee, Natasha Whelan and Jill Birch, along with all the other people who worked behind the scenes to turn the words into pages, and the pages into this book.

Beyond the people that work with me directly, I would also like to thank my supportive family, including Jennifer, Andrew, Dad and Cosmo, as well as my extended family, including the mothers and grandmothers and step grandmothers who all play a part.

And finally, I'm thankful to my agent, Neil Salkind, who encourages me, is my biggest fan, my mentor, and my part-time therapist. I am happy that Neil is retiring and I wish him the best (even though a huge part of me wishes he didn't have to retire at all). From now on I'll have to refer to Neil as my friend, not my agent; but no matter how I refer to him from now on, I am thankful to be on his shortlist and welcome our continued communications.

Publisher acknowledgements:

The publishers are grateful to the following for permission to reproduce copyright material:

Adobe product screenshots reprinted with permission from Adobe Systems Incorporated. Microsoft screenshots reprinted by permission of Microsoft Corporation.

Contents at a glance

Contents

Top 10 Laptop & Tablet Tips

1 Getting started

2 Explore Windows 8's unique features

6 Explore the social networking apps

7 Explore media apps

8 Access and use available online stores

9 Learn desktop basics

10 Use the Internet Explorer Desktop app

11 Explore desktop apps

12 Configure network sharing

13 Enable and use accessibility options

14 Manage, protect and troubleshoot your laptop

15 Tips for Over 50s tablet users

Top 10 Laptop & Tablet Problems Solved

Top 10 Laptop & Tablet Tips

Tip 1: Use a Microsoft account

When you set up your Windows 8 laptop or tablet, you were prompted to create and/or log in with a Microsoft account. If you opted *not* to do this or were unable to, then you created a local account instead. We suggest you use a Microsoft account; a Microsoft account is shown here.

Your account

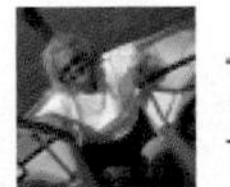

Joli Ballew
joli_ballew@hotmail.com

- **Microsoft account** – A Microsoft account is a personal but global account you use to log in to your Windows 8 computer. When you use this kind of account, Windows 8 will automatically configure certain apps with personalised information, and your preferences and settings will be available no matter what Internet-enabled Windows 8 computer you log on to. You must use a Microsoft account to access features like SkyDrive, Calendar and the Store, among others.
- **Local account** – This is a personal account you create and use to log on to your Windows 8 computer that is only associated with that computer. Your account settings and preferences don't 'follow' you from one Windows 8 computer to another like a Microsoft account can. You can't access SkyDrive, Calendar, the Store and other apps using a local account.

HOT TIP: It's never too late to switch from a local account to a Microsoft account. You do this from PC Settings.

ALERT: If you want to get the most possible from Windows 8 and you want to be able to access all of the apps, you must use a Microsoft account.

Tip 2: Access the default charms

Charms are a new feature of Windows 8. You probably haven't seen any charms yet because they are hidden by default. Charms are quite unique and let you easily configure settings, share information, view devices and search for data, among other things. You can access the default charms in many ways.

- Using touch, place your thumb in the middle of the right side of the screen and flick left (inward).
- On a keyboard, use the key combination Windows key + C.
- Using a mouse or touch pad, move the cursor to the bottom or top right corner of the screen, and when the transparent charms appear, move the cursor upward or downward.

HOT TIP: If you're using a touch screen on a tablet, use your thumb and flick inward from the right edge of the screen to bring up the charms. On a touch screen monitor (such as one you might connect to a small laptop), try your right index finger instead.

DID YOU KNOW?

The Shut Down command is available from the Settings charm, from the Power icon that appears there.

Tip 3: Change the screen resolution

If the items on the desktop are too small for you to see comfortably, follow these steps to change the screen resolution.

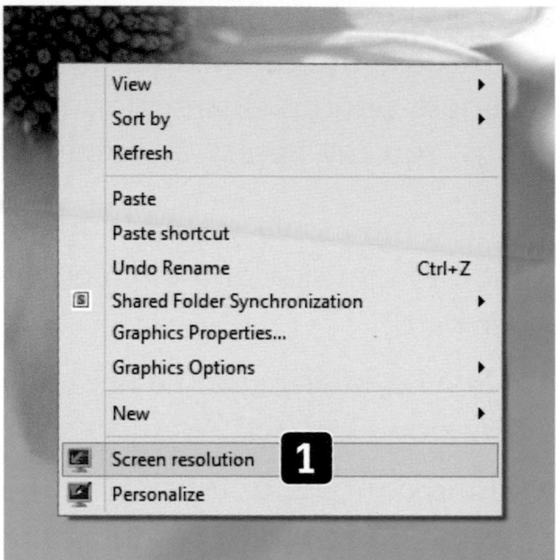

1. Right-click an empty area of the desktop and click Screen Resolution.
2. Move the slider to 1366 × 768. Click Apply.
3. If you like the resolution, keep it. If not repeat this process until you find one you like.

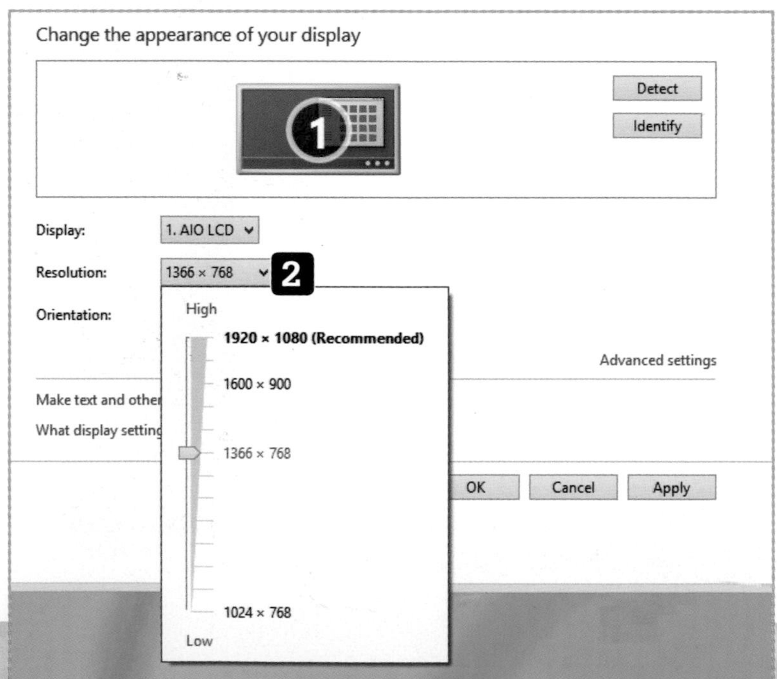

DID YOU KNOW? The lower the resolution, the larger the items on your screen appear.

ALERT: Some features of Windows 8 won't work if the resolution is below 1366 × 768.

Tip 4: Add a tile to the Start screen

There are more windows, apps, system tools, desktop applications, and so on available than appear on the Start screen by default. There's the Calculator, for instance, and Windows Media Player, Control Panel, Windows Explorer and WordPad, to name a few. You can add any item to the Start screen to have easier access to it.

1. Right-click an empty area of the Start screen. On a touch screen, flick upward from the bottom of the screen.
2. Click All apps.
3. Right-click (or tap, hold and drag downward) an item you'd like to add.

4. From the bar that appears at the bottom of the page click Pin to Start. (This will change to Unpin from Start after you do.)

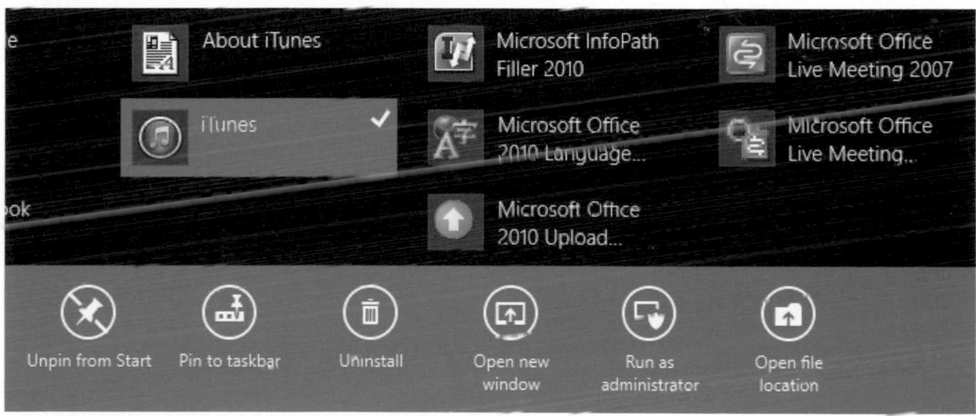

5. Return to the Start screen and locate the new tile. It will be placed on the far right. You may want to drag it left to reposition it.

DID YOU KNOW?
You can open an app from the All Apps screen by clicking it once.

HOT TIP: Go ahead and add tiles for apps, applications, system tools, windows and other items that you know you'll use often. You may want to add Control Panel if you're familiar with that feature, for instance.

Tip 5: Add formatting to an email

Mail, like other apps, is streamlined. Thus, the formatting options are hidden away in the Mail toolbar. You access those options with a right-click of a mouse or track pad, or a flick upward with your finger on a touch screen. Once the options are available, you apply them as you would any formatting tools in any word processing program. You can only format text in the body of the email, though; you can't format text in the subject line.

DID YOU KNOW?
If you apply formatting options without any text selected, those options will be applied to all future text until you change them. If you select text and then apply formatting, the formatting is only applied to the selected text.

1. While composing an email, click in the body of the email (where you type your message).
2. Right-click to see the formatting options. (Note that you can click More to see additional options.)
3. Click any formatting option (perhaps Bold) and then click another (perhaps Italic).
4. Click Font and choose a new font and font size.
5. Type a few words in the body of the email.

ALERT: If the new font choices aren't applied when you type, try clicking in a new line, pressing Enter to go to a new line, or click under the signature. Sometimes this type of application of the formatting tools is a little tricky.

Tip 6: Import pictures from a digital camera

You can put photos on your computer in lots of ways, but the easiest way is to use the Photos app. The Photos landing page offers an option to add a device to *see* photos that are on them, but if you right-click while on that page, the option to *Import* those photos appears.

1. Connect your camera, insert a memory card or connect an external drive that contains photos.
2. Open the Photos app, and click any back buttons as necessary to access the landing page.
3. Right-click the landing page to access the toolbar.
4. Click Import.
5. By default, all of the photos are selected as shown here, provided they have not already been imported. Right-click to deselect photos.

DID YOU KNOW?
When you import photos, you copy them to your laptop.

HOT TIP: Create a descriptive name for the folder that will hold the imported photos; don't just accept the default name offered.

6 Type a name for the folder these pictures will be imported to, and then click Import.

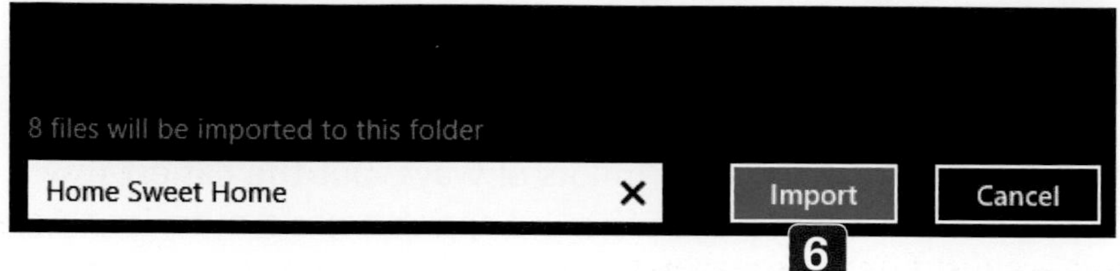

7 Click Open album (not shown) to view the photos.

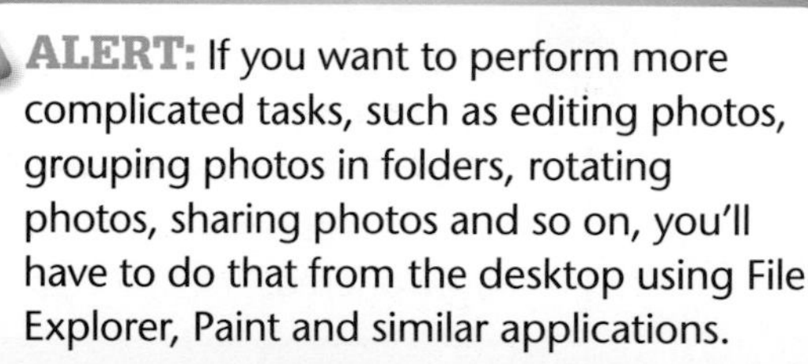

ALERT: If you want to perform more complicated tasks, such as editing photos, grouping photos in folders, rotating photos, sharing photos and so on, you'll have to do that from the desktop using File Explorer, Paint and similar applications.

Tip 7: Get a free app

There are thousands of free apps. Some, like Netflix and Audible, require you to be a member to access content. Others may include ads and offer an ad-free version for a price. Some free apps let you make in-app purchases to buy, for example, more farm animals, gaming 'lives', additional content and so on. Some free apps are simply awesome, and are just fine on their own.

1. From the Start screen, click or tap Store.
2. If necessary, click any back buttons to get to the starting page, and then, under Spotlight, click Top free.

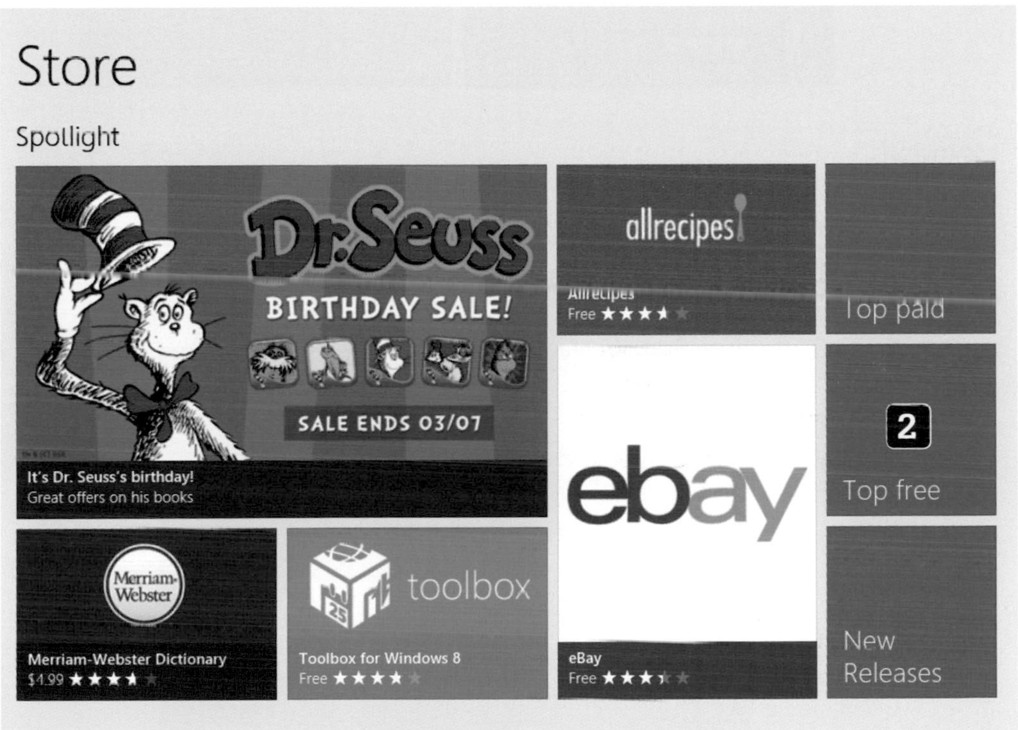

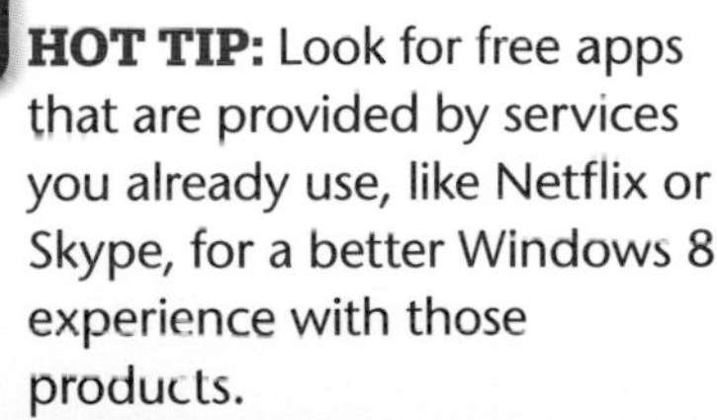
HOT TIP: Look for free apps that are provided by services you already use, like Netflix or Skype, for a better Windows 8 experience with those products.

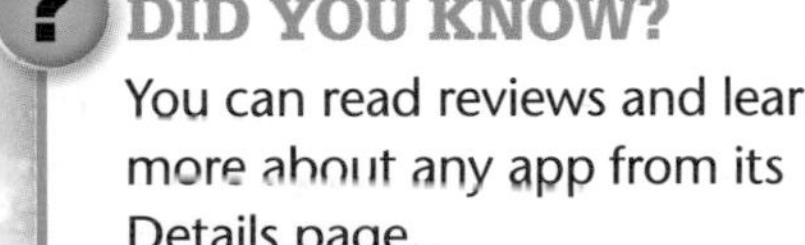
DID YOU KNOW?
You can read reviews and learn more about any app from its Details page.

3 Click any app that interests you. These are all very popular.

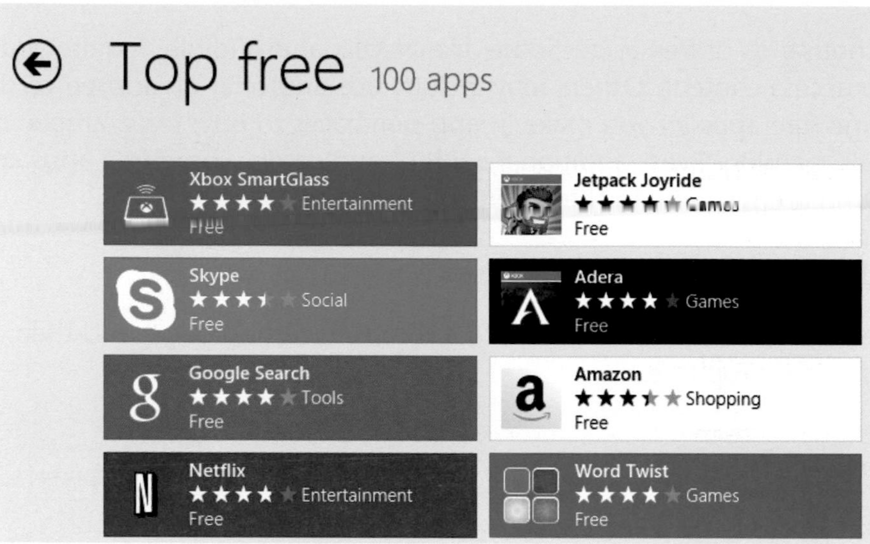

4 Click Install.

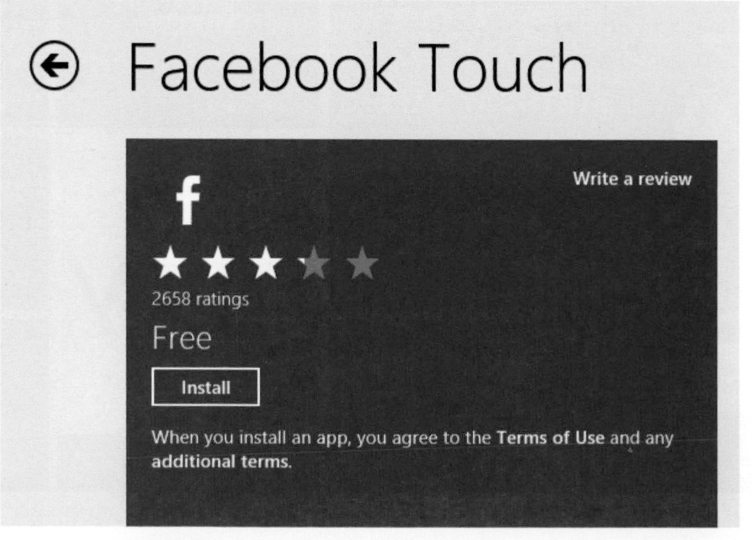

HOT TIP: It's OK to try any free app; you can easily uninstall it if you don't like it.

Tip 8: Add an item to the taskbar

Since there isn't a Start button, locating an item while you are on the desktop requires you tap the Windows key on the keyboard, type what you want to find on the Start screen, and click the result to open it. It's much easier to add items you use often to the taskbar. When you do, you won't have to leave the desktop to find what you need. This is called 'pinning' an item. You can only pin desktop applications though; you can't pin Start screen apps to the taskbar.

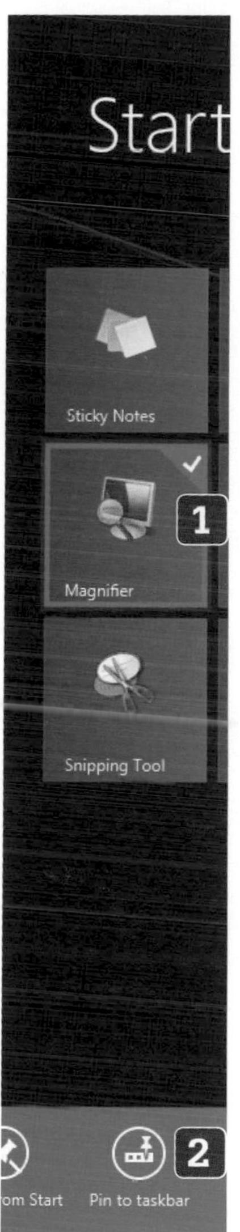

1. From the Start screen (or the All Apps screen) right-click an item you'd like to add to the taskbar.
2. Click Pin to taskbar. If you don't see this option, it can't be pinned.
3. Repeat as desired, and then note the new items that are pinned.

HOT TIP: As you get to know Windows 8 and learn which desktop apps you use most, pin them to the taskbar. You may want to pin Windows Media Player, Sticky Notes, Help and Support and others.

HOT TIP: Once an item is pinned to the taskbar, you only have to click or tap it one time to open the related application.

Tip 9: Copy data from another computer

You can access shared data only when you are connected to the network it is shared on. Thus, while sharing may work in many instances, if you're going to be away from your network you'll want to copy necessary data so you will have it with you. There are many ways to do this. We prefer to set up two windows, one that has the data to copy and the other that contains the place to copy it to, and then drag data to copy it.

1. Use File Explorer on your laptop to open a window to hold the files you want to copy.

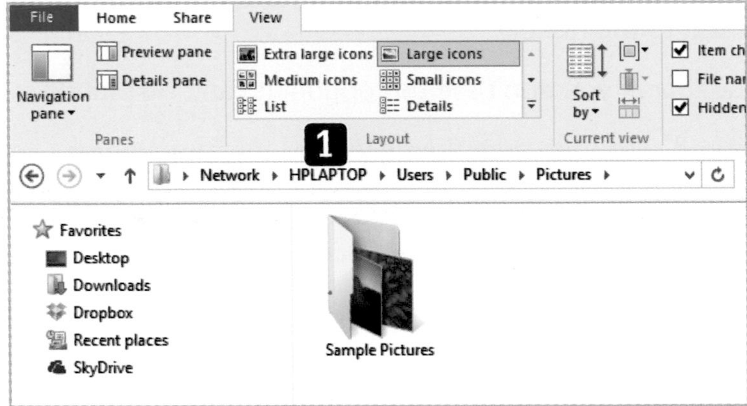

2. Right-click the File Explorer icon and click File Explorer to open a second File Explorer window.
3. Use this second File Explorer window to locate the data you want to copy. You'll have to click Network in the Navigation pane to browse to and locate the data.

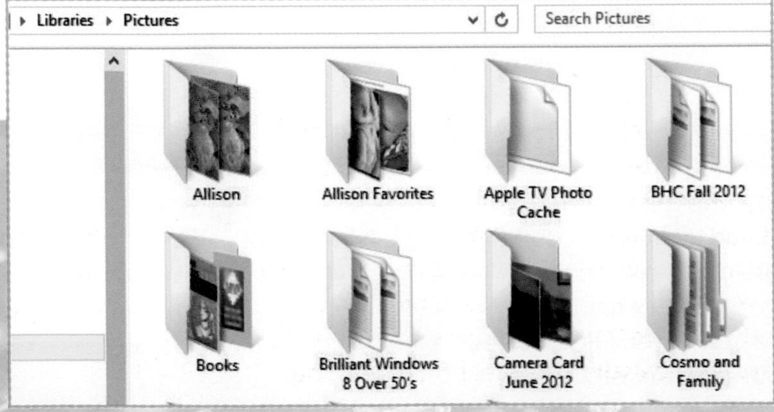

4. Hold down the Ctrl key and select the items in this second window to copy.
5. Right-click and drag the data from the second File Explorer window into the first.
6. Let go and choose Copy here.

DID YOU KNOW?

There are a lot of rules to learn if you want to drag and drop data using a left-click, and the rules are hard to remember. With a left-click you aren't prompted to move or copy when you let go of the mouse; in fact, one or the other will happen automatically based on the circumstances. However, when you drag and drop with a right-click you are always prompted to move or copy the data, and you have to make a choice before anything happens. This is much safer and easier than guessing.

ALERT: What you see when you perform this task and what is shown here will differ greatly!

Tip 10: Enable Airplane mode

During aeroplane takeoffs and landings, you are prompted to turn off all electronic devices. However, once you have the go ahead that it's OK to use 'approved electronic devices' you can turn on your laptop and use it, provided you enable Airplane mode.

1. Click Windows key + I.
2. Click the Network icon.
3. Move the slider for Airplane mode from On to Off.

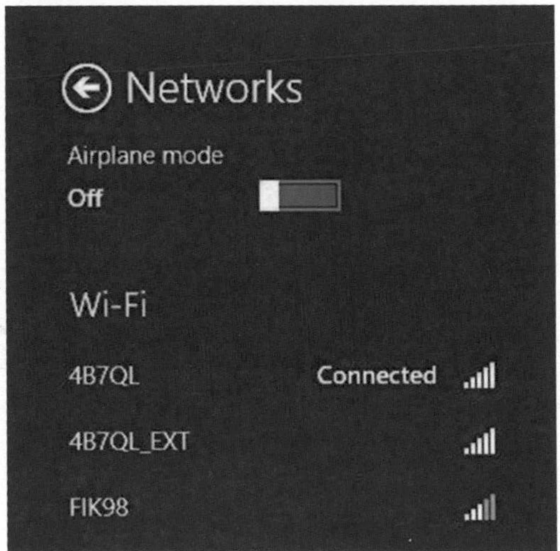

HOT TIP: Another way to enable Airplane mode is to type Airplane at the Start screen, click Settings, and then click Turn airplane mode on or off.

WHAT DOES THIS MEAN?

Airplane mode shuts down all network communications as well as cellular connections, theoretically so your transmissions won't interfere with the aeroplane's transmissions.

1 Getting started

Introduction

A laptop computer is a portable device; thus, your laptop differs from a traditional desktop computer in many ways. It comes with a battery you can charge, use and recharge; a touch pad or similar piece of hardware that works like a mouse; and an onscreen keyboard (thanks to Windows 8). If you purchased a high-end model, you may even have a touch screen. If you're new to laptops, you may not have any experience with these features; that's OK; it's easy to learn.

Most laptops and tablet computers have features desktop computers offer. Almost all come with USB ports, an Ethernet port, a CD/DVD drive and an old-fashioned keyboard, among other things. And of course, all devices run an operating system, in our case some version of Windows 8.

In this chapter you'll learn what kind of device you own (it may be a tablet computer and not an actual laptop, for instance). After that, you'll power on your device, work through any set up processes, and learn to use a few of the features unique to Windows 8, including the functionality associated with the Windows key. You'll also learn how to access the traditional desktop you may already be used to. If you want to, you can go straight to the desktop every time you use the computer; that's fine with us!

HOT TIP: You don't have to have a laptop to use this book, you can have a tablet or an ultrabook.

ALERT: The Windows 8 operating system will be updated regularly. This means that what you see in this book and what you see on your computer might vary if you've installed those updates. This book was written before any updates were created. It's OK though; you can still use this book!

Know what kind of device you own

You probably purchased and own a standard laptop. However, you might have purchased a tablet, netbook or ultrabook instead, and you may not really understand the differences between them. It's important to know what kind of device you own and what edition of Windows 8 is installed on it, so that you'll know which features of the Windows 8 operating system and what kind of hardware are available to you. This laptop runs Windows 8 Pro with Media Center and has limited touch support, as detailed in Control Panel.

- **Laptop (or Netbook)** – Laptop computers run a full version of Windows 8, and you'll have access to all of the features available in the operating system. Laptops come with a keyboard and some type of pointing device (track pad, track ball, touch pad and so on). A good laptop can replace a desktop computer.
- **Ultrabook** – These are thin laptops. Because of that, they often don't have space

DID YOU KNOW?

The outside of the box your device came in shows what kind of device you purchased. If you don't have the box, you may own a user's manual.

for an Ethernet port or a CD/DVD drive. Other ports may be missing too. Ultrabooks generally run a full version of Windows 8.

- **High-end tablet** – High-end tablets almost always run a full version of Windows 8, but you may not have access to a physical keyboard, specialty ports, and other laptop hardware. Some tablets can be attached to a dock that contains these features though, but docks are often sold separately. Likewise, you can generally connect Bluetooth devices like keyboards and mice, if desired.
- **Simple tablet** – Simple tablets are often installed with Windows 8 RT. This is not the full version of Windows 8 that is installed on laptop computers. If you have a computer that runs Windows 8 RT, you'll notice as you use the device that some features are unavailable.

HOT TIP: If you have a tablet and don't have a keyboard, you'll have to rely on touch techniques to navigate it, and you'll see tips for doing so throughout this book.

Explore the battery

There are several items that have to do with the battery, and they're probably all located on the underside or back of your laptop. Before you turn the laptop upside down to look at them, make sure you turn it off and unplug it.

1. If the computer is turned off, skip to step 3.
2. If the computer is turned on, press and hold the Windows key on the keyboard and then tap the I key. Click or tap Power and then Shut Down.

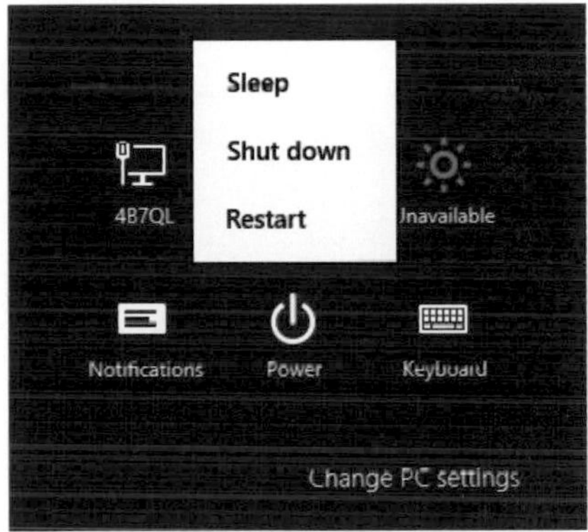

3. Unplug the laptop from the wall outlet and remove the power cable. Set the power cable aside.
4. Close the laptop's lid and carefully turn the laptop upside down and place it on a desk or table.
5. If there is a battery bay with a door, you'll have to open it to access the battery.
6. If there is not a battery bay with a door, the battery may slide or snap to connect and disconnect.

HOT TIP: Your laptop may be configured to shut down when you press the Power button, although often it's configured to simply go to sleep.

DID YOU KNOW?
Tablets may not have a battery bay, and the battery may not be removable.

WHAT DOES THIS MEAN?

Battery bay: This holds the computer's battery. Sometimes you have to use a screwdriver to get inside the battery bay, but most of the time you simply need to slide out the compartment door.

Plug in the power cable

A power cable is the cable that you will use to connect the laptop to the wall outlet (power outlet). When you connect the power cable to both the laptop and the power outlet, the laptop will use the power from the outlet and charge the battery at the same time. When you unplug the laptop from the power outlet, the laptop will run on stored battery power.

1 Locate the power cord. It may consist of two pieces that need to be connected.

2 Connect the power cord to the back or side of the laptop as noted in the documentation.

3 Plug the power cord into the wall outlet.

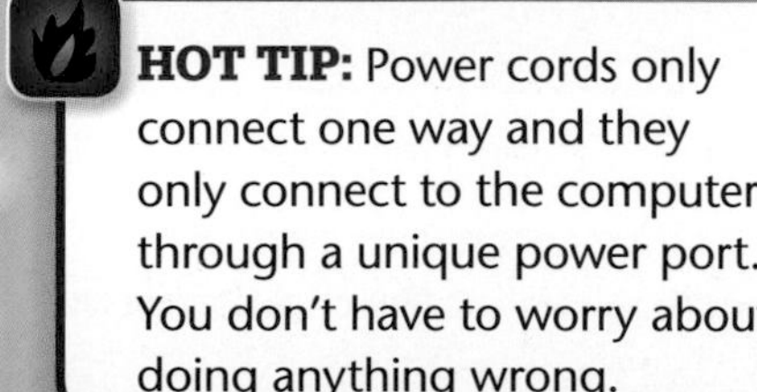

HOT TIP: Power cords only connect one way and they only connect to the computer through a unique power port. You don't have to worry about doing anything wrong.

DID YOU KNOW?
You can connect and disconnect the power cable at any time, even when the computer is running.

Recognise USB ports

USB ports, or universal serial bus ports, offer a place to connect USB devices. USB devices include mice, external keyboards, mobile phones, digital cameras and other devices, including USB flash drives.

1. Locate a USB cable. The length and shape depend on the device, although one end is always small and rectangular.

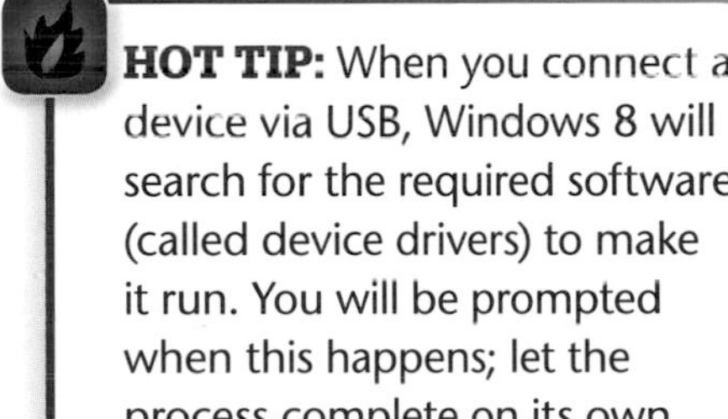

HOT TIP: When you connect a device via USB, Windows 8 will search for the required software (called device drivers) to make it run. You will be prompted when this happens; let the process complete on its own.

2. Plug the rectangular end of the USB cable into an empty USB port on your laptop.

3. Connect the other end to the USB device.
4. Often, you'll need to turn on the USB device to get Windows 8 to recognise it, but not always.

HOT TIP: FireWire is often used to connect digital video cameras, professional audio hardware, and external hard drives to a computer. FireWire ports are larger than USB ports and move data more quickly.

WHAT DOES THIS MEAN?

A **flash drive** (or thumb drive) is a portable storage unit. You can use it to back up your important files easily.

Locate the Ethernet port

You use an Ethernet port to physically connect your laptop to your local network. If you have a cable modem, router or other high-speed internet device at home, you can use Ethernet to connect to it. Ethernet connections are often faster than wireless ones, but the gap is lessening. Extremely thin laptops such as ultrabooks may not have an Ethernet port, and you'll have to connect wirelessly.

1. Locate an Ethernet cable. They are often blue, although they can be grey, white or some other colour.
2. Connect the cable to both the PC and the Ethernet outlet on a router or cable modem.

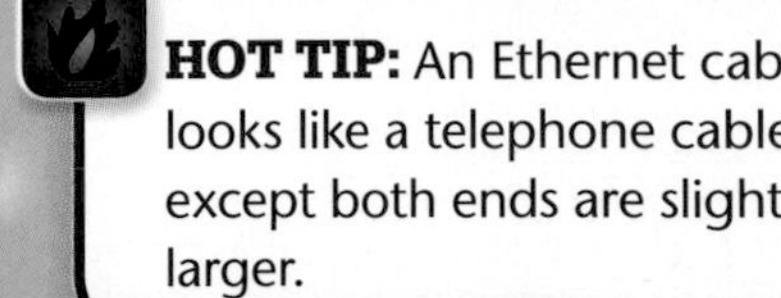

HOT TIP: An Ethernet cable looks like a telephone cable, except both ends are slightly larger.

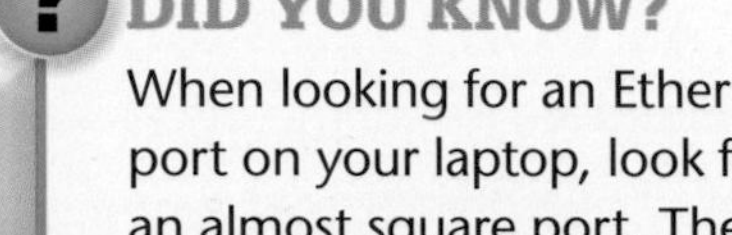

DID YOU KNOW?
When looking for an Ethernet port on your laptop, look for an almost square port. The Ethernet cable will snap in.

Connect headphones

Most laptops come with built-in speakers, cameras and microphones. However, you may want to connect headphones for privacy. You may also need to connect headphones to more clearly hear system sounds, music, and the sounds that accompany videos and movies, especially when you're in a public place or on an aeroplane.

1. If necessary, turn on the headphones.
2. Connect the headphones to the applicable port. You'll see a picture of a set of headphones on it.

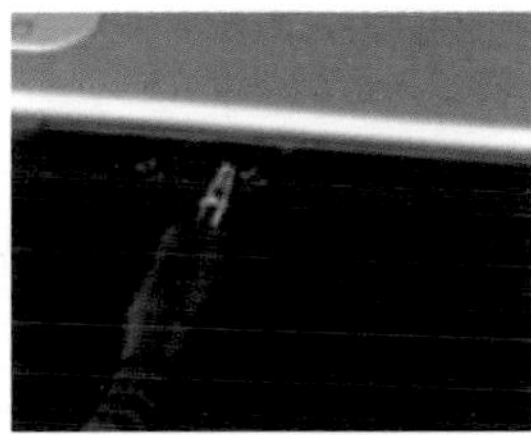

3. If prompted, work through any set up processes.

DID YOU KNOW?
You may see two sound ports. Line-in jacks bring data into the laptop; line-out jacks port data out to external devices such as speakers or headphones.

DID YOU KNOW?
You may find volume controls on the outside of your laptop, and there may be volume options on the keyboard. The first time you play music or video on your laptop try pressing the F9, F10 and F11 keys to see what happens.

ALERT: You probably don't need to purchase expensive headphones. Inexpensive headphones work just fine for most users.

Locate additional ports

You'll see other ports not mentioned here depending on the make and model of your laptop. You may see ports that enable you to connect an external monitor, a FireWire device or SD cards, among other things. On a standard sized laptop you'll probably also see a CD/DVD drive bay.

1 Turn the laptop and view all sides of it.

2 View all of the available ports.

3 Refer to your user's guide to explore these ports. Here is a serial port.

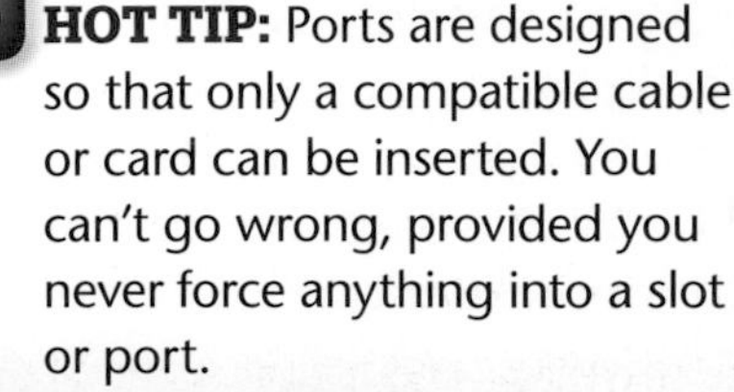

HOT TIP: Ports are designed so that only a compatible cable or card can be inserted. You can't go wrong, provided you never force anything into a slot or port.

DID YOU KNOW?

A serial port can be used to connect your laptop to an external monitor, even a very old one.

Start Windows 8

Before you can use your laptop you have to press the power button. The first time you turn on a new laptop, you'll have to work through the Windows 8 setup process.

1. If applicable, open the laptop's lid.
2. Press the power button.
3. If applicable, work through the setup process. If you are prompted to work through this process, refer to the next page in this book.
4. When the Lock screen appears, click anywhere on it, and type your password.
5. The startup process is complete when you see the Start screen. Part of a Start screen is shown here.

DID YOU KNOW?
Starting a computer is also called 'booting' it. If a computer won't boot there are various troubleshooting tools available.

ALERT: Although it isn't mandatory, during the setup process, create or input a Microsoft account. This enables you to use all of the features built in to Windows 8.

Follow the setup instructions

When you set up your laptop for the first time, you are prompted to make a few choices. Some of these are listed here.

- The colour of the Start screen.

- Which settings to use. For now, choose Use express settings.
- Which network, if applicable, to connect to, and whether or not to share your data on that network.

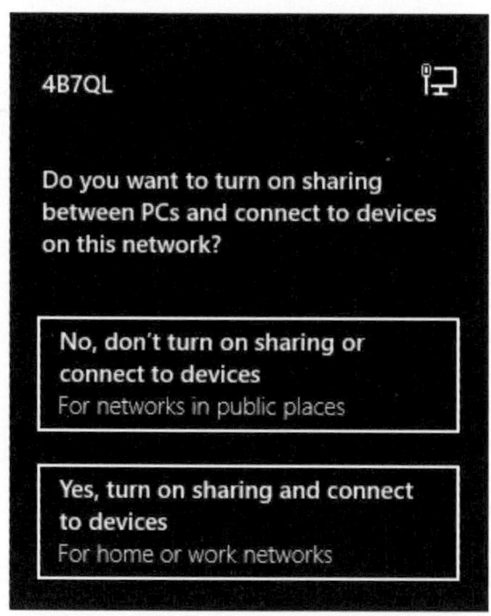

- Sign in/User name choice. If possible, use this time to create and/or input a Microsoft account.

SEE ALSO: Chapter 2, refer to the section Understand the new jargon for more information on the Microsoft account.

DID YOU KNOW?
If you don't already have a Microsoft account you can get one during the setup process.

Explore the Start screen

Once you gain access to the Start screen, your computer is ready to use. You'll probably see the default set of tiles on that screen, so what you see will differ from what you see here.

HOT TIP: If you use a tablet that runs Windows 8 RT, you'll see Microsoft Office apps on the Start screen.

1 Position your mouse at the bottom of the screen; a scroll bar appears. Use this to access apps that run off the screen on the right. (You can flick your finger across a touch screen.)

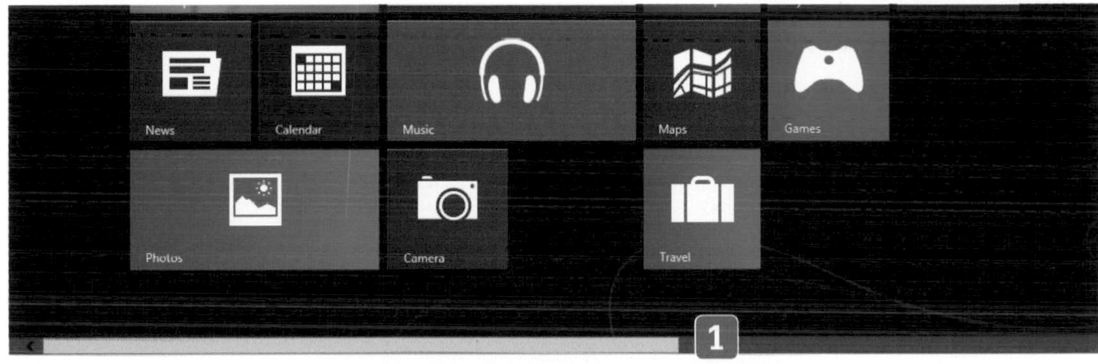

2 If you click or tap a tile, the related app opens. Try Travel.

3 To return to the Start screen from any app:

- Move the cursor to the bottom left corner of the screen and click the Start screen thumbnail that appears, or
- Tap the Windows key on the keyboard or on the device itself (if one exists).

HOT TIP: To view all of your apps, right-click an empty area of the screen and click All Apps. On a touch screen, flick up from the bottom.

HOT TIP: If you are using a mouse you can use the scroll wheel on it to move around in the Start menu.

Use the touch pad

Most laptops come with a touch pad. You'll use this to move the cursor around the screen. Most of the time you can click on the bottom left or bottom right of that touch pad to perform left and right mouse clicks.

1. Place your finger on the touch pad and move it around. Notice the cursor moves.
2. If there are buttons, for the most part the left button functions in the same way as the left button on a mouse and the right button functions the same way as the right button on a mouse.

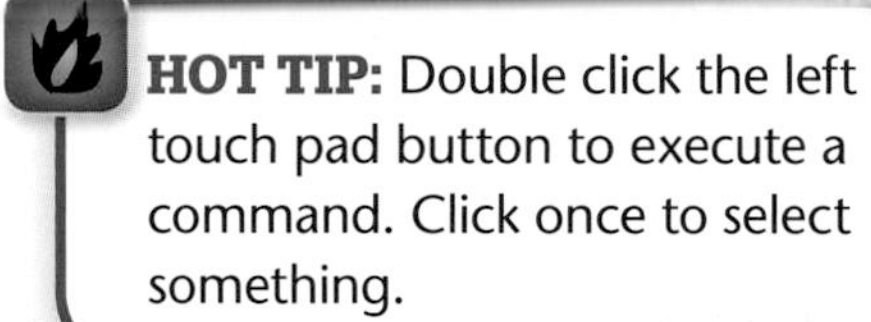

HOT TIP: Double click the left touch pad button to execute a command. Click once to select something.

3. If there is a centre button, often this is used to scroll through pages. Try clicking and holding it to move up, down, left or right on a page.

HOT TIP: Click the right touch pad button to open contextual menus to access Copy, Select All and similar commands. It may not be a button though; it may just have a small line to delineate it.

ALERT: Keep your fingers and hands clean when using the touch pad – it has a sensitive surface.

Access the desktop

If you've ever used a computer, you've worked at the desktop, the traditional computing environment. Your Windows 8 laptop or tablet also offers a desktop – which you access from the Desktop tile. You may be more comfortable here and prefer not to use the Start screen at all; that is OK with us!

1. Use any method to access the Start screen if you aren't already on it. (You can tap the Windows key on a keyboard.)
2. From the Start screen, click or tap Desktop.
3. Note the Desktop features:
   - A The Recycle Bin.
   - B The Taskbar (with icons for open files and programs).
   - C The Internet Explorer icon (the program is open here).
   - D The File Explorer icon (we've opened File Explorer here).
   - E The Notification area.
   - F Various items stored on the desktop itself.

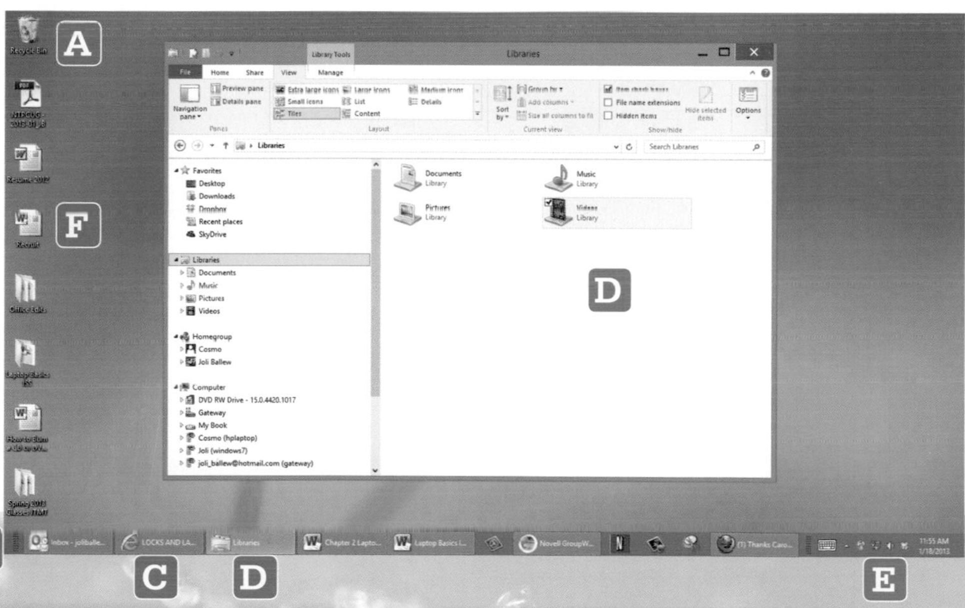

? DID YOU KNOW?
You can use the keyboard icon in the Notification area to access an onscreen keyboard.

! ALERT: The Start button is no longer available on the taskbar, at least at the time this book was published. If you'd like to access something a bit like it, press the Windows key + X key combination.

Change the screen resolution

While at the desktop, note how large or small the icons are. Click the folder icon at the bottom of the screen (on the taskbar) to see the size of the items there. If the items are too small for you to see comfortably, follow these steps to change the screen resolution.

1. Right-click an empty area of the desktop and click Screen resolution.
2. Move the slider to 1366 × 768. Click Apply.
3. If you like the resolution, keep it. If not repeat this process until you find one you like.

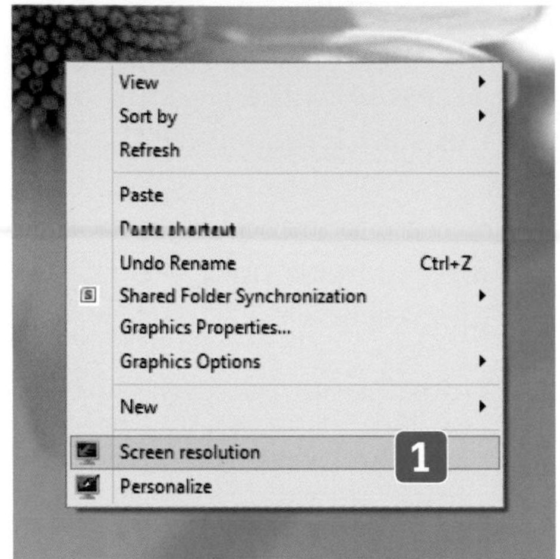

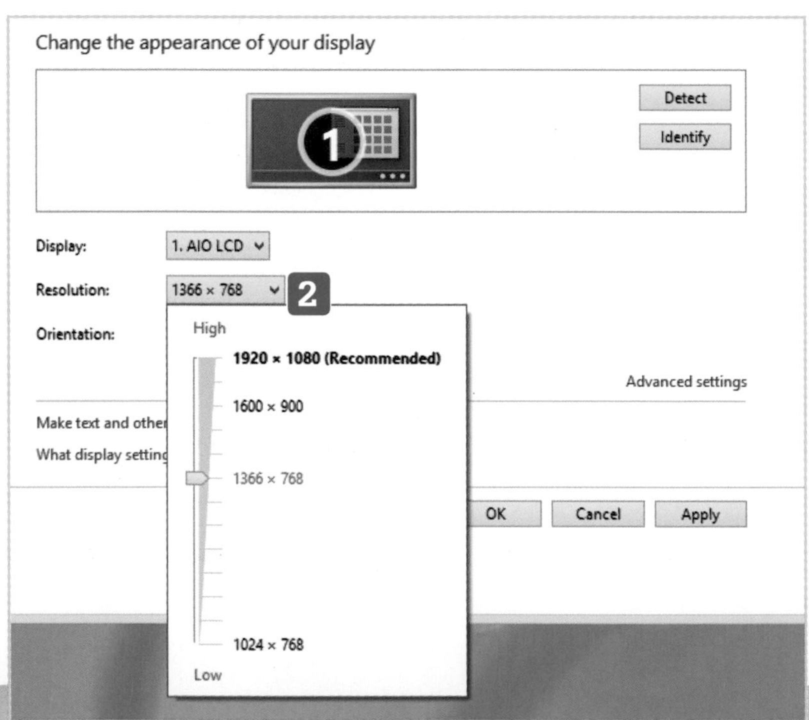

DID YOU KNOW?
The lower the resolution, the larger the items on your screen appear.

ALERT: Some features of Windows 8 won't work if the resolution is below 1366 × 768.

Use the Windows key

All Windows-compatible keyboards offer a Windows key. It is on the left side, at the bottom, between the Ctrl key and the Alt key. Most touch-only tablets have a button with the Windows logo on it that serves the same purpose. The Windows key plays a 'key role' in Windows 8. Here are a few things you'll use this key for:

- Press the Windows key to return to the Start screen from anywhere.

- Press the Windows key + I to access the command to shut down the computer. You'll choose from the available Power choices.

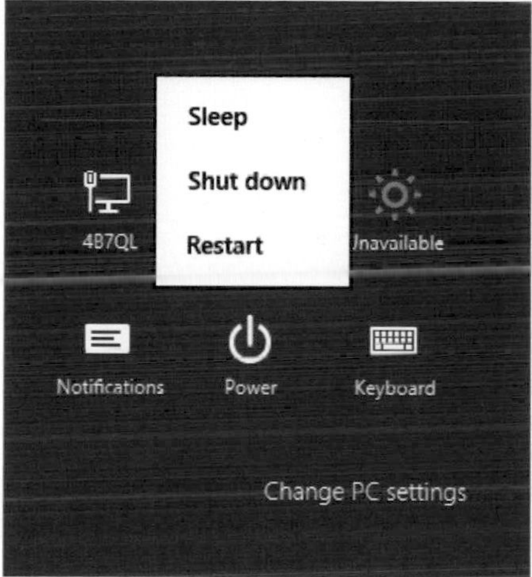

- Press Windows + F to search for a file.
- Press Windows + X to open a shortcut menu similar to the old Start button.

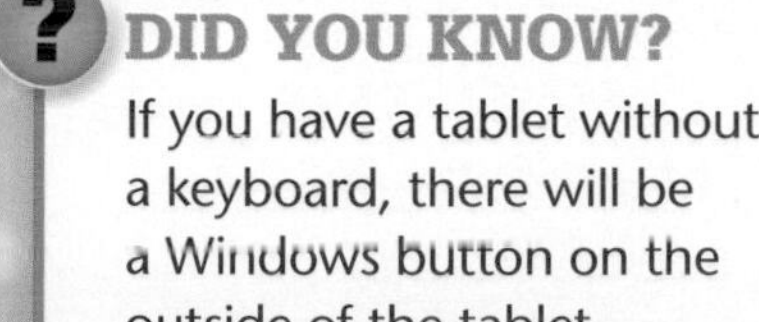

DID YOU KNOW?

If you have a tablet without a keyboard, there will be a Windows button on the outside of the tablet.

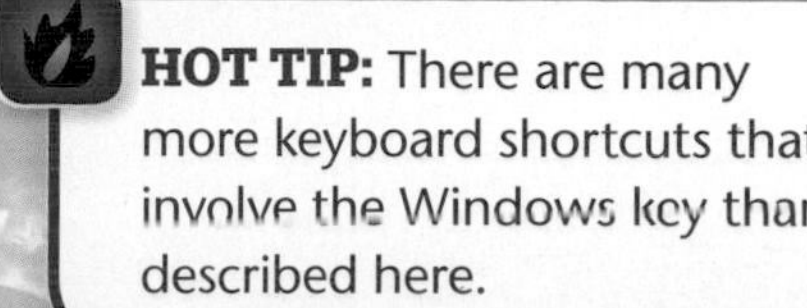

HOT TIP: There are many more keyboard shortcuts that involve the Windows key than described here.

2 Explore Windows 8's unique features

Introduction

Windows 8 is a new breed of operating system. As you learned in Chapter 1, it has a Start screen that holds tiles for the available apps, and it has a special tile to allow you to access the traditional desktop. The Start screen is a completely new concept for Microsoft (and new to you too).

Beyond the Start screen there are many other new features, most of them hidden away in neat little toolbars and 'hot corners' you access by performing specific touch gestures or mouse clicks. As an example of the latter, in Chapter 1 you learned that you could move your cursor to the bottom left corner of any Windows screen and click the thumbnail that appears. This movement lets you return to the Start screen from anywhere. The other three corners are 'hot' too.

In this chapter you'll learn about these new features as well as the new jargon (terminology) that accompanies them. You'll learn about hot corners, special mouse clicks, charms and apps, to name a few others.

Use a Microsoft account

When you set up your Windows 8 laptop or tablet, you were prompted to create and/ or log in with a Microsoft account. If you opted *not* to do this or were unable to, then you created a local account instead. We suggest you use a Microsoft account; a Microsoft account is shown here.

- **Microsoft account** – A Microsoft account is a personal but global account you use to log in to your Windows 8 computer. When you use this kind of account, Windows 8 will automatically configure certain apps with personalised information, and your preferences and settings will be available no matter what Internet-enabled Windows 8 computer you log on to. You must use a Microsoft account to access features like SkyDrive, Calendar and the Store, among others.
- **Local account** – This is a personal account you create and use to log on to your Windows 8 computer that is only associated with that computer. Your account settings and preferences don't 'follow' you from one Windows 8 computer to another like a Microsoft account can. You can't access SkyDrive, Calendar, the Store and other apps using a local account.

HOT TIP: It's never too late to switch from a local account to a Microsoft account. You do this from PC settings.

ALERT: If you want to get the most possible from Windows 8 and you want to be able to access all of the apps, you must use a Microsoft account.

Understand the new jargon

There are a few terms to understand before you jump in to Windows 8. You'll see these terms throughout the book.

- **Lock screen** – You must bypass the Lock screen before you can unlock the computer. To unlock your computer you input your unique password, password picture pattern, or PIN after bypassing it. This is a Lock screen.

> **? DID YOU KNOW?**
> You can right-click an empty area of the Start screen to view all of the available apps. If you use a touch screen, flick upward from the bottom instead.

- **Start screen** – The Start screen appears after you unlock the computer. It holds tiles that you use to open apps, programs, folders and so on.

- **Start screen app** – A simple program that enables you to do something quickly and easily, like check email, send a message, check the weather or surf the internet. *Apps*, as they are referred to, offer less functionality than full-fledged programs (*Desktop apps*), and are more like what you'd see on a smartphone or an iPad. Here is the Internet Explorer app.

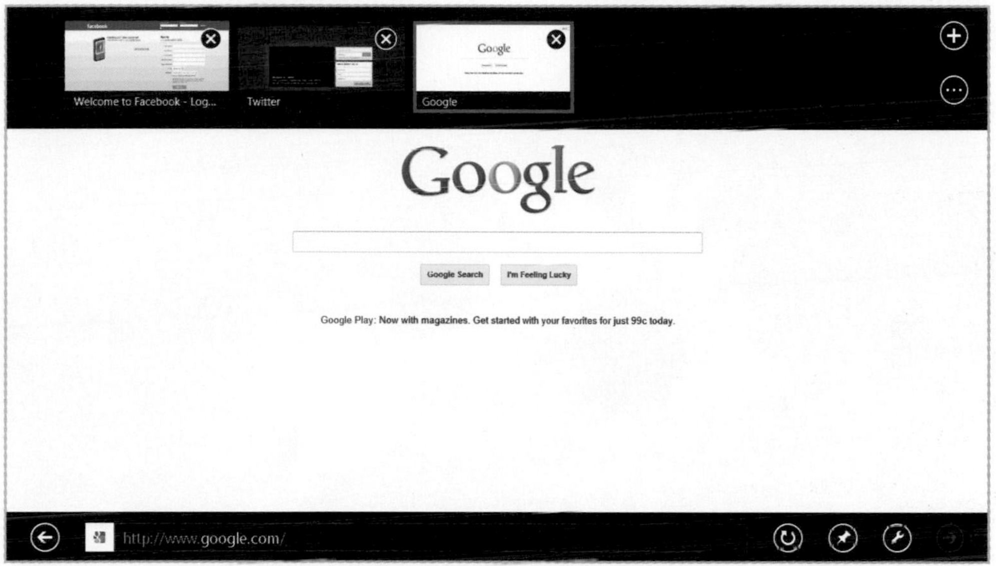

- **Desktop app** – These types of apps are the traditional programs you may already be familiar with. Desktop apps are complete programs like Paint, Notepad, Windows Media Player, Internet Explorer, and similar third-party programs such as Adobe Reader. They open on the *desktop*. Here is the Internet Explorer desktop app; you can see the traditional desktop behind it.

- **Desktop** – The desktop is the traditional computing environment complete with the taskbar, desktop background, shortcuts to programs, and so on. If you've ever used a computer you've used the desktop. This is what my desktop looks like.

DID YOU KNOW?
Some applications have two versions. For instance, there is an Internet Explorer app that is available from the Start screen, and an Internet Explorer Desktop app available from the desktop.

HOT TIP: We believe the majority of Desktop apps are on their way out and that new, more streamlined Start screen-type apps will eventually take their place. Thus, if keeping up with the latest technology is important to you, when there are two versions of an app available (such as is the case with Internet Explorer), use the app available from the Start screen.

Log in to Windows 8

The Lock screen appears when you turn on or wake up your Windows 8 computer. You must bypass the Lock screen and input your password in the resulting log in box before you can use your computer.

1. If you have a touch screen, use your finger to swipe upward from the bottom or touch the screen. If you have a mouse or physical keyboard do any of the following:
   - Swipe upward with the mouse.
   - Tap the Space bar on the keyboard.
   - Click anywhere on the screen.
2. Type your password or PIN and tap Enter or the keyboard, or, type your password and tap or click the right facing arrow.

3. The Start screen appears.

DID YOU KNOW?
You can tap or click the icon that looks like an eye that appears in the Password window after you've entered a letter or two to see the actual characters (instead of the dots that appear by default).

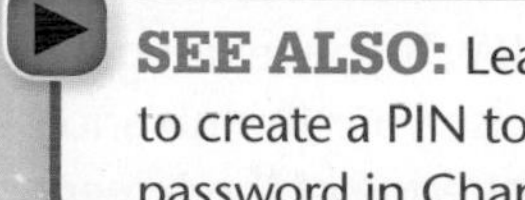

SEE ALSO: Learn how to create a PIN to replace a password in Chapter 3.

Access the default charms

Charms are a new feature of Windows 8. You probably haven't seen any charms yet because they are hidden by default. Charms are quite unique and let you easily configure settings, share information, view devices and search for data, among other things. You can access the default charms in many ways.

- Using touch, place your thumb in the middle of the right side of the screen and flick left (inward).
- On a keyboard, use the key combination Windows key + C.
- Using a mouse or touch pad, move the cursor to the bottom or top right corner of the screen, and when the transparent charms appear, move the cursor upward or downward.

HOT TIP: If you're using a touch screen on a tablet, use your thumb and flick inward from the right edge of the screen to bring up the charms. On a touch screen monitor (such as one you might connect to a small laptop), try your right index finger instead.

DID YOU KNOW?

The Shut Down command is available from the Settings charm, from the Power icon that appears there.

Explore the default charms

As you saw on the previous page, there are five charms. What you see when you click each may differ depending on what you're doing when you click them. For instance, if you click the Share charm while on the Start screen, you'll be notified there's nothing available to share there. If you click the Share charm while in Maps, you can share the location or directions you've looked up with others via email or other options.

- **Search** – To open the Search window where you can type what you're looking for. Note the categories: Apps, Settings, Files. What's shown in the left side of the screen changes when you start typing your search term.

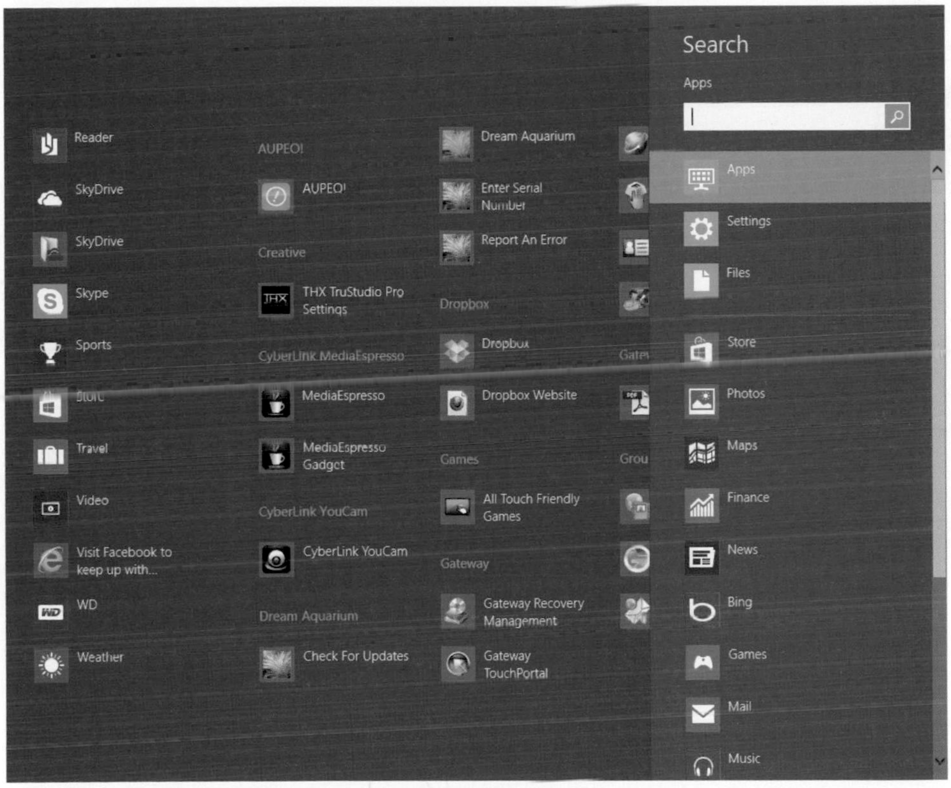

> ? **DID YOU KNOW?**
> You can access charms from anywhere in Windows 8, even the desktop or while in an app.

> **HOT TIP:** From the Settings charm, click or tap Change PC settings to access the PC Settings screen (or hub). You can make changes to your computer there including creating a PIN, changing the Lock screen picture, adding users and so on.

- **Share** – To share something with others, such as a map to a location.

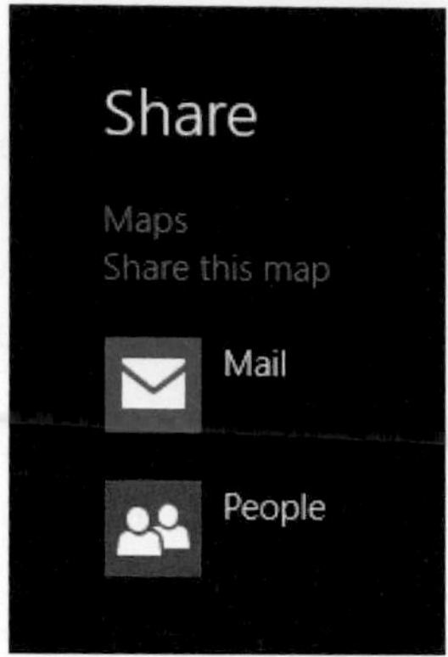

- **Start** – To access the Start screen.
- **Devices** – To access devices that can be used with the open app, window or program.
- **Settings** – To access settings available with the open screen, app, program and so on. You'll use this charm to join networks, change the volume, shut down the computer, and more.

Use the Weather app

Another new feature of Windows 8 is the Start screen apps. Some are simple to use and others are simpler! One of the easiest to use is the Weather app. Its tile is on the Start screen.

1. From the Start screen, click the Weather tile.

2. If prompted, click Allow to let the Weather app learn your location.
3. Review the information offered.
4. Use the scroll bar to view additional information including but not limited to various regional maps, historical weather information and the hourly forecast for your area.

DID YOU KNOW?
If you use a Microsoft account and configure the Weather app on one computer, when you log on to another Windows 8 computer using that account, your app settings will be synced.

HOT TIP: If you have a touch screen, use your finger to flick left and right to access other areas of the Weather app.

DID YOU KNOW?
You can right-click or flick upward from the bottom to access the Weather app's personalised toolbar (which holds charms specific to the app). This is discussed next. You can use these to manipulate the information shown in it, such as changing from Celsius to Fahrenheit.

Explore an app's toolbar

While in any app you can right-click with a mouse or touch pad, or flick up or down with a finger (on a compatible touch screen), to access the toolbar that is specific to that app. This toolbar holds charms unique to the app. In the case of the Weather app, you can add new places, see world weather, change your current location, and more.

1 Open the Weather app as outlined on the previous page.

2 Right-click with a mouse.

3 Note the toolbar across the top.

4 Note the toolbar across the bottom.

5 Click or tap any charm on either toolbar to view information and make changes. This is World Weather.

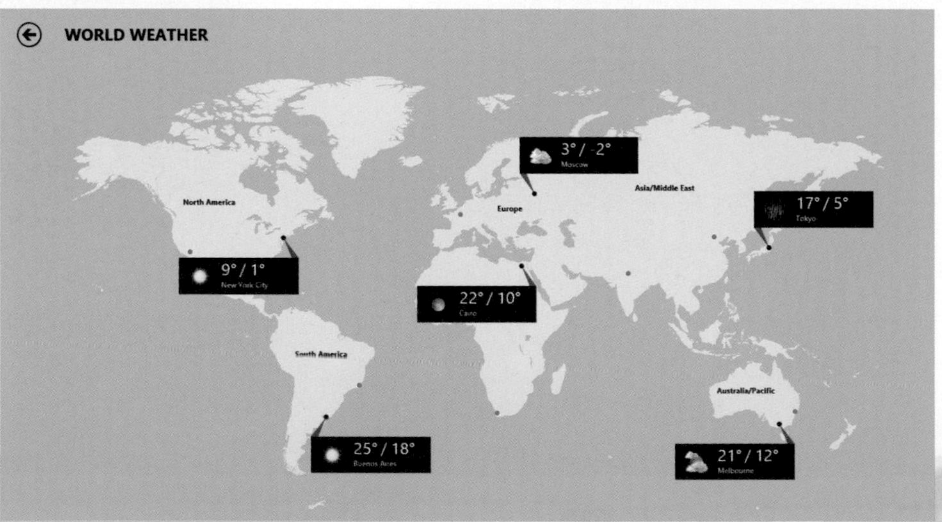

HOT TIP: As you explore apps for the first time, right-click to explore their toolbars too.

DID YOU KNOW?

Some apps will only offer a toolbar across the bottom or the top, and may not offer them in both places.

Use the Travel app

The Travel app is another of the easiest to use apps, and is packed with information about places you may want to visit or read about. One of the most outstanding features is the ability to explore cities in 360 degree views. As with other apps, you can right-click or flick upwards to access the app's charms.

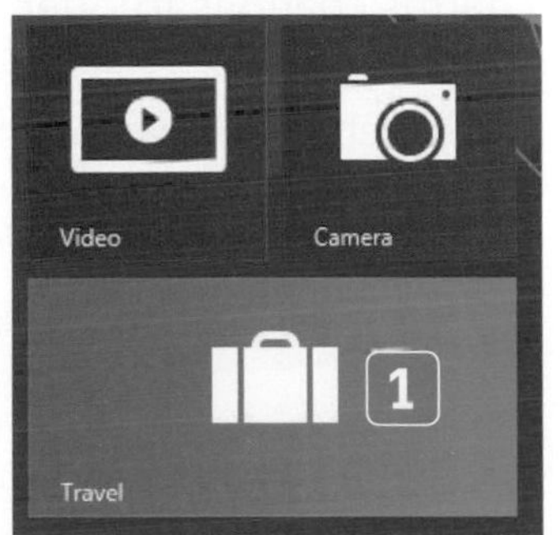

1 From the Start screen, click Travel.

2 Use the scroll bar on the screen or the wheel on your mouse to move through the information.

3 Click any item to view it; click the resulting 'back' button to return.

4 Locate the Panoramas section, specifically any item with 360 degrees on it. Click the item.

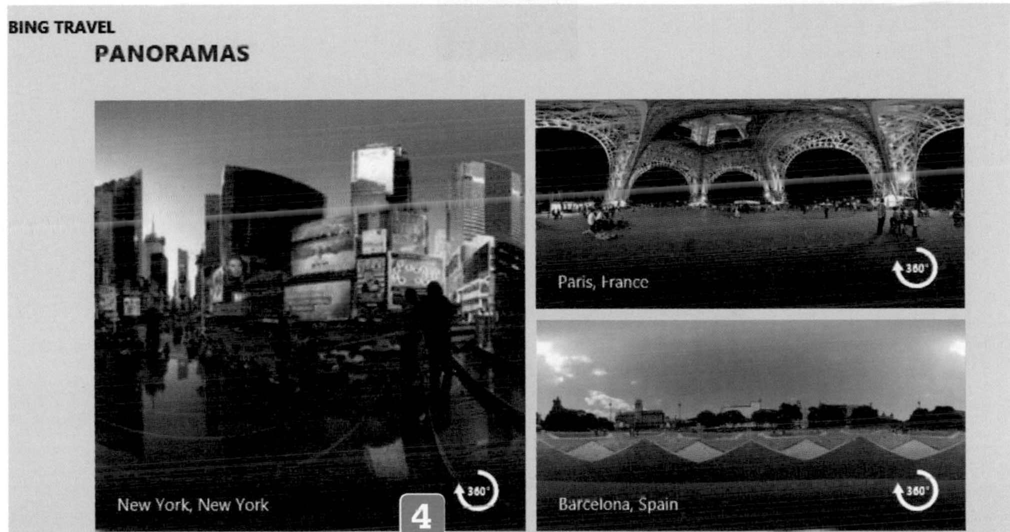

5 Use your finger or mouse to drag on the image to move it around on the screen.

HOT TIP: When you access a city from the Featured Destinations section, you'll have access to an overview of the city, photos, a list of attractions, and more.

DID YOU KNOW?
While in any app (in this case Travel) you can access the previously used app (in this case, Weather) by moving the mouse cursor to the top left corner and clicking. If you use touch only, flick inward from the left middle edge.

Explore an app's default charms

You learned that the five default charms are Search, Share, Start, Devices and Settings. You also know various ways to view them, including the key combination Windows + C and positioning the mouse in the top right or bottom right hot corner. When you access these charms while inside an app though, what you see when you click those charms changes to offer information and settings for the app you are in.

1. Open the Travel app as outlined on the previous page.
2. Access the default charms using any method (perhaps Windows key + C).
3. Click the Search charm.

4. Type a destination and click the result.

5. Access the charms again and, this time, click Share. Note the ways you can share this information.

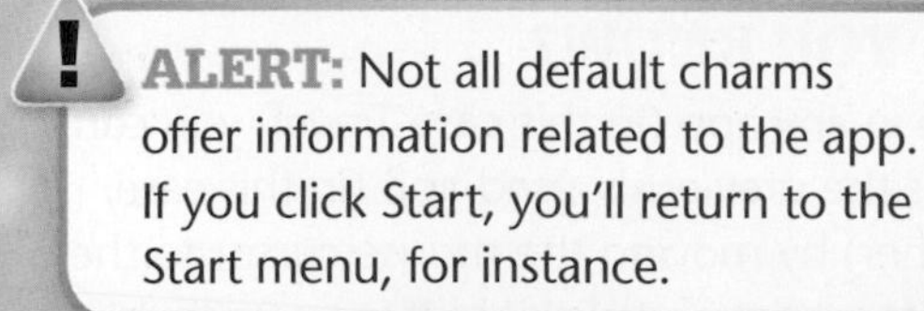

ALERT: Not all default charms offer information related to the app. If you click Start, you'll return to the Start menu, for instance.

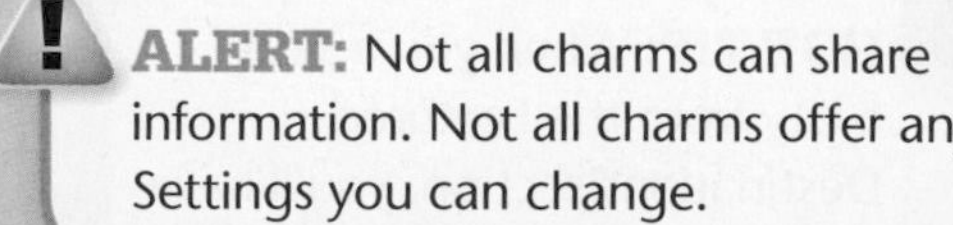

ALERT: Not all charms can share information. Not all charms offer any Settings you can change.

Search for a location with Maps

You can use the Maps app to locate a place or get directions from one place to another. By default, Maps will use your current location as the starting point, provided you allow it to access your position when prompted. You can use the Share charm to share the information you obtain with others.

1 From the Start screen, click Maps.

2 Right-click or swipe upward from the bottom to access the available Maps charms.

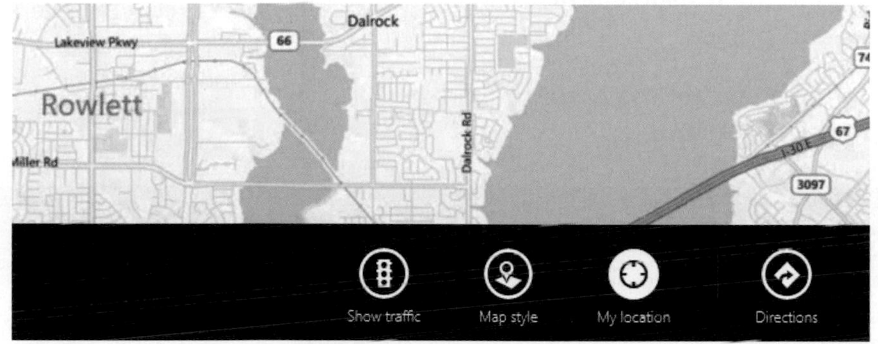

3 Explore the following, then click Directions:

- Show traffic – To view the current flow of traffic as green, yellow or red. Green means traffic is moving; red means it's extremely slow.
- Map style – To switch from the default Road view to Aerial view.
- My location – To have Maps place a diamond on the map to indicate where you are or to recalculate your location.
- Directions – To get directions from one place to another.

4 Leave your starting address as your current location and type an ending address.

5 Press Enter on the keyboard.

6 Right-click to access the option to clear the map of the directions on it.

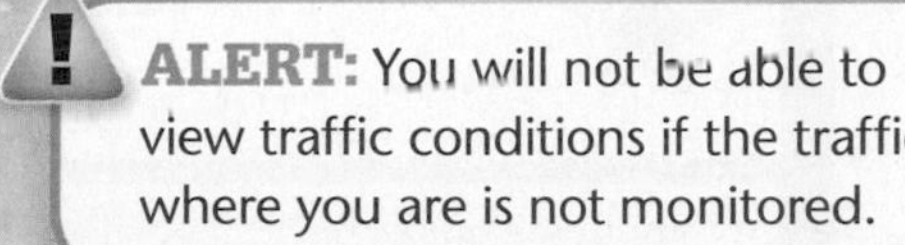

ALERT: You will not be able to view traffic conditions if the traffic where you are is not monitored.

HOT TIP: Click My location, and then click Map style, Aerial view. Zoom in (double-click or use pinch) to view a picture of your own home, business or location as it appears from the sky!

Get the latest sports news and follow a team

Like most apps, the Sports app also offers a host of information. There are articles, photos, and the ability to add your favourite teams so you can follow them easily through the app.

1. From the Start screen, click Sports.
2. Scroll through the available articles, news, schedules and photos.
3. On the far right, locate the Favorite Teams section. Click the + sign.

HOT TIP: To remove a team from your list of favourite teams, click Favorite Teams, then right-click the team to remove. Click Remove.

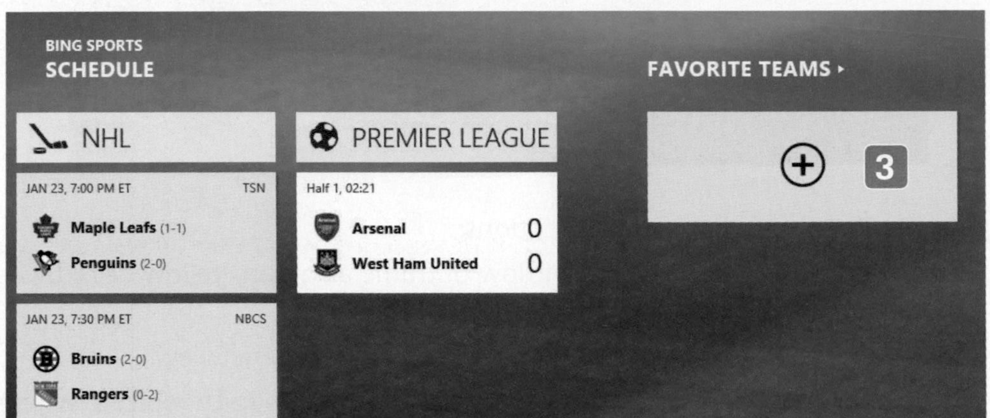

4. Type the team to follow and repeat as desired. Click Add if applicable.
5. Click Cancel when finished.
6. Note the new entries; you can now click any of these to learn more.

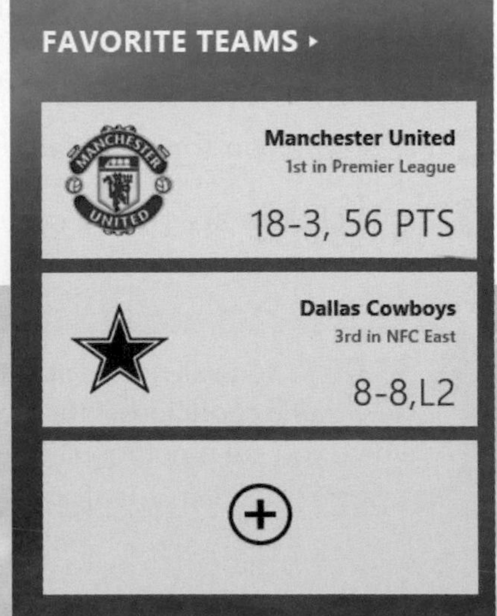

DID YOU KNOW?

You can position your mouse in the bottom right corner of the Sports app and click the dash that appears to access a list of available categories (such as Top Story, News, Schedule and Favorite Teams).

View your personal calendar

The Calendar app lets you input calendar data, including major events, goals, birthdays, appointments and so on, which are ultimately synced with your Microsoft account *in the cloud*. Because the data is synced to third-party computers that are connected to the internet, any changes you make to the calendar from other compatible devices are automatically synced too. This also means calendar data will be up-to-date no matter how many devices you use, and that you can access the calendar data from anywhere.

1. From the Start screen, click Calendar.
2. Right-click with a mouse or flick upward from the bottom of the screen with your finger to access the Calendar's toolbar and related charms.

3. Explore Day, Week and Month by clicking them each one time. Click Today.
4. Click New.
5. Note the option to create a new event. If desired, input data and information and click the Save icon.

? DID YOU KNOW?
You can view your calendar from almost anywhere. It's on the web at https://calendar.live.com/.

HOT TIP: The Calendar tile on the Start screen is *live*. This means that as appointment and event dates draw near, the tile will show the information on the Start screen. You'll learn more about live apps shortly.

Move among open apps

At some point you'll find that you have quite a few apps open at once. That's OK, because open apps don't use any system resources when you aren't using them. However, you do need to know how to get back to those apps when you are ready to use them again. Although you can always return to the Start screen and tap the app's tile, there are better ways.

If you have a keyboard and mouse, try these techniques while on any screen or in any app:

- Hold down the Alt key and press the Tab key to show a row of open apps. Press Tab repeatedly until you get to the app you want to use, then let go.

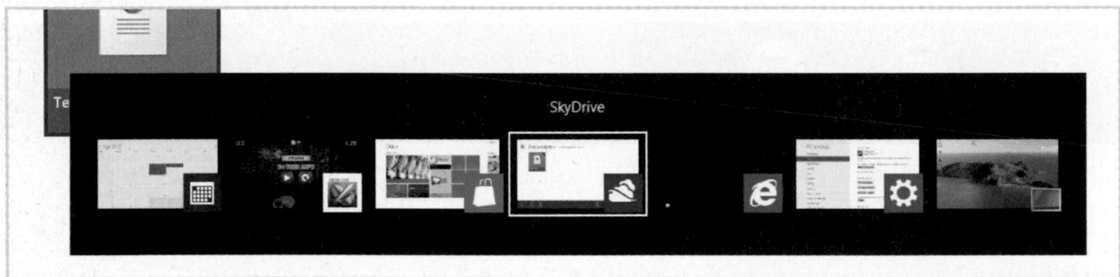

- Position your mouse in the top left corner of the screen to view and click the last used app, or drag the mouse downward slowly to view the other available apps to access those.

DID YOU KNOW?
Try the Windows + Tab key combination too. You may be able to move through apps that way as well.

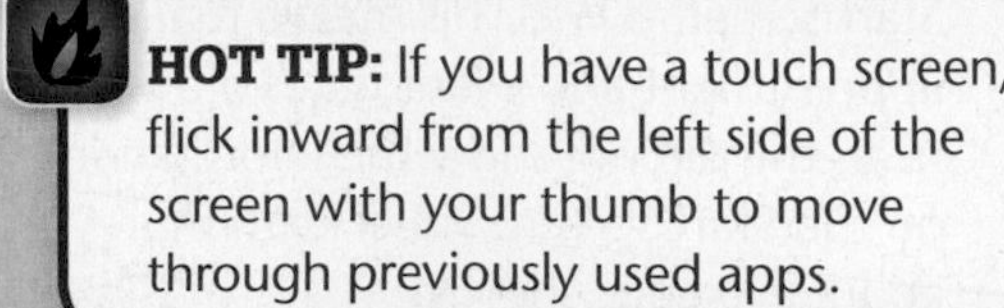

HOT TIP: If you have a touch screen, flick inward from the left side of the screen with your thumb to move through previously used apps.

3 Personalise the Start screen

Introduction

You know that the Start screen offers access to apps, and if you've been following along from the start you've even tried a few of them (Weather, Travel, Maps and Calendar). After you've used apps for a while though, you may decide you don't need all of them on the Start screen; perhaps you don't like some of them, have desktop editions you prefer to their app counterparts, or know you simply won't ever use them. It's easy to remove and add tiles.

You may have already decided that you don't want anything at all to do with apps, ever. (Although we hope not!) If this is the case, you will probably want to remove almost everything that is there now and move the Desktop tile to the top left. You can then add tiles for desktop apps you use most often, like Microsoft Office Word, Paint, Internet Explorer and Photoshop Elements, to fill the rest of the screen. You can do that as well. (You can even add tiles for contacts, websites and folders.)

Once you've positioned the tiles the way you want them, you can personalise the tiles even more. You can make some smaller, for instance. You can also enable or disable 'live' tiles, the technology that makes the tiles show up-to-date information on them. After that you can change the screen background and even create a PIN to access the Start screen more quickly at log on.

Move tiles on the Start screen

As you become more familiar with apps, you may find you use some quite often and others rarely, if ever. It's easy to move the tiles for the apps you use often to the left side of the Start screen for easier access and move others farther away.

1. At the Start screen, click and hold on a tile to move.
2. Drag the tile to a new area of the screen and drop it there.
3. When you drag an app away from its current 'group' you'll see a thick line. You can opt to group like apps together.

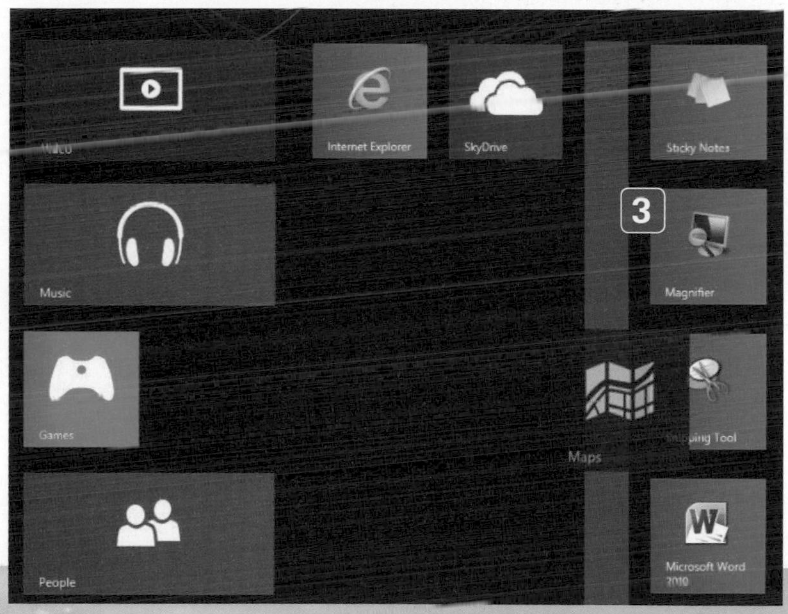

HOT TIP: If you have a touch device, you'll have to touch, hold and drag a little downward to start to move the tile, and then continue dragging until you have it at its new location. Remove your finger to drop it there.

SEE ALSO: Learn how to name a group of tiles later in this chapter.

Add a tile to the Start screen

There are more windows, apps, system tools, desktop applications, and so on available than appear on the Start screen by default. There's the Calculator, for instance, and Windows Media Player, Control Panel, Windows Explorer and WordPad, to name a few. You can add any item to the Start screen to have easier access to it.

1. Right-click an empty area of the Start screen. On a touch screen, flick upward from the bottom of the screen.
2. Click All apps.

3. Right-click (or tap, hold and drag downward) an item you'd like to add.
4. From the bar that appears at the bottom of the page click Pin to Start. (This will change to Unpin from Start after you do.)

5. Return to the Start screen and locate the new tile. It will be placed on the far right. You may want to drag it left to reposition it.

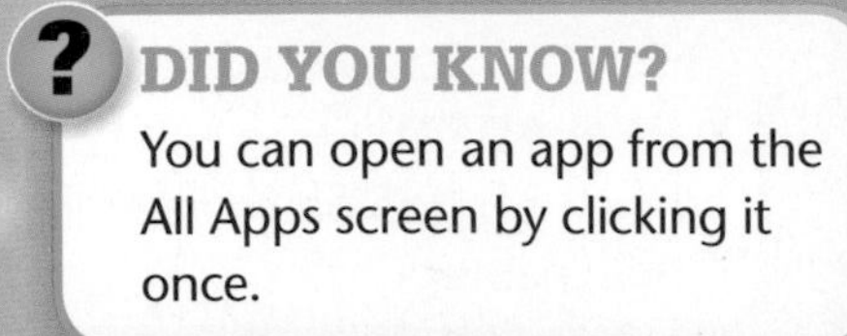

DID YOU KNOW?

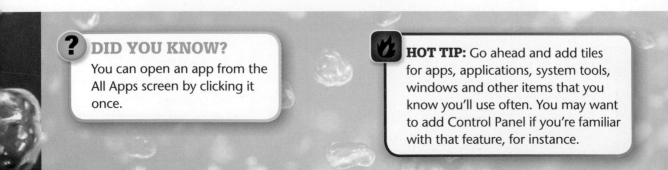

You can open an app from the All Apps screen by clicking it once.

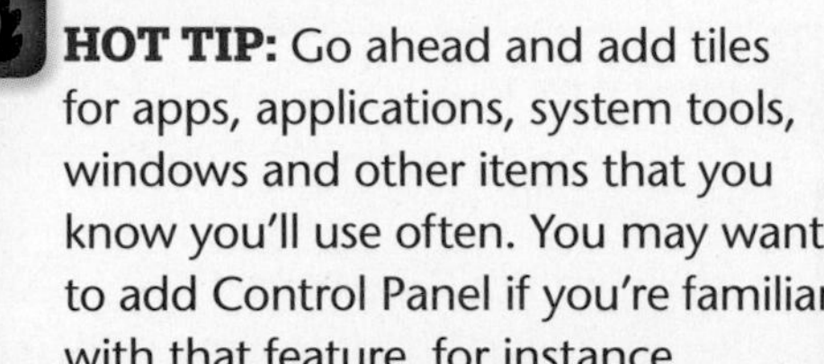

HOT TIP: Go ahead and add tiles for apps, applications, system tools, windows and other items that you know you'll use often. You may want to add Control Panel if you're familiar with that feature, for instance.

Remove a tile from the Start screen

You remove an unwanted tile from the Start screen by selecting it and then choosing Unpin from Start. If you like, you can select multiple tiles to remove at once.

1. Right-click or tap, hold and drag downward on any tile you'd like to remove.
2. Repeat as desired to select additional tiles.
3. Click or tap Unpin from Start.

HOT TIP: After you've removed unwanted tiles, reposition what's left by dragging the remaining tiles to the desired positions.

DID YOU KNOW?

When you remove a tile from the Start screen you don't uninstall it. You can always access it (and even add it back) from the All Apps screen.

Turn live tiles on or off

You may have started to notice that most of the apps you've explored thus far (including Weather, Calendar and Travel) become 'live' after you use them. That means they show up-to-date information on the Start screen. Here Weather, Sports and Finance are live. If this bothers you, you can disable the live feature.

1 Note the tiles that are currently live. (Three of the four tiles shown here are live.)

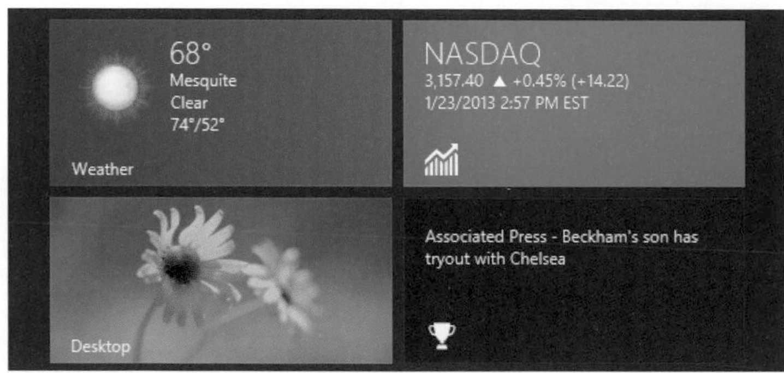

2 Right-click the live tile you want to turn off.

3 Click Turn live tile off.

4 Repeat these steps but click Turn live tile on to undo this.

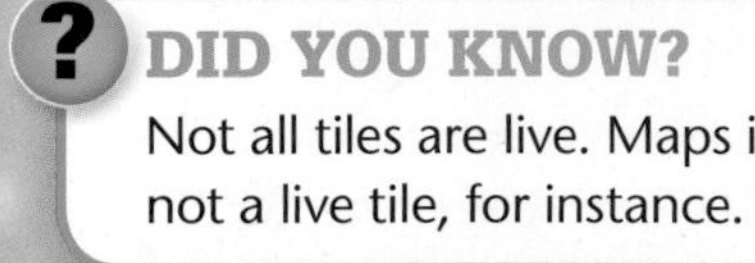

DID YOU KNOW?
Not all tiles are live. Maps is not a live tile, for instance.

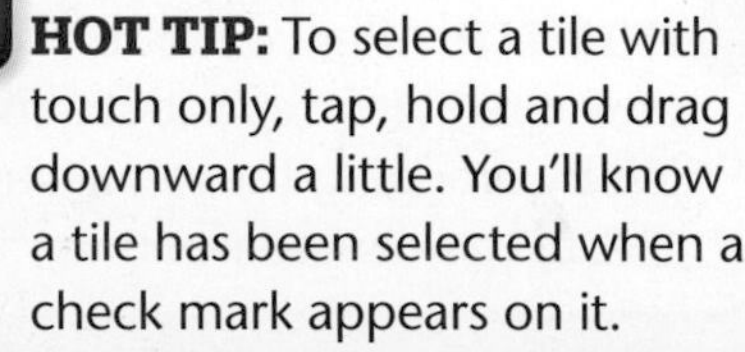

HOT TIP: To select a tile with touch only, tap, hold and drag downward a little. You'll know a tile has been selected when a check mark appears on it.

Make app tiles larger or smaller

You can make large, rectangular tiles smaller and square. In the future additional options will be available. You may want to make larger tiles smaller so that you can fit more tiles in the Start screen viewing area (so that you don't have to scroll so much).

1. Right-click a rectangular tile.
2. Click Smaller.

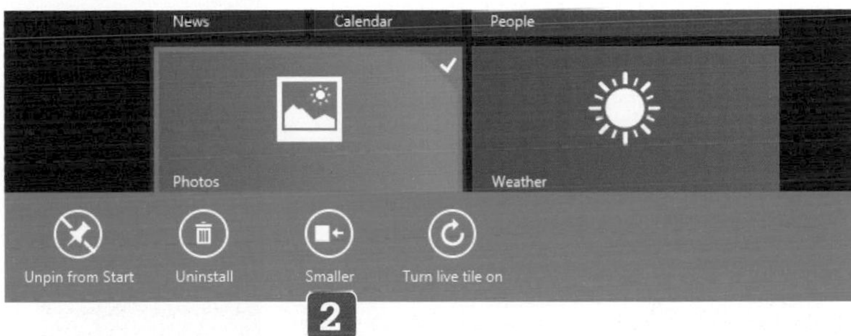

3. To undo this, repeat and click Larger.
4. Repeat as desired. Here most of the tiles are small.

Change the Start screen background

When you set up your Windows 8 computer, you chose the colour of the Start screen's background (we chose green but sometimes revert to blue). You can change the colour from the PC settings interface (also called the PC settings hub).

1. Bring up the charms and click Settings. (You can use the keyboard shortcut Windows key + C, flick in from the right side of the screen using your thumb, or position the cursor in the bottom right or top right corner of the screen.)
2. Click Change PC settings.
3. In the left pane click Personalize; in the right pane click Start screen.

4. Move the slider to the desired colour and click the desired design.

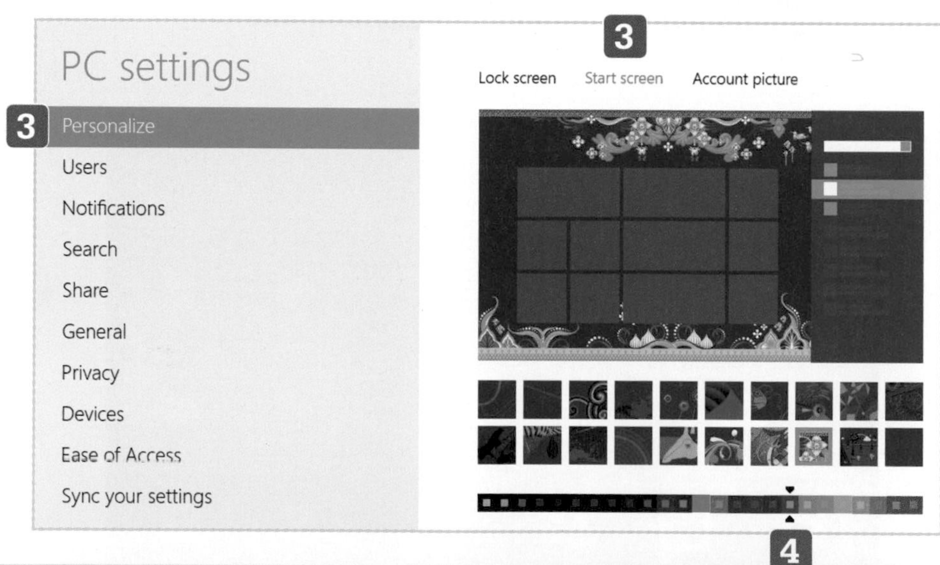

? DID YOU KNOW?

If you use a Microsoft account to log in to your Windows 8 computer, and if you make changes to how your computer looks as outlined in this chapter, then when you log on to any other Windows 8 computer or tablet with that same Microsoft account, those changes will be applied there too.

HOT TIP: Notice when you change the Start screen background the colour of the categories in the PC settings hub changes too.

Name a group of apps

The last bit of personalising left to do is to name the groups of apps you've created. If you haven't yet finalised your Start screen layout, do so before continuing by dragging and dropping and removing and adding the apps and desktop apps you want to have access to from the Start screen.

1 Click the – sign in the bottom right corner of the Start screen.

2 Right-click a group of apps and click Name group on the toolbar that appears.

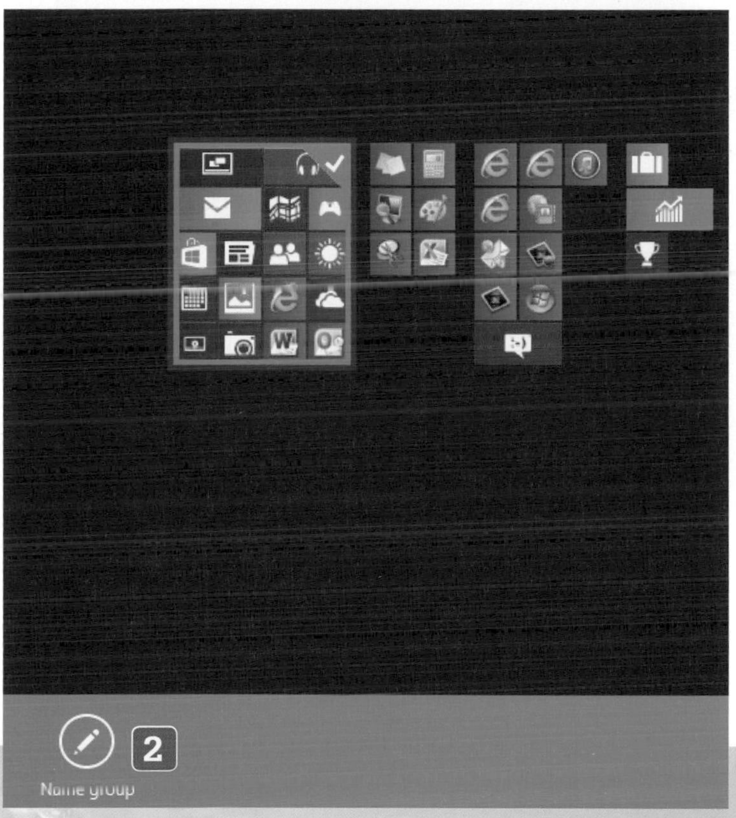

? DID YOU KNOW?

You can remove the name of a group by repeating the steps here. When you're ready to name the group, simply delete what is there so it is blank and click Name.

3 Type the name for the group and click Name.

4 Click once on an empty area of the screen to return to the default view.

5 Note the new name.

? DID YOU KNOW?

You can add even more items to the Start screen than have been introduced here. For instance, you can add a tile for a folder that you can only access from the desktop. You'll learn how to add additional items throughout this book as the need arises.

Create a PIN for faster access to the Start screen

When you log in to your Windows 8 device, you have to type a password. This can become tiring after a while, especially if you don't have a physical keyboard. Even if you do have a keyboard, typing a complex password still takes time and can be difficult if your hands are arthritic, cold or large. You can change your login requirements so that you need only enter a numeric personal identification number (PIN) instead.

1. At the Start screen, type PIN. (If you don't have access to a physical keyboard, from the Settings charm, tap Keyboard and tap Touch keyboard and handwriting panel.)
2. On the right side of the screen, click Settings.
3. Click Create or change PIN.

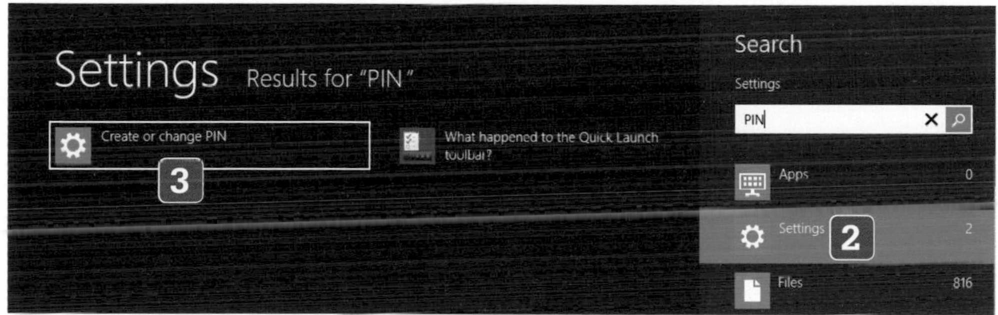

4. Click Create a PIN.
5. Type your current password, click OK, and then enter the desired PIN two times.
6. Click Finish.

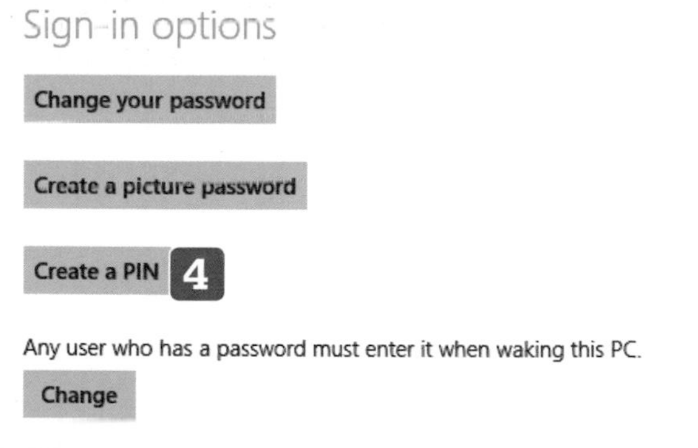

HOT TIP: You create a PIN in PC settings. You can use this same interface to configure many of the personalisation tasks you'll find in this chapter and others.

HOT TIP: When creating a PIN try to avoid things like 12345 or 9876. Avoid using your birthday too. (Make it at least a little difficult to guess!)

4 Use the Internet Explorer Start screen app

Introduction

The Internet Explorer Start screen app is a great option for surfing the internet on a laptop or a tablet. It is clean and streamlined, and is not cluttered with tabs, menu bars and similar elements. Like other apps, it has hidden toolbars that you can access with a right-click or a flick upward on a touch screen, if and when you do need access to the available features. Because of this, you are able to use your entire screen to view web pages.

Because it is so streamlined, though, Internet Explorer (IE) doesn't offer all of the features you may be used to in a web browser. It's more like a web browser you'd use on an iPad or a smartphone. If you need more than what IE offers, you will want to use the traditional version of Internet Explorer. You can find that on the desktop (just like in the olden days!). In this chapter we'll focus on the IE app, the app you'll find on the Start screen. You'll learn about the desktop version in Chapter 10.

Know what you get from the IE Start screen app

Windows 8 comes with two versions of Internet Explorer. One is an app on the Start screen, and one is an application that opens on the desktop. Here are some of the major differences between them.

- Anytime you click a link in an email, message, document and so on, the IE app (the one on the Start screen) will open. It is the default.
- The IE app is available from the Start screen and its tile is shown here, but the desktop version is not (although you can add it if you want).
- The IE app is a better option on tablets, laptops and computers with small screens than its full-version counterpart, because the IE app was built to offer a full-screen browsing experience in a limited space.

- The IE app on the desktop is a traditional application that looks and acts much like its predecessor. It opens on the desktop.
- Sometimes, you will have to switch from the IE app to the desktop version if a web page won't function properly, such as when unsupported technologies are required; to access a group of favourites or home pages you've set; or to access traditional menus including File, View, Tools and so on.

HOT TIP: Even if you are uncomfortable at first, get to know the IE app. Once you are used to it, you'll find it's a much better fit for your laptop than the traditional version.

DID YOU KNOW?

View on the desktop is an option in the IE Start screen app. This means you can use the app until you need the other version, and then switch to it easily.

Explore the Internet Explorer app

You open the Internet Explorer app by clicking or tapping its tile on the Start screen. When the app opens, look for the features listed here. You must right-click or flick upward from the bottom of a touch screen to access these features. By default, nothing shows on the screen but the website itself.

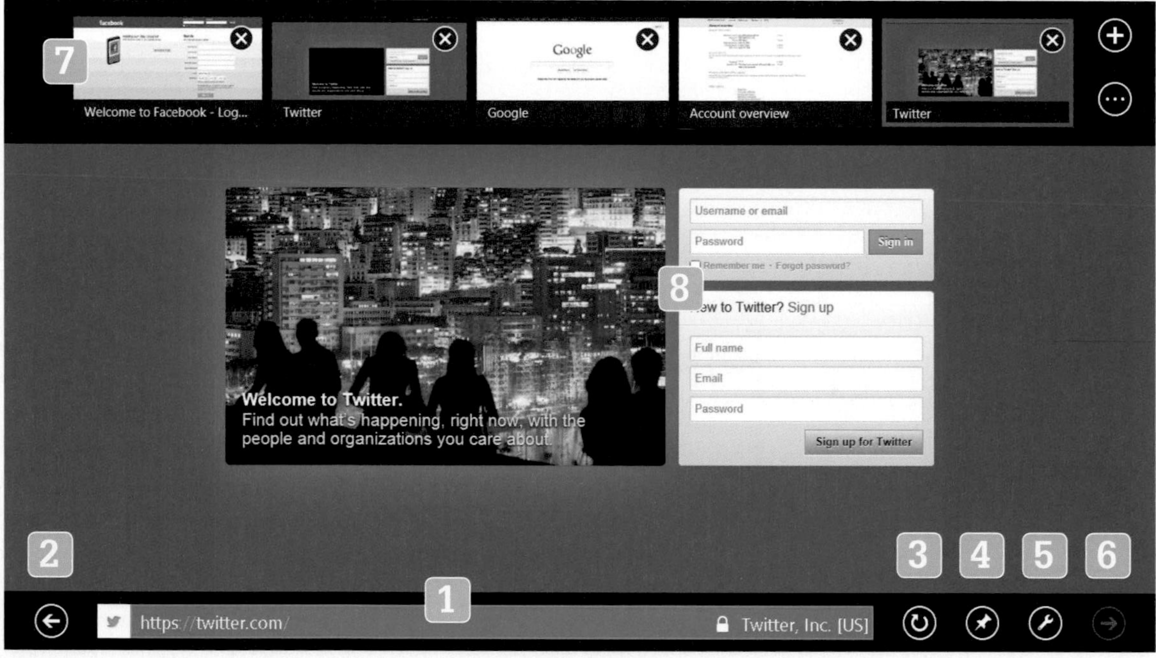

1. Address bar. Here we've navigated to https://twitter.com.
2. Back. Use this to return to the previously visited web page.
3. Refresh. Use to reload the web page.
4. Pin to Start. Click to create a tile for the web page on the Start screen.

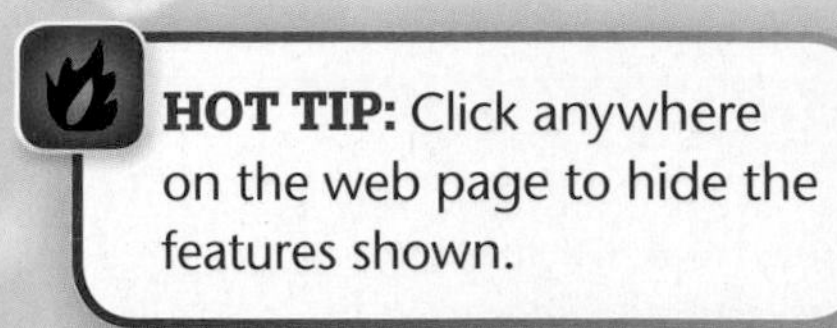

HOT TIP: Click anywhere on the web page to hide the features shown.

5 Page Tools. Click to find something on a page, view the website in the Desktop app, and more.

6 Forward. Click to move to a previously visited page. This is available only after clicking the Back button.

7 Tabs. Click any thumbnail to return to a previously tabbed website. Note the option to remove the thumbnail (X), and the options to open and close tabs (+ and …).

8 Content. This is the web page content.

DID YOU KNOW?

If you position your cursor in the middle of the left or right side of the page, transparent Back and Forward arrows appear.

Visit a website

There are several ways to visit a website, including clicking links on other web pages, in emails and in messages. You can also navigate to a website by typing its name in the Address bar.

1. From the Start screen, click the Internet Explorer tile.
2. Click once in the Address Bar. (Right-click if it's not visible.)
3. Type the desired web address.
4. If you've visited the page before, it will appear above the Address bar and you can click it. If not, simply press Enter on the keyboard or click the right-facing arrow.

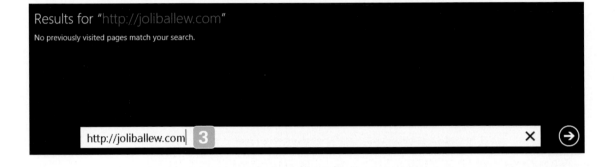

HOT TIP: Navigate to a second and third website using the Address bar, and then practise using the Back and Forward buttons and arrows.

DID YOU KNOW?
After you've used the IE app for a while, the app will determine what websites you visit most. Then, when you click inside the Address bar, thumbnails will be available to quickly access those sites.

Manage tabs with the hidden toolbar

You saw the tabs on the hidden toolbar on the previous page. You use these features to manage open websites and to open and close tabs. Before you continue on, navigate to several websites from the Address bar or using any method desired.

1. Right-click the screen.
2. Click the X by any tab to close it.

3. Click the + sign to open a new, blank page, and type the desired address or choose from the thumbnails that appear.

4. Right-click again, and click the three dots (...). Note the options and explore as desired.

? DID YOU KNOW?
If you opt to open a new tab using the InPrivate option (available from the ellipses from Tab tools), IE won't remember the website in its History list, and won't save anything else related to your visit either.

HOT TIP: To close all of your open tabs quickly, right-click, click the Tab tools icon (...), and click Close Tabs.

Pin a website to the Start screen

If there's a website you visit often you can pin it to the Start screen. Then you can simply click the tile to open the IE app and go directly to it.

1. Use the IE app to navigate to a website.
2. Right-click to show the toolbars.
3. Click the Pin to Start charm and click Pin to Start.
4. If desired, type a new name for the website.
5. Click Pin to Start again.

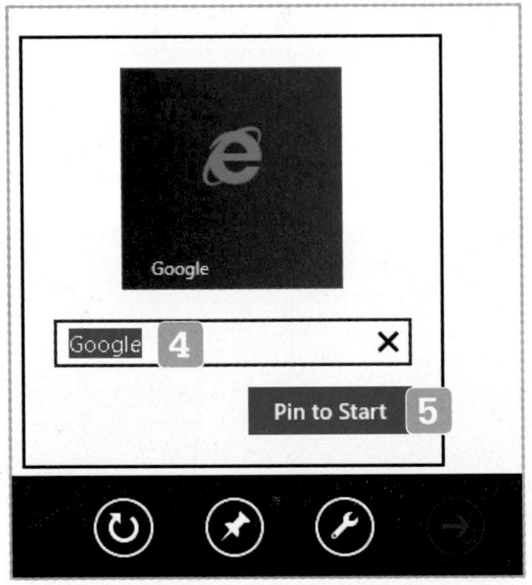

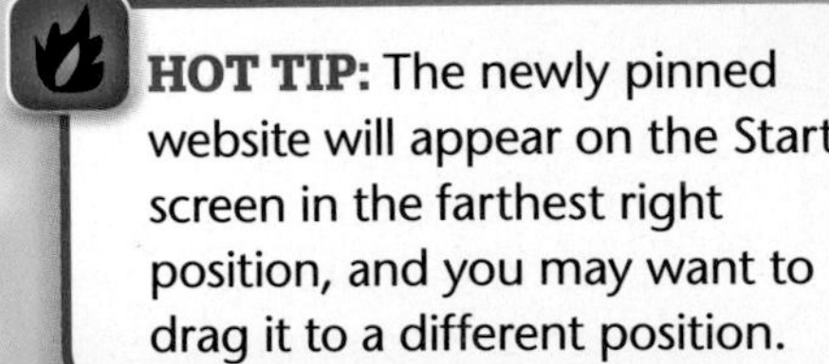

HOT TIP: The newly pinned website will appear on the Start screen in the farthest right position, and you may want to drag it to a different position.

DID YOU KNOW?
If you use a Microsoft account to log in to Windows 8, when you log in to another Windows 8 machine your Start screen configuration will be available there too.

Explore Settings

You can configure settings for the IE app from the Settings charm. These include the ability to delete your browsing history, enable or disable the ability for websites to ask for your physical location, and more.

1. Open the IE app and, using any method, bring up the charms. You can use Windows key + C.
2. Click Settings.
3. Click Internet Options.

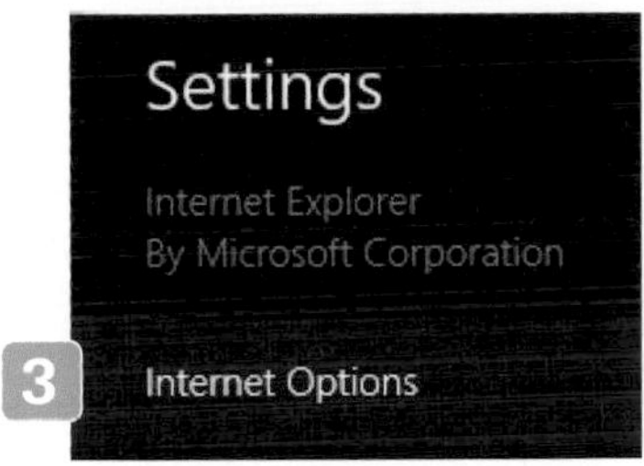

4. Explore the options.

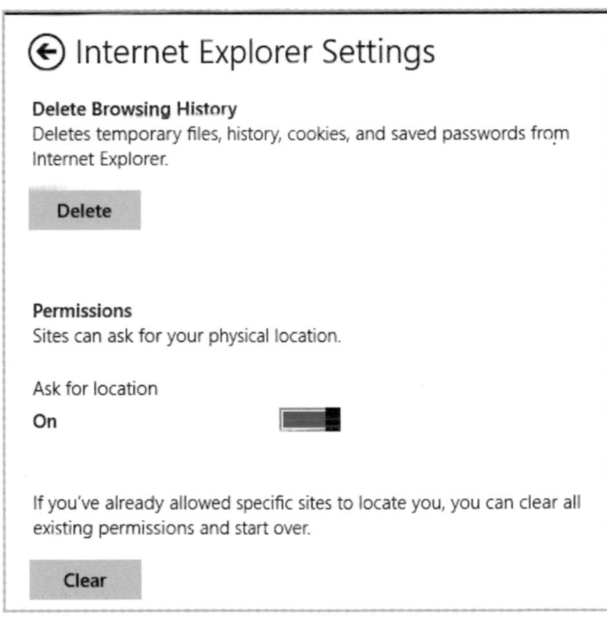

Internet Explorer Settings
Delete Browsing History
Deletes temporary files, history, cookies, and saved passwords from Internet Explorer.
Delete
Permissions
Sites can ask for your physical location.
Ask for location
On
If you've already allowed specific sites to locate you, you can clear all existing permissions and start over.
Clear

DID YOU KNOW?
Permissions is another option from the Settings charm while in the IE app. Here you can enable or disable notifications.

HOT TIP: You can zoom in and out from the Internet Explorer Settings area.

5 Get your email with the Mail app

Introduction

Windows 8 comes with only one built-in option for managing email, the Mail app. Because it is an app and not a full-fledged desktop application, it offers minimal features when compared to programs like Windows Live Mail or Microsoft Office Outlook. It is meant to be that way though, and because of its minimalistic approach it is streamlined and easy to use.

If you have already signed in to your Windows 8 laptop or tablet with a compatible Microsoft account like one from Hotmail.com or Live.com, Mail is already set up. If you have a third-party email account, you'll have to add that manually. Once your email accounts are ready, accessing new mail and composing your own is a simple process.

Access email

If you are logged on with a Microsoft account, the Mail app is already set up and ready to use.

1. Locate the Mail icon on the Start screen and click it.

2. Explore the Inbox and folders.
3. If you see mail there, click once to read it.

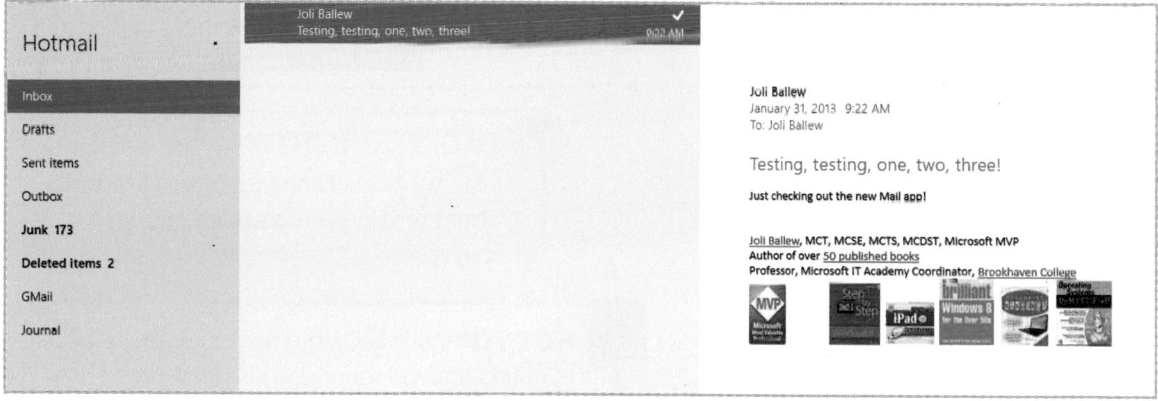

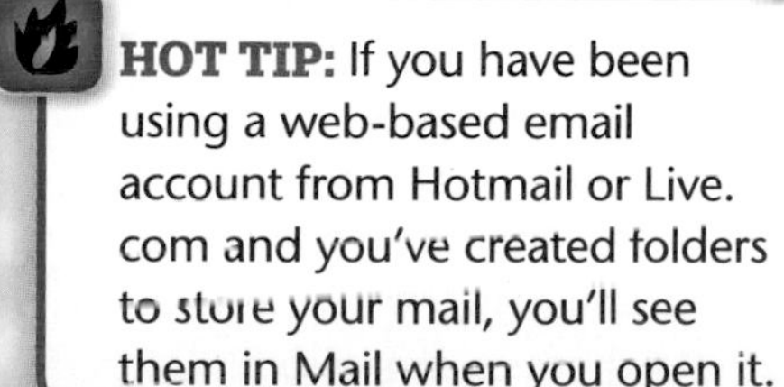

HOT TIP: If you have been using a web-based email account from Hotmail or Live.com and you've created folders to store your mail, you'll see them in Mail when you open it.

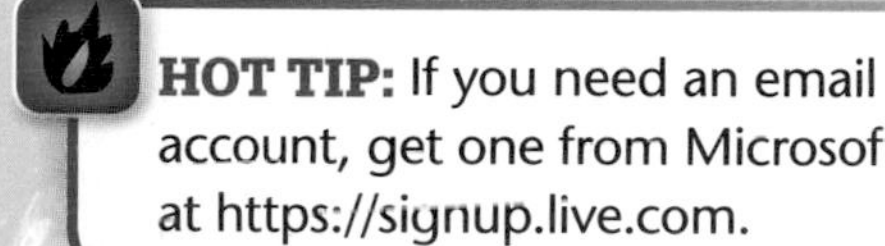

HOT TIP: If you need an email account, get one from Microsoft at https://signup.live.com.

Set up a third-party email account

If you use an email account you obtained from an entity other than Microsoft (such as Gmail), you'll have to set up the account manually. You access the option to add an account from the Settings charm while inside the Mail app.

1. Open Mail and then access the charms. You can use the Windows key + C or flick inward from the right side of a touch screen. Click Settings.
2. From the Settings options, click Accounts.
3. Click Add an Account (not shown).
4. Choose the type of account to add.
5. Type the required information when prompted, including your email account and password.
6. Click Connect.
7. If you receive an email that requires you to finish setting up your account, follow the directions provided to do so.

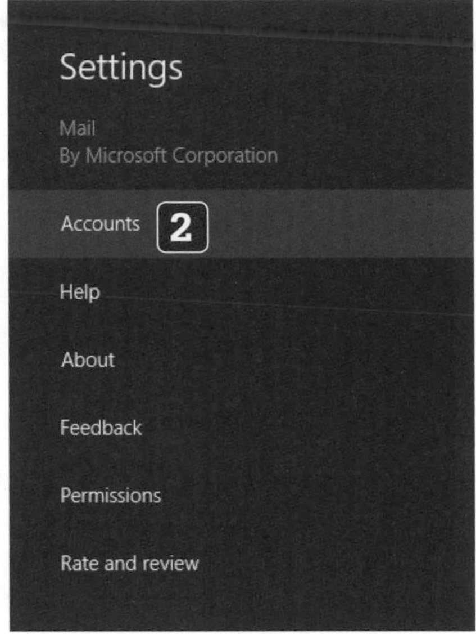

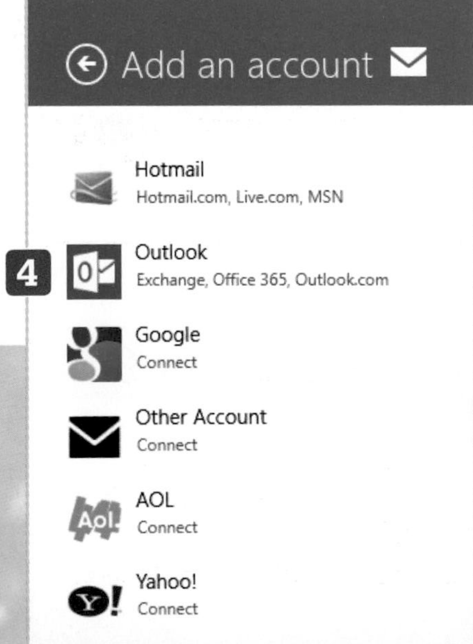

DID YOU KNOW?
Mail supports Exchange email accounts. These are corporate email accounts.

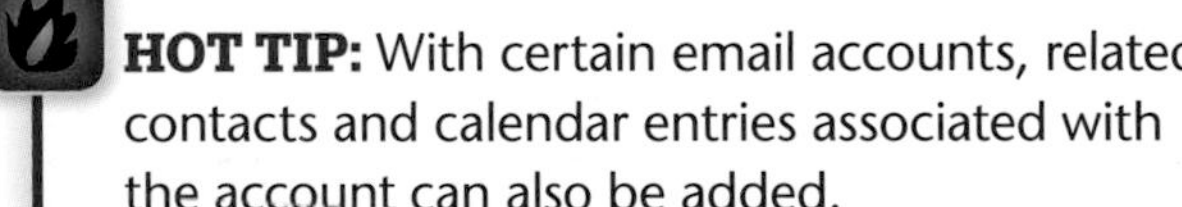

HOT TIP: With certain email accounts, related contacts and calendar entries associated with the account can also be added.

HOT TIP: At the website for Gmail, Hotmail, Live Mail and so on, create folders (or labels) for organising email you want to keep (perhaps Travel, Grandkids and Hobbies). You'll see those folders in the Mail app the next time you log on, and you can move related mail into them to organise it.

Read email

The Mail app gets email on its own; you don't have to do anything except to wait for email to arrive. If you want to check for email manually though, you can click the Sync charm any time you want.

1. If you have more than one email account configured, select the account to use.

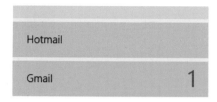

2. Right-click the screen or flick upward to view the charms. Click Sync.

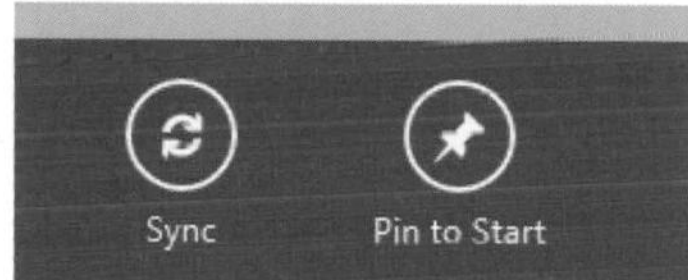

3. Click the email to read.

ALERT: Each email account you configure has its own Inbox; email from multiple accounts isn't grouped together in one folder, at least at the time this book was published.

HOT TIP: Always delete email immediately after you read it if you don't need to keep it for future reference. This will help keep your inboxes clean and tidy.

WHAT DOES THIS MEAN?

Inbox: This folder holds mail you've received.

Outbox: This folder holds mail you've written but have not yet sent (or has not been sent).

Sent Items: This folder stores copies of messages you've sent.

Deleted Items: This folder holds mail you've deleted.

Drafts: This folder holds messages you've started and saved but not completed. Click the X in a new message and click Save draft to put an email in progress here.

Junk: This folder holds email that is probably spam. You should check this folder occasionally, since Mail may put email in there you want to read.

Compose and send a new email

You compose an email message by clicking the + sign in the upper right hand corner of the Mail interface. You input who the email should be sent to and the subject, and then you type the message. If you prefer, you can click the + sign that is located just to the right of the To line, and choose your recipient(s) from the People app (which you'll learn about in the next chapter).

1. Click the + sign.

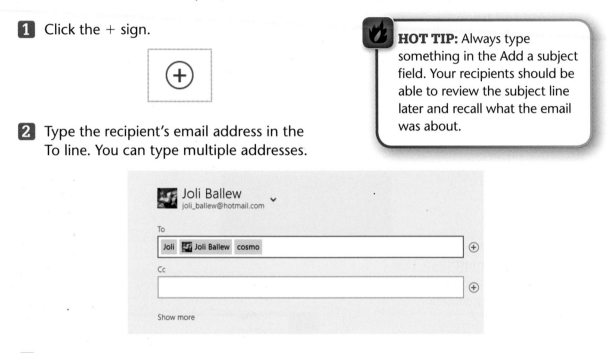

2. Type the recipient's email address in the To line. You can type multiple addresses.

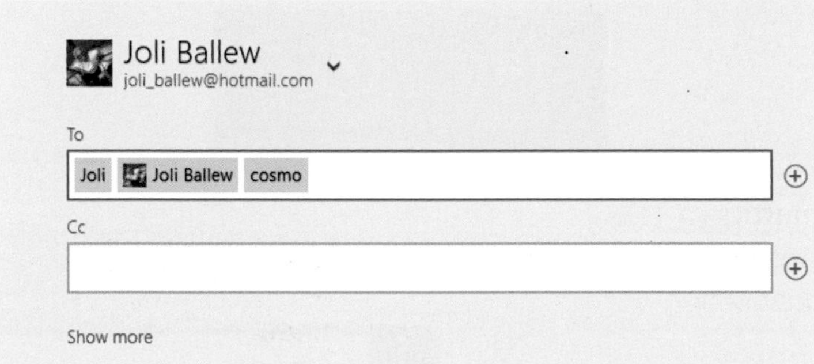

3. Type a subject in the Add a subject field.
4. Type the message in the body pane under the subject field.
5. Click the Send icon.

HOT TIP: Always type something in the Add a subject field. Your recipients should be able to review the subject line later and recall what the email was about.

HOT TIP: You can compose emails even when you aren't connected to a network (such as when you are on a plane or away from a wi-fi network) and the emails will remain in your Outbox until a connection is available. They'll be sent automatically.

DID YOU KNOW?

If you want to send the email to someone and you don't need them to respond, you can put them in the CC line. This is a carbon copy.

If you want to send the email to someone and you don't want other recipients to know you have included them in the email, click Show More. Then, add the address in the resulting Bcc line. This is a blind carbon copy.

Add formatting to an email

Mail, like other apps, is streamlined. Thus, the formatting options are hidden away in the Mail toolbar. You access those options with a right-click of a mouse or track pad, or a flick upward with your finger on a touch screen. Once the options are available, you apply them as you would any formatting tools in any word processing program. You can only format text in the body of the email, though; you can't format text in the subject line.

DID YOU KNOW?

If you apply formatting options without any text selected, those options will be applied to all future text until you change them. If you select text and then apply formatting, the formatting is only applied to the selected text.

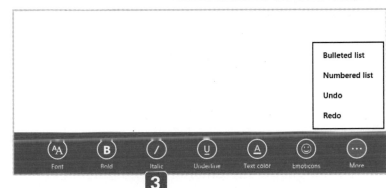

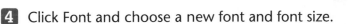

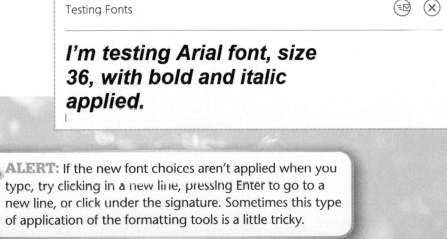

1. While composing an email, click in the body of the email (where you type your message).
2. Right-click to see the formatting options. (Note that you can click More to see additional options.)
3. Click any formatting option (perhaps Bold) and then click another (perhaps Italic).

Bulleted list
Numbered list
Undo
Redo
Font Bold Italic Underline Text color Emoticons More
3

4. Click Font and choose a new font and font size.
5. Type a few words in the body of the email.

Testing Fonts
I'm testing Arial font, size 36, with bold and italic applied.

ALERT: If the new font choices aren't applied when you type, try clicking in a new line, pressing Enter to go to a new line, or click under the signature. Sometimes this type of application of the formatting tools is a little tricky.

Respond to an email

You have a few options when responding to email you receive. You can forward the email to someone, reply to the sender, or reply to everyone the email was sent to (if there were multiple recipients).

1. Select the email you want to respond to.
2. Click the respond button, and then click the appropriate option.

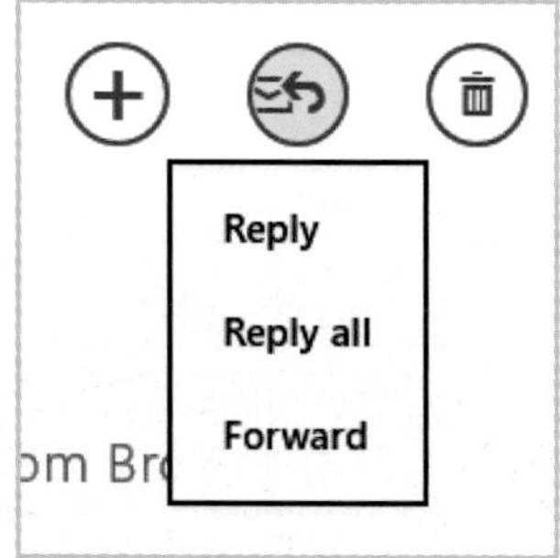

3. If desired, change the subject, and then type the message in the body pane.
4. Click Send.

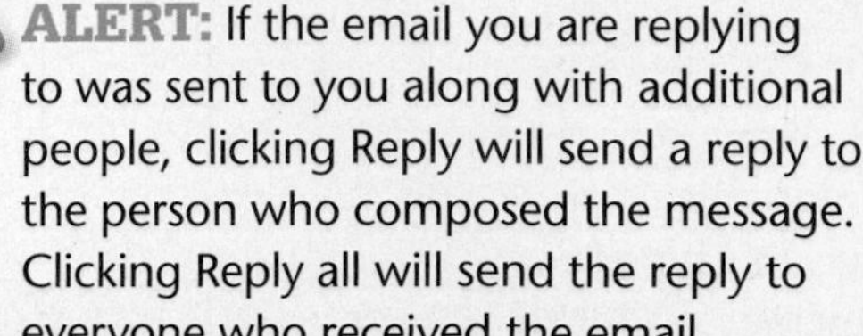

ALERT: If the email you are replying to was sent to you along with additional people, clicking Reply will send a reply to the person who composed the message. Clicking Reply all will send the reply to everyone who received the email.

HOT TIP: Mail offers formatting tools that you can use to change the font, font colour, font size and more. See previous sections.

Print an email

Sometimes you'll need to print an email. You access your printer from the Devices charm. Since it's likely that you do not have a printer attached to your laptop or tablet, you'll have to look for a shared printer.

1. Select the email to print.
2. Bring up the default charms (Windows key + C will show these) and click Devices.
3. Select the printer to use (not shown). We'll choose a printer that is shared from a Windows 7 desktop computer.
4. Configure the print options and click Print.

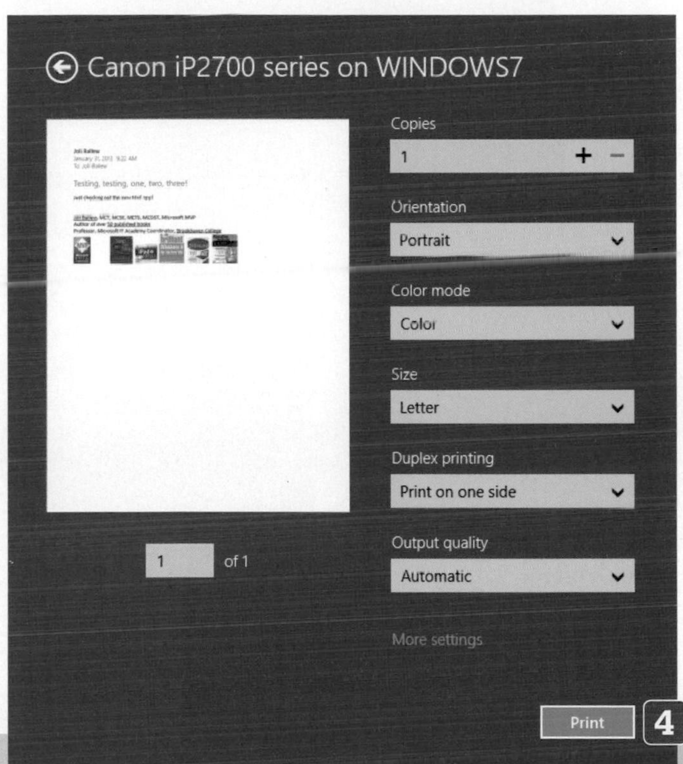

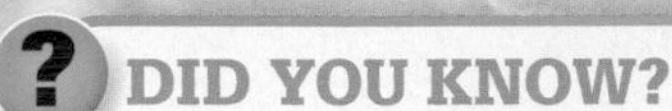

DID YOU KNOW?

If using a mouse or track pad is difficult for you, the keyboard shortcut Ctrl + P will open the Print window. From there, select the printer and configure printer options, then print.

Attach something to an email

Although email that contains only a message serves its purpose quite a bit of the time, often you'll want to send a photograph, a short video, a document or other data. When you want to add something to your message other than text, it's called adding an attachment.

HOT TIP: When searching for your attachments, click Go Up as needed to locate the folder that contains what you'd like to attach.

1. Click the + sign to create a new mail message; select the recipients, type a subject, and compose the email.
2. Right-click the screen and click Attachments.

3. Locate the file to attach and click it. You can select multiple files.
4. Click Attach (not shown).

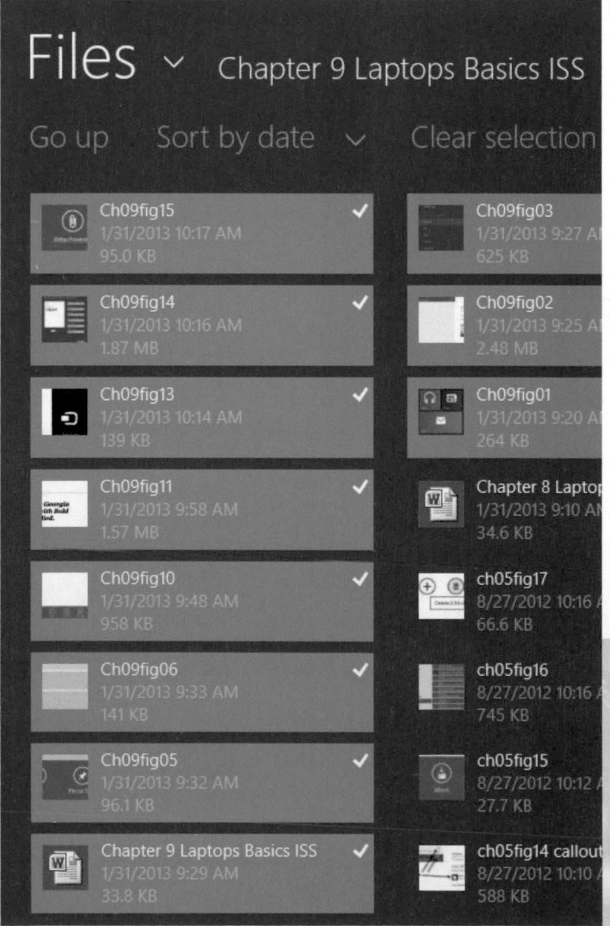

ALERT: Anything you attach won't be removed from your computer; instead, a copy will be created for the attachment.

ALERT: Don't send too many files in one email (in fact, what is shown here is quite a lot); it may take a long time to send and a long time to receive.

View an attachment in an email

If an email you receive from someone else contains an attachment, you'll see a paperclip. To open the attachment, first select the email, and then click the attachment to open. If you are prompted to download the rest of the message, do that too.

1. Click the email that contains the attachment.

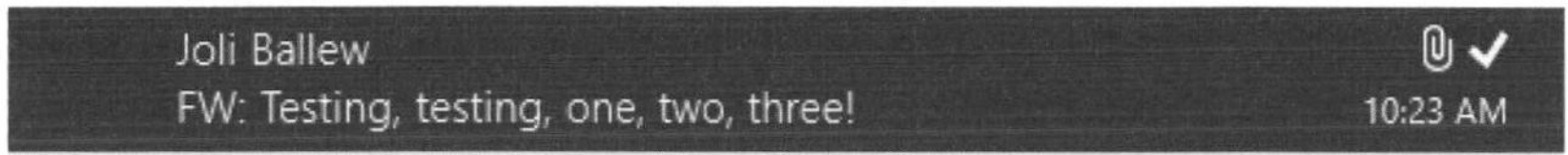

2. If applicable, click Download to download the attachment(s) to your laptop.

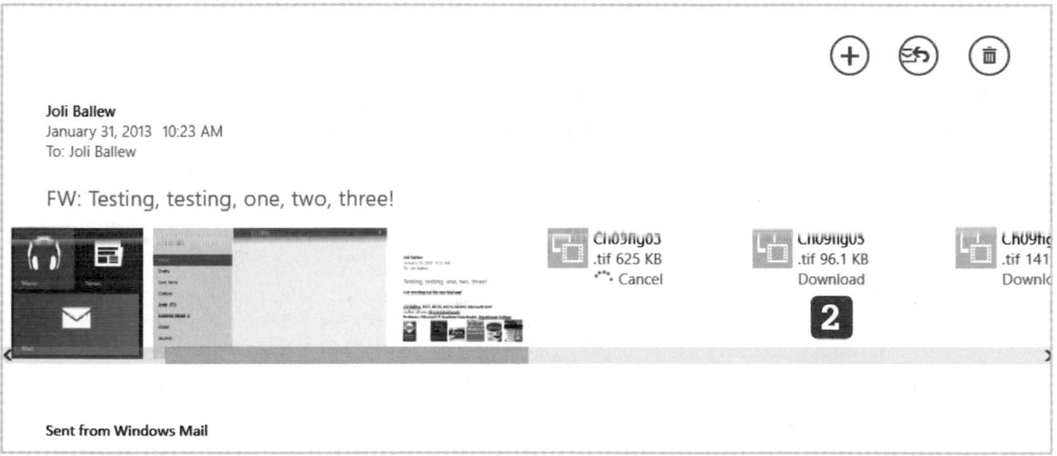

3. Once the download has completed, click the attachment name and choose to open the Item.

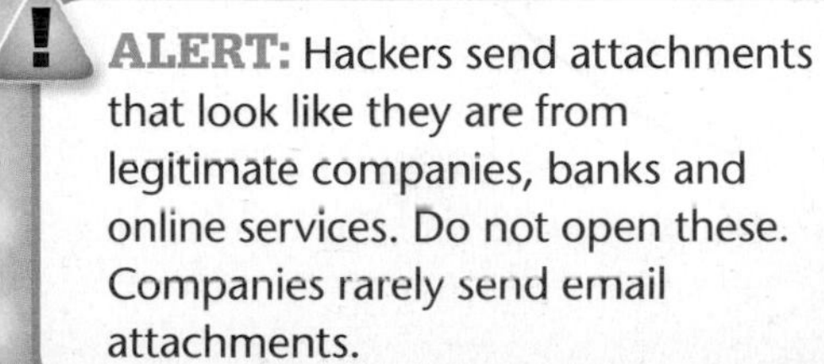

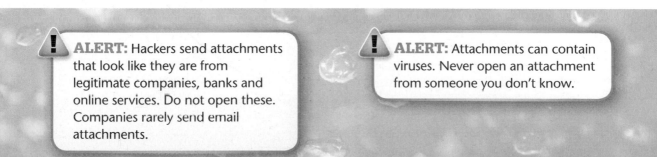

ALERT: Hackers send attachments that look like they are from legitimate companies, banks and online services. Do not open these. Companies rarely send email attachments.

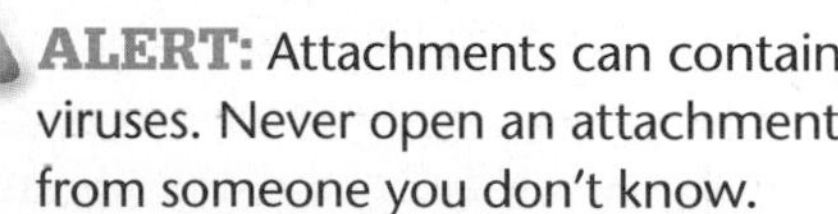

ALERT: Attachments can contain viruses. Never open an attachment from someone you don't know.

View junk email

All email accounts have some version of a *junk* folder. If an email is suspected to be spam, it gets sent there. (Spam is another word for junk email.) Unfortunately, sometimes email that is actually legitimate gets sent to the junk folder. Therefore, once a week or so you should look in this folder to see whether any email you want to keep is in there.

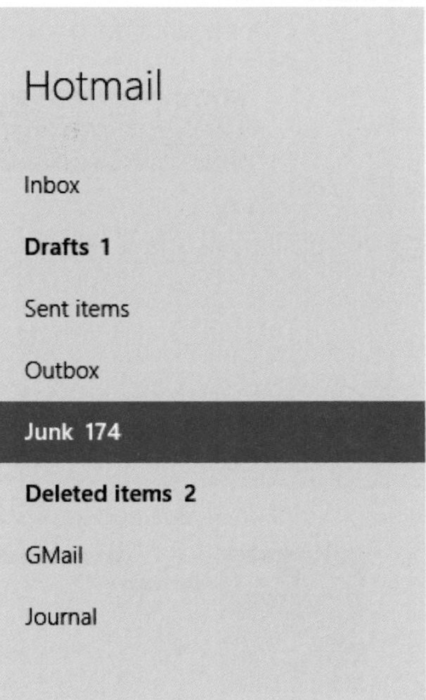

1. Click the junk folder one time. (Depending on the email account you use, it may say Junk Email, Junk, or something else.)
2. Use the scroll bars if necessary to browse through the email in the folder.
3. If you see an email that is legitimate, click it once.
4. Right-click to access the charms, and click Move.

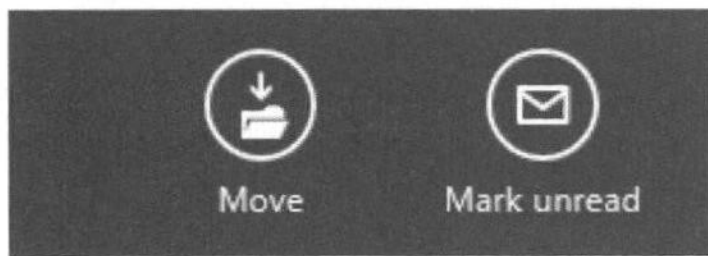

5. Click Inbox.

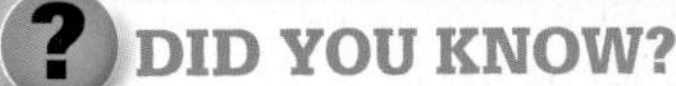

DID YOU KNOW?
The Mail app doesn't have all of the features that full-fledged programs do (such as Microsoft Office Outlook), so it's not possible to, say, add contacts from an email (easily), create subfolders, and so on.

ALERT: Mail requires routine maintenance which generally involves deleting email from various folders. You'll learn how to delete items in a folder next.

Delete email in a folder

It's easy to delete a single email: click the email one time and then click the Trash icon. It's a little more difficult to delete more than one email at a time.

1. Click any folder that contains email you'd like to delete. You may want to choose Sent Mail, Inbox, or even Junk.
2. Click the first entry in the list to delete, hold down the Shift key, and then click the last. This will select these two emails and all the ones in between.

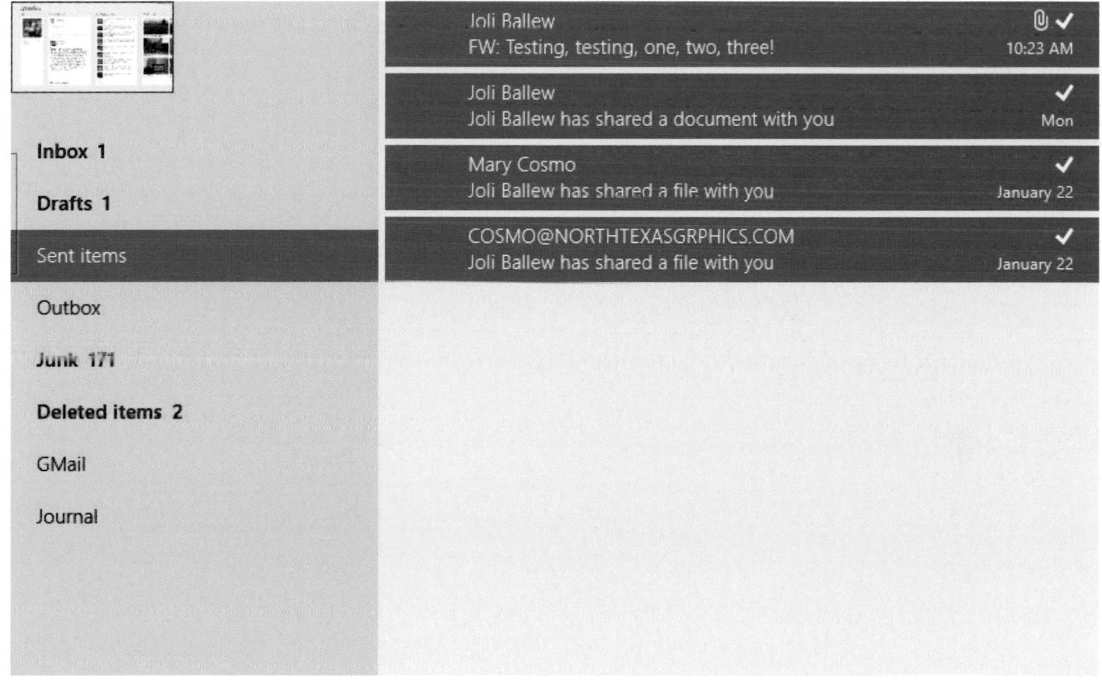

3. Click the Trash icon.

HOT TIP: If you use an email provider that lets you create folders on their website, do so. Those folders will appear in Mail. You can then move email you want to keep to them, and you won't have to delete them!

4. Repeat Step 1. This time, hold down the Ctrl key while selecting individual emails.
5. Click the Trash icon.

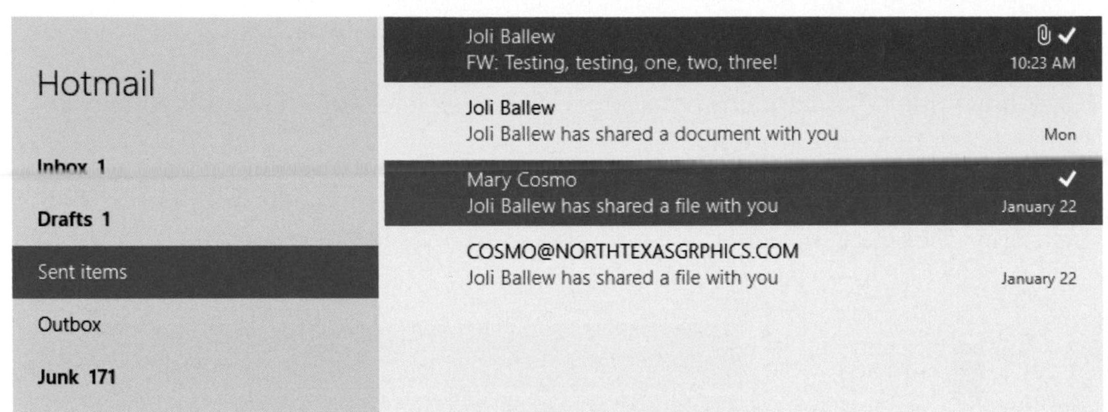

DID YOU KNOW?

Even if you delete an important email and decide you want it back, you can get it in the Deleted Items folder (at least until you empty that folder).

6 Explore the social networking apps

Introduction

Windows 8 offers two apps to help you keep in touch with others. One is Messaging, the other, People. Messaging lets you communicate using instant text messages. People lets you communicate with others through social networks such as Facebook and Twitter. There are additional apps you can obtain, such as Skype, to allow for even more ways to communicate. Skype, for instance, lets you hold video chats.

Get to know the Messaging app

You use the Messaging app to exchange instant messages with people you know. Instant messages are sort of like the text messages you may already be familiar with (which are sent from phone to phone through cellular connections), but instant messages are generally sent from computer to computer (or app to app) and use an available internet connection instead. Here are some other fun facts:

- Instant messages you send and receive using the Messaging app are text only. You can't send pictures or videos (at least not when this book was published).
- You can send instant messages from your computer to various smartphones, iPads and other devices (and back), but both devices must have a compatible messaging app installed on them.
- An instant message is sent over the internet, and thus no cellular connection is required.
- If you have a Microsoft account, the Messaging app may already be set up and ready to use.
- The Messaging app has its own tile on the Start screen.

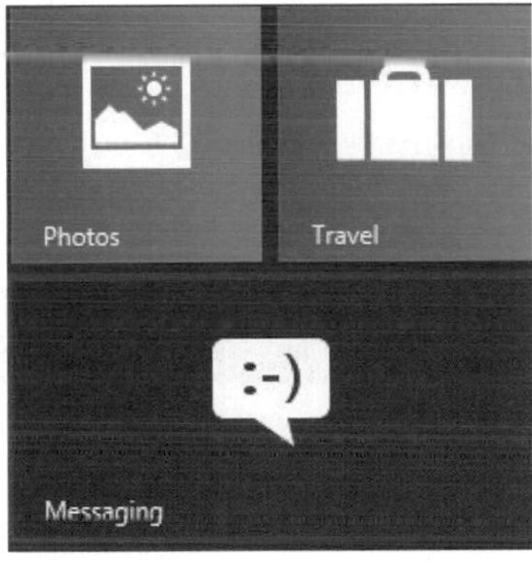

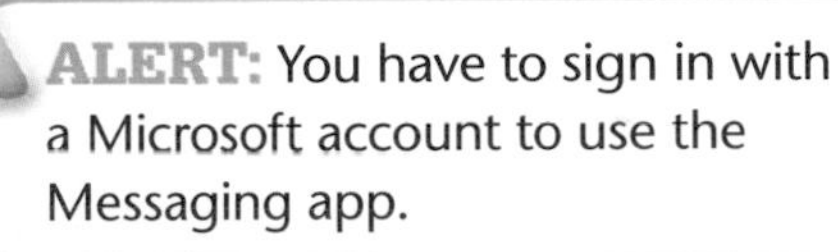

ALERT: You have to sign in with a Microsoft account to use the Messaging app.

HOT TIP: You can add a Facebook account to the Messaging app to communicate with your Facebook contacts. Read on to learn how.

Add social accounts to the Messaging app

Although you can use your Microsoft account (Messenger account) to communicate using the Messaging app, you can add others. If you have a Facebook account, for instance, you can add it and communicate with your Facebook friends. Currently these are the only two networks that are supported, but we expect more to be added soon.

1. Open the Messaging app from the Start screen.
2. If you see a message from the Windows team, Messaging is already set up for Messenger. If not, input your Microsoft account credentials.
3. To add your Facebook account:
   - Access the default charms (Windows key + C or flick inward from the right side of the screen).
   - Click the Settings charm and then click Accounts.
   - Click Add an account.
   - Choose Facebook from the resulting list.
   - Click Connect and input the required information.

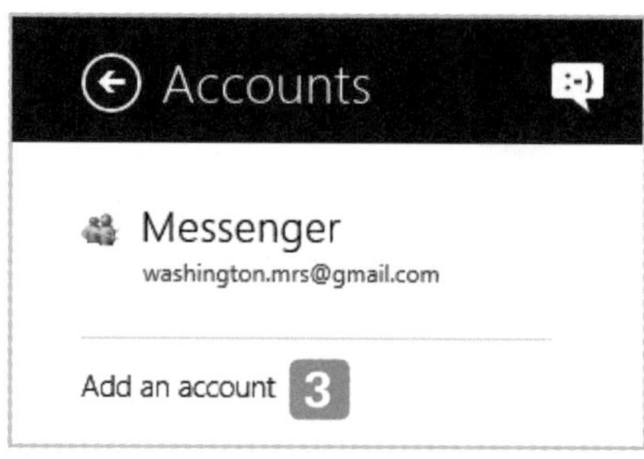

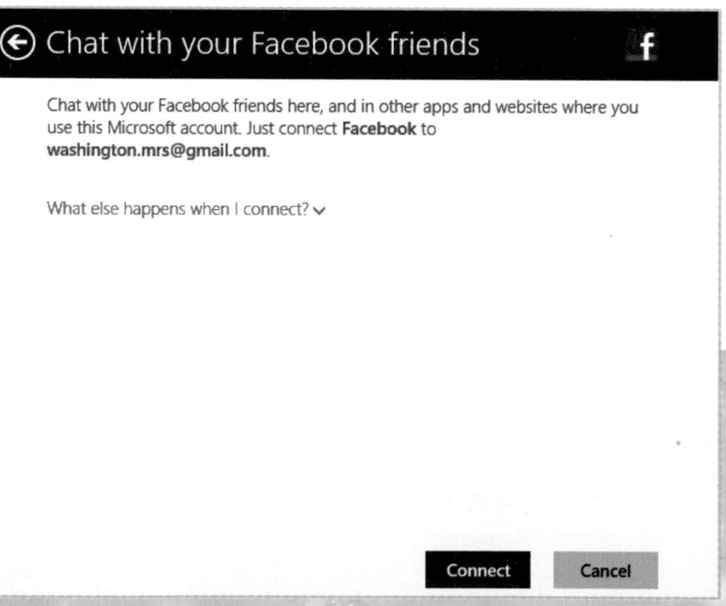

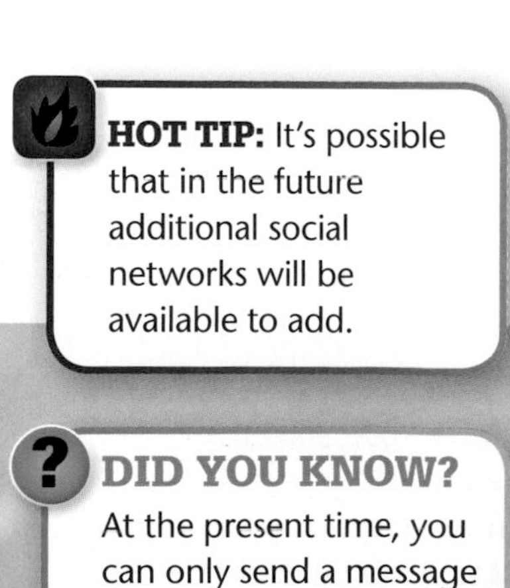

HOT TIP: It's possible that in the future additional social networks will be available to add.

DID YOU KNOW?

At the present time, you can only send a message to a Facebook friend if they are online.

Send an instant text message

Once you have a few contacts, you can start a conversation with one of them. It doesn't matter if they are Messenger contacts or Facebook contacts. To start a new conversation with someone (also called a 'thread'), follow these steps.

1 With the Messaging app open, click the + sign to start a new message.

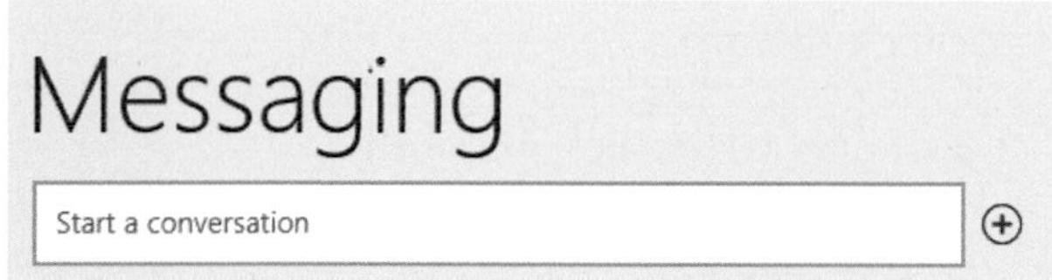

2 The People app will open; choose the desired contact and click Choose.

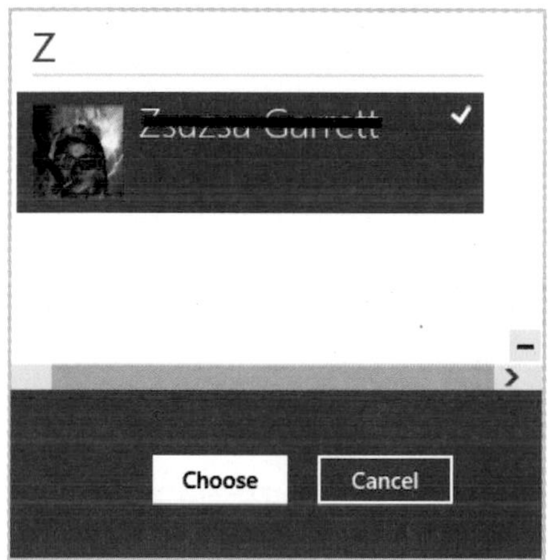

3 Type your message in the text message window and press Enter. Your message will appear at the top of the page.

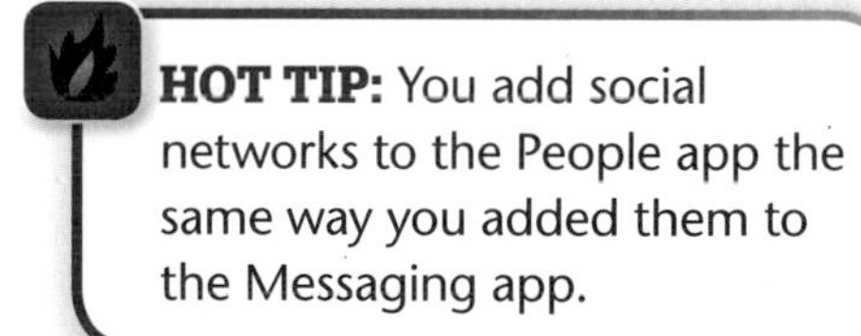

HOT TIP: You add social networks to the People app the same way you added them to the Messaging app.

DID YOU KNOW?
If you close the Messaging app and reopen it later, it will be just as you left it.

ALERT: An instant message is not the same thing as a text message. Instant messages are generally sent from computer to computer, or device to device, while simple texts are sent using cell phones.

Set up the People app

Like the Messaging app, you can add information about the social networks you belong to. When you do, you can see your friends' status updates, access their contact information, send them email and messages, and more. To get started, open the People app from the Start screen.

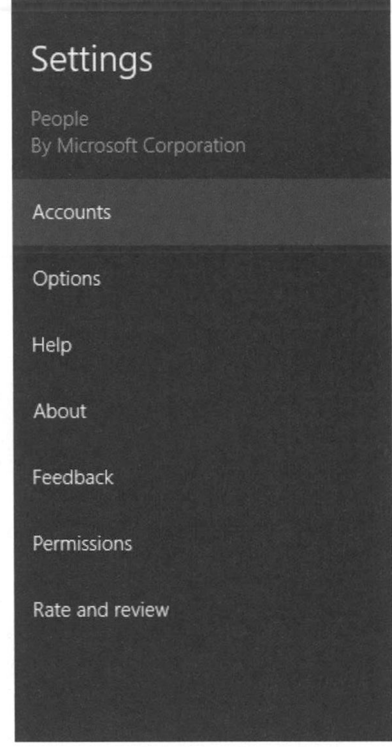

1. With the People app open, access the default charms (Windows key + C or flick inward).
2. Click the Settings charm and then click Accounts.
3. Click Add an account.
4. Choose the account from the resulting list.
5. Click Connect and input the required information.
6. Repeat to add all of your social accounts.

HOT TIP: You may not have to input this information if you've already input it for other apps. Once you tell Windows 8 something, it remembers it!

DID YOU KNOW?

If you position your mouse in the bottom right corner of the People app and click the – sign that appears, the screen will change from the large tiles you currently see for your contacts to small, alphabetic tiles you can use to go directly to that group of contacts. Click any tile to return to the default view.

View and edit contacts

The information you have for a contact may need to be updated manually if a person changes their phone number or email account, moves to a new address or gets a new job, among other things.

1. Locate the contact to edit in the People app.
2. Click the name of the contact so that it appears in its own screen (possibly with a social networking update to the right of it).

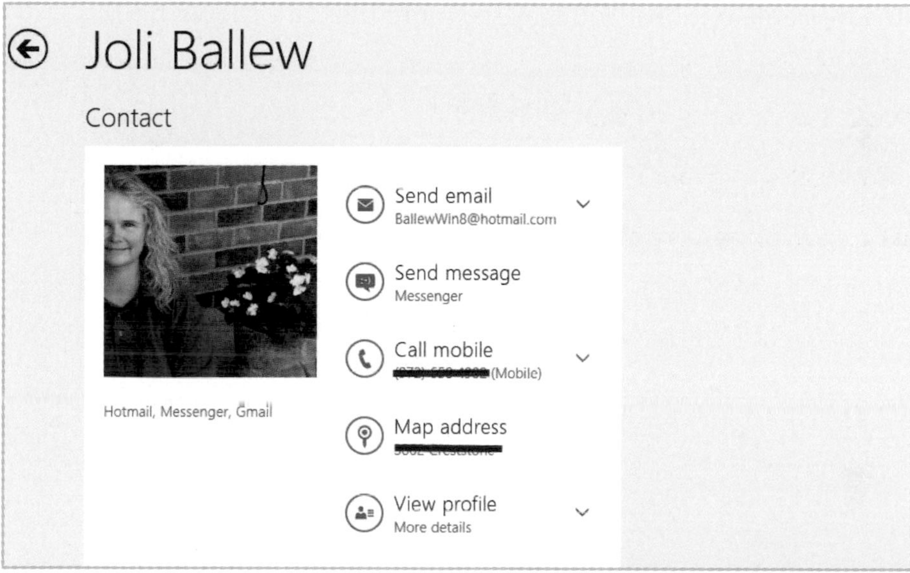

3. Right-click or flick upward and click Edit.

4. Replace or add data as required and click Save.

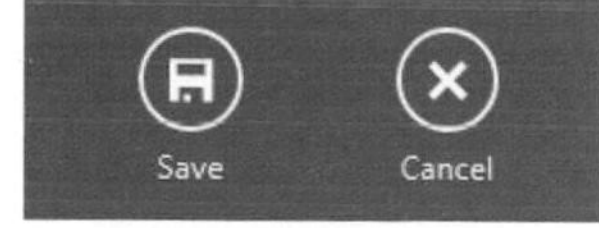

DID YOU KNOW?

Changes made by a contact may automatically appear in the People app if the contact makes those changes from a compatible social network you also belong to (and have added to the People app).

Connect with a contact

There are so many ways to communicate with a contact it would be difficult to try to describe them all. You can send an instant message or an email, call them on the phone, visit them in person, and so on. The People app puts all compatible options in one place.

1. Open the People app.
2. Locate the contact and click the contact name one time.
3. Note the available options. You may see more than are shown here.

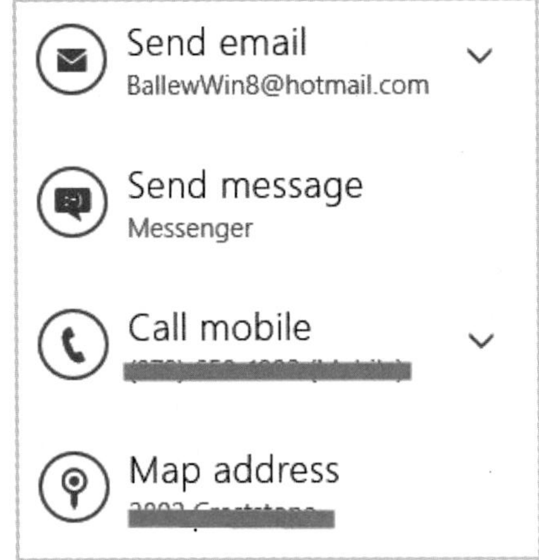

4. Click the contact option to use and continue as necessary.

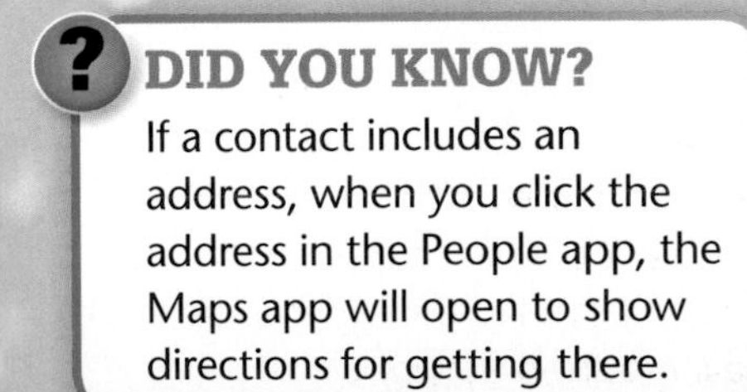

DID YOU KNOW?
If a contact includes an address, when you click the address in the People app, the Maps app will open to show directions for getting there.

HOT TIP: If you want to 'call' someone from the People app using your laptop or tablet, you'll have to get the Skype app.

Update your status on Facebook

You can update your Facebook status and compose a tweet (using Twitter, another social networking technology) from inside the People app.

1. Open the People app and click Me. (You may have to click a Back arrow or scroll left first.)
2. Click the arrow available under the What's new section (if applicable).

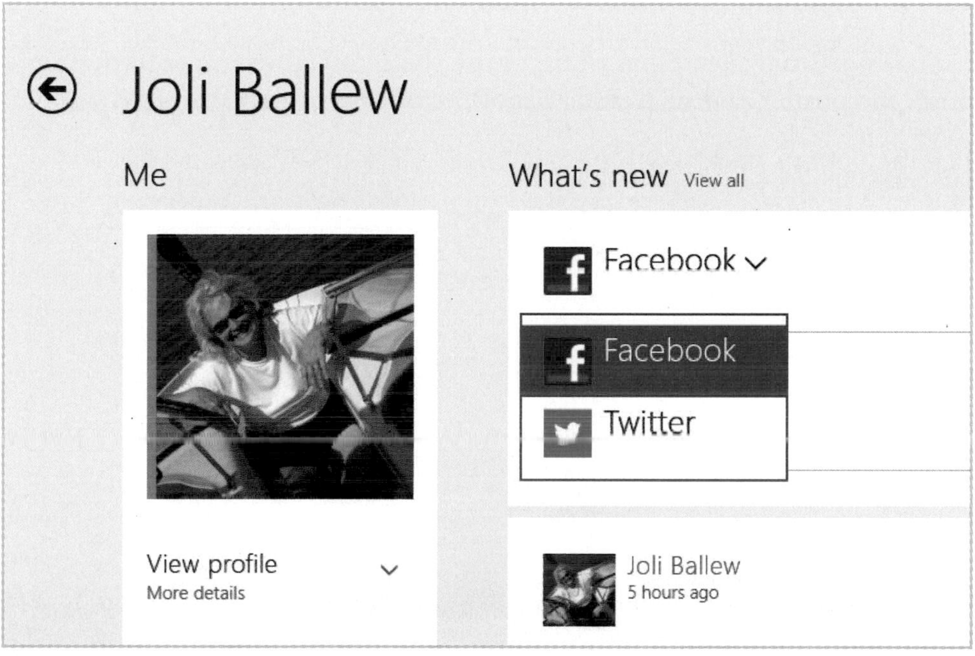

3. Select Facebook, Twitter or another available option.
4. Type your update or tweet as applicable.

HOT TIP: You can 'like' and comment on Facebook posts, and retweet and reply to Twitter entries from inside the People app.

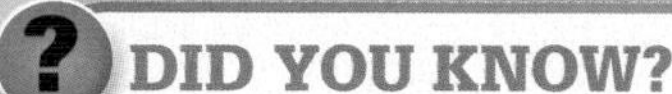

DID YOU KNOW?

At the time this book was written, you could only update your status on Facebook or tweet on Twitter. We expect more technologies to become available soon though.

View others' social networking updates

You view others' updates, posts and tweets from the What's new option (available under the Me option you just explored). You can click any option available under an entry to reply, like or respond to it, as applicable. If you have signed in with multiple social networks, you can filter what you see from the toolbar.

1. Open the People app and click the What's new tab.
2. Use your finger to flick left and right, or use the scroll wheel on your mouse to move through the posts. (There's a scroll bar at the bottom of the screen as well.)
3. Notice the options under each post or tweet. Click to respond as desired.
4. Right-click or flick upward and click Filter.
5. Choose which social network(s) you'd like to view.

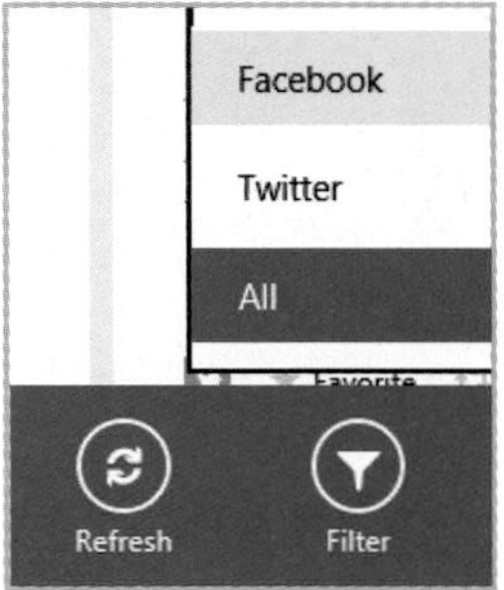

DID YOU KNOW?
The Refresh button, available next to Filter on the People toolbar, will refresh the information shown under What's new.

HOT TIP: To filter your contacts list by certain social networks, from the Settings charm, click Options and review the settings.

Get Skype

Skype is an app that lets you hold video conversations with others who also use Skype. You'll need to get Skype if you don't already have it, and then contact those who also use Skype to become a contact.

1. From the Start screen, click Store.
2. Use the Windows key + C to access the charms and click Search.
3. Type Skype in the search box; click Skype (shown second in the list here).

4. Click Install.
5. Click Install and type your Microsoft account and password if prompted.
6. From the Start screen, click Skype to open it.

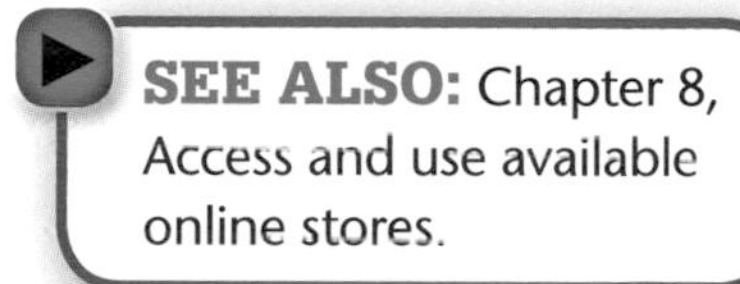

SEE ALSO: Chapter 8, Access and use available online stores.

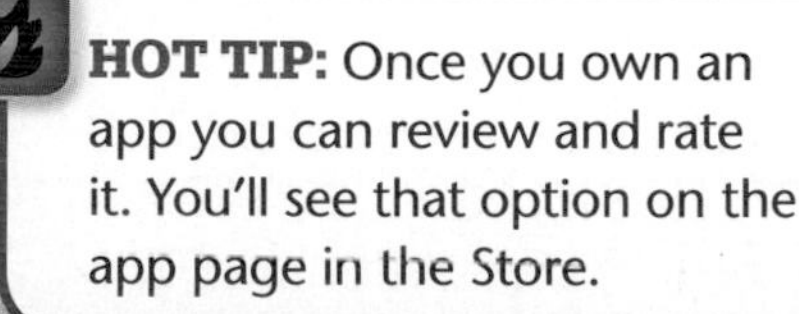

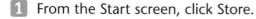

HOT TIP: Once you own an app you can review and rate it. You'll see that option on the app page in the Store.

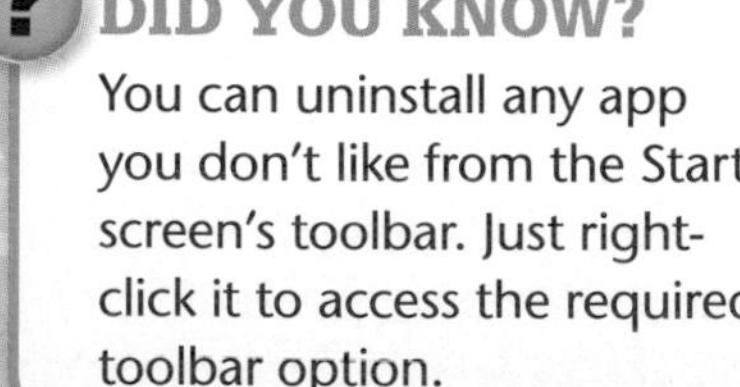

DID YOU KNOW?
You can uninstall any app you don't like from the Start screen's toolbar. Just right-click it to access the required toolbar option.

Initiate a Skype video chat

You will need to have at least one contact that also uses Skype if you want to try it out. You can right-click the Skype interface and click Add contact if you want to try to add contacts from your People app. Or, you can tell others your Skype name and ask them to add you. Whatever the case, once you have a Skype friend, you can call them.

1. Open Skype from the Start screen.
2. Click any contact you'd like to Skype with.
3. Note the options available:
   - A Video chat.
   - B Phone call.
   - C Add others to the conversation.
   - D Instant message.
4. Click any option and follow any prompts to get started.

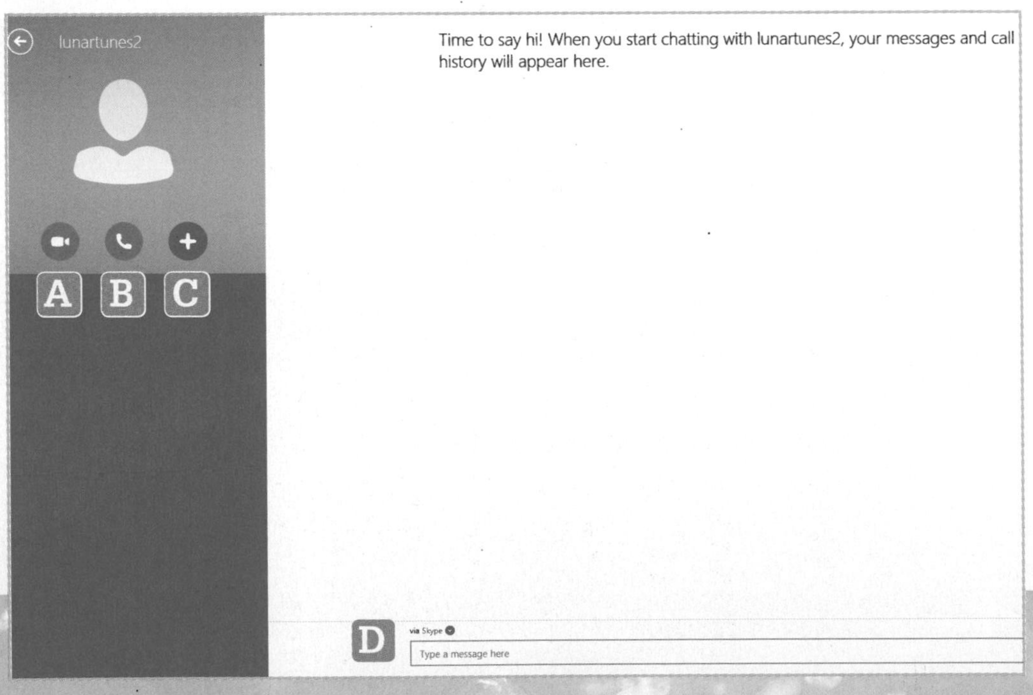

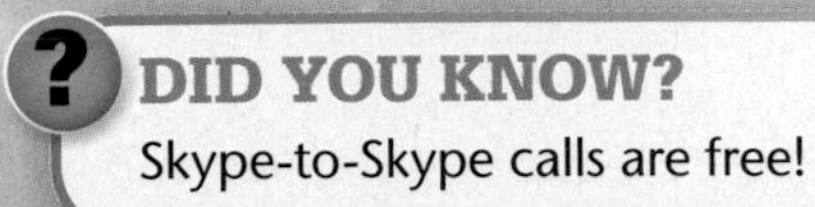

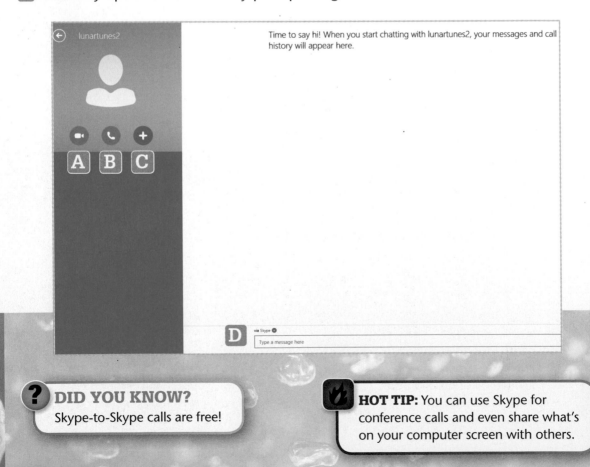

DID YOU KNOW?
Skype-to-Skype calls are free!

HOT TIP: You can use Skype for conference calls and even share what's on your computer screen with others.

7 Explore media apps

Introduction

Windows 8 comes with three distinct media apps. There's a Photos app a Music app, and a Video app. You can use these apps to access and view your media in various ways. You can watch a slide show of your favourite photos, for instance. You can play a song or album that you've copied to your laptop or tablet. You can watch a movie or a TV programme too, provided that the media is on your laptop or can be accessed from it.

Explore the Music app

The Music app, available from the Start screen, offers access to the music you have on your laptop or tablet. You can use this app to play music, add songs and albums to the 'now playing' list and view information about an artist, among other things. If you have a Microsoft account, you can also access the Microsoft Store where you can purchase more music online.

1. From the Start screen, click the Music tile.
2. If you have music in your Music library, you'll see it under My Music. (Scroll to the left end of the app.)

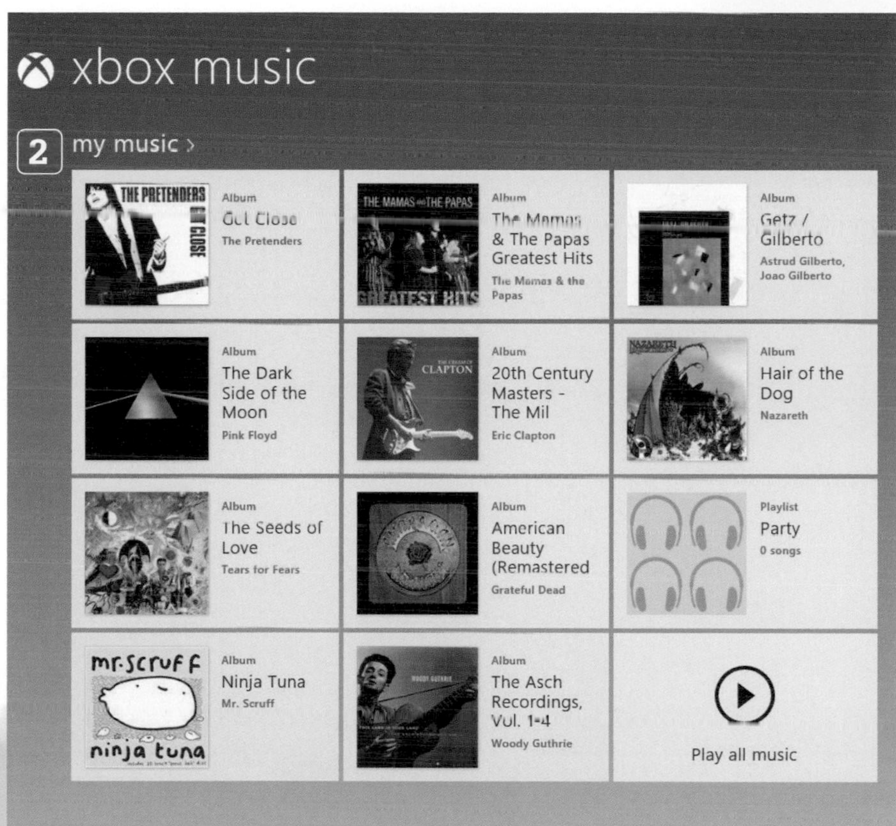

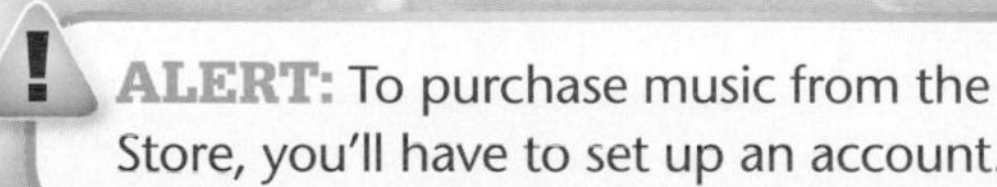

ALERT: To purchase music from the Store, you'll have to set up an account.

3 Use the scroll bar, the scroll wheel on your mouse, or flick with your finger to see the other Music options, including the ability to browse the Store for new releases.

HOT TIP: With the Music app open, use the key combination Windows + C to access the charms, and click Settings, then Preferences. From there you can configure options for the Music app.

HOT TIP: From the Music app, click xbox music store and, once inside, choose a song and click Preview to hear a sample.

Play a song

If you have music in your Music library you can play it from the Music app. If you don't have any music, you can copy music files from another computer you own.

1. Open the Music app and, under My Music, click as necessary to locate a song to play.
2. Click the song and click Play.
3. Repeat. As you add songs, click Add to now playing.

4. Explore the playback options at the bottom of the screen (the control area). You may have to flick up or right-click to access these.

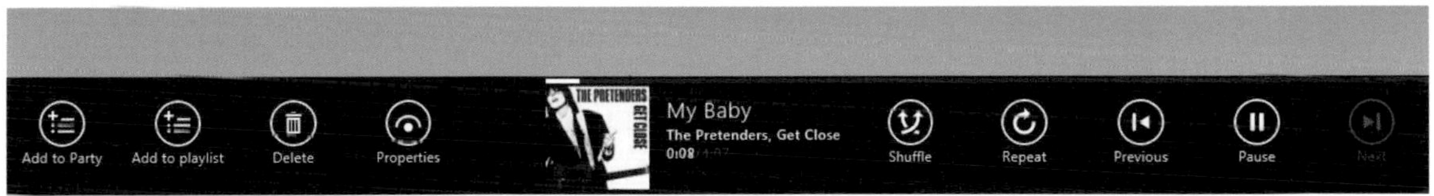

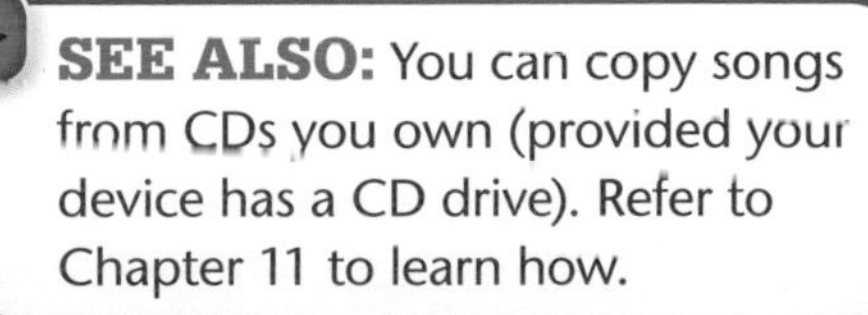

SEE ALSO: You can copy songs from CDs you own (provided your device has a CD drive). Refer to Chapter 11 to learn how.

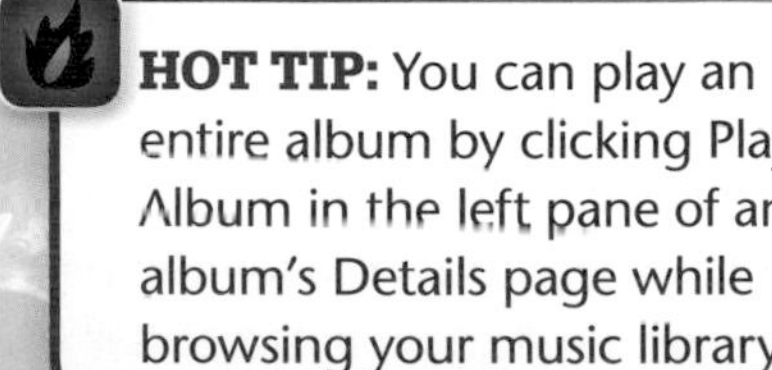

HOT TIP: You can play an entire album by clicking Play Album in the left pane of an album's Details page while browsing your music library.

5 Click the album cover from the control area to view additional information; click all of the icons to see what they offer. Note the Back button.

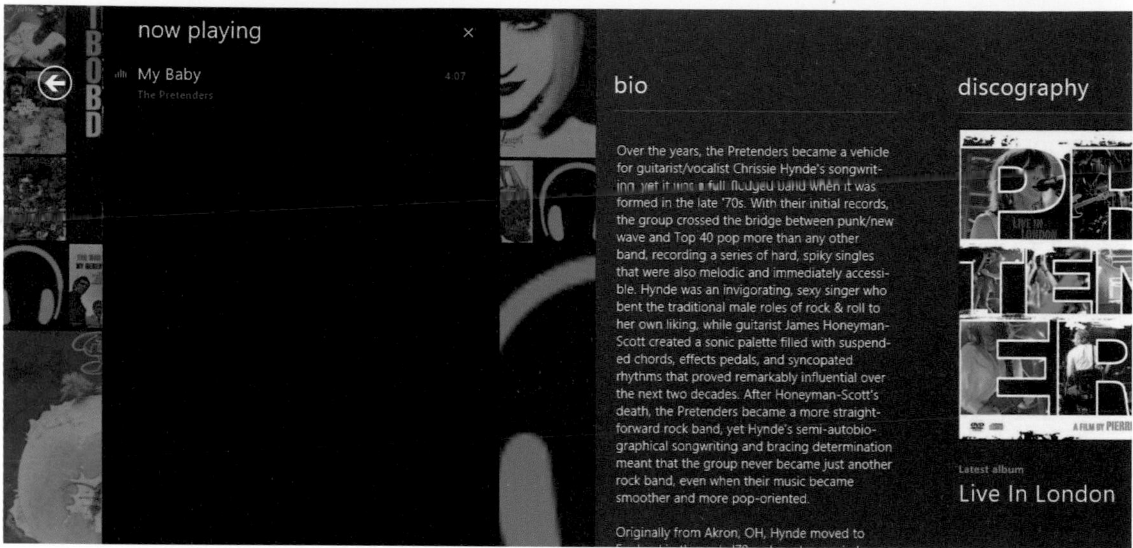

DID YOU KNOW?

When you return to the Start screen after using the Music app for the first time, the tile will be live and will show a thumbnail of the song that is playing.

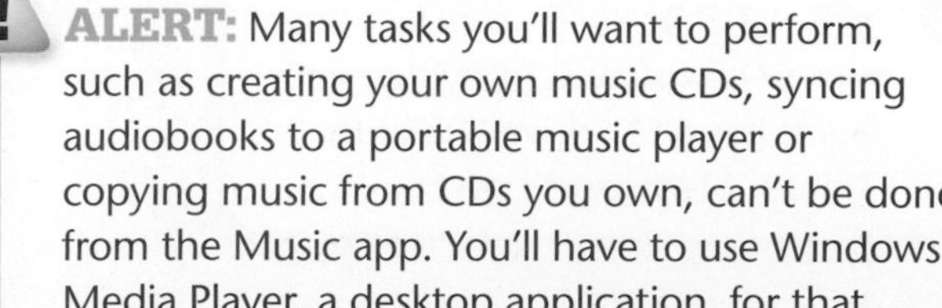

ALERT: Many tasks you'll want to perform, such as creating your own music CDs, syncing audiobooks to a portable music player or copying music from CDs you own, can't be done from the Music app. You'll have to use Windows Media Player, a desktop application, for that.

Explore the Photos app

The Photos app, available from the Start screen, is a great place to view your photos. The app separates your photos by what's stored on your computer, and what is stored in various places on the internet. If you've created subfolders to organise your photos, those subfolders will appear too.

1. From the Start screen, click Photos.

2. Note the folders that already appear. This is the landing page.

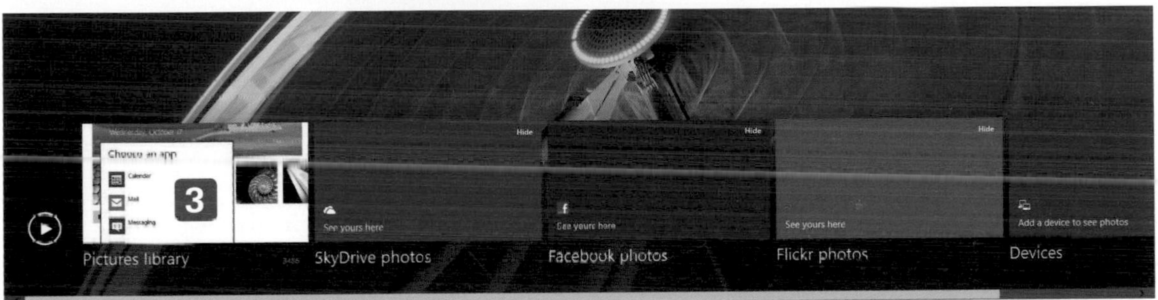

3. Click the Pictures library. (My Pictures library holds screen shots for this book!)
4. If you see subfolders, click them to access the pictures stored there.
5. Click or tap the screen and then the Back arrow to return to previous screens.

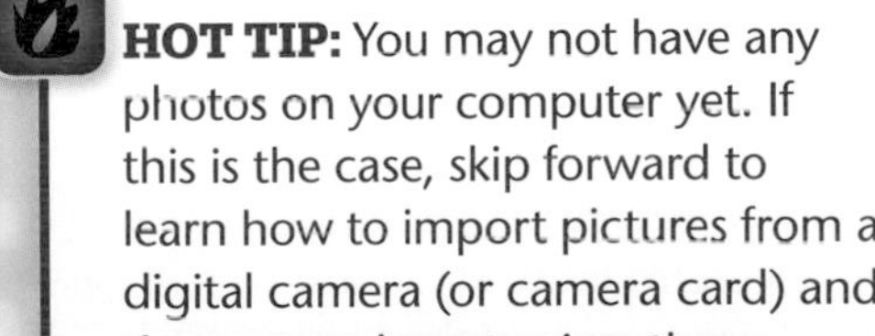

HOT TIP: You may not have any photos on your computer yet. If this is the case, skip forward to learn how to import pictures from a digital camera (or camera card) and then return here to view them.

ALERT: When you save pictures to your computer, make sure to save them to the Pictures library. This will make your pictures easy to find in the Photos app.

View a photo

As you navigate the Photos app, clicking folders and subfolders, you'll see the photos you've stored on your laptop or are available from it. While in folders in subfolders, the photos are in preview mode. You can view them this way or click them to view them in full screen mode. We'll explore both here.

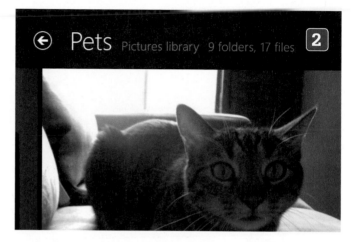

1. Open the Photos app from the Start screen.
2. Click the Pictures library.
3. If applicable, click any subfolder. You'll see photos in Preview mode.
4. Click any photo to view it in full screen mode.
5. Use the arrow that appears in the middle of the left side, shown here, to move back one photo. Use the arrow that appears on the right (not shown) to move forward one photo.
6. Click once on the screen to show the Back arrow, shown here in the top left corner, to move back one folder. Repeat as needed to return to the Photos landing page.

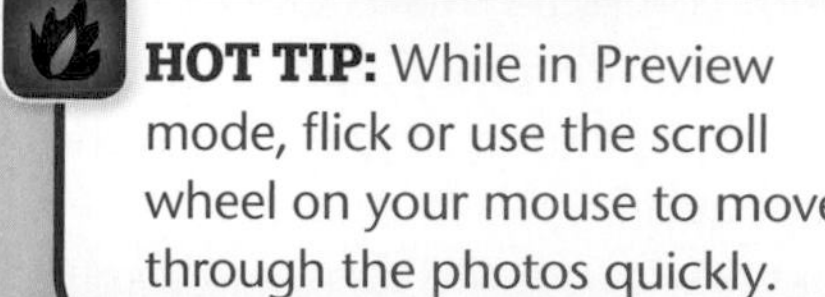

HOT TIP: While in Preview mode, flick or use the scroll wheel on your mouse to move through the photos quickly.

HOT TIP: At the Photos landing page, click SkyDrive photos, Facebook photos or Flickr photos to make the photos you have stored there appear in the Photos app.

Import pictures from a digital camera

You can put photos on your computer in lots of ways, but the easiest way is to use the Photos app. The Photos landing page offers an option to add a device to *see* photos that are on them, but if you right-click while on that page, the option to *Import* those photos appears.

1. Connect your camera, insert a memory card, or connect an external drive that contains photos.
2. Open the Photos app, and click any back buttons as necessary to access the landing page.
3. Right-click the landing page to access the toolbar.
4. Click Import.

5. By default, all of the photos are selected as shown here, provided they have not already been imported. Right-click to deselect photos.

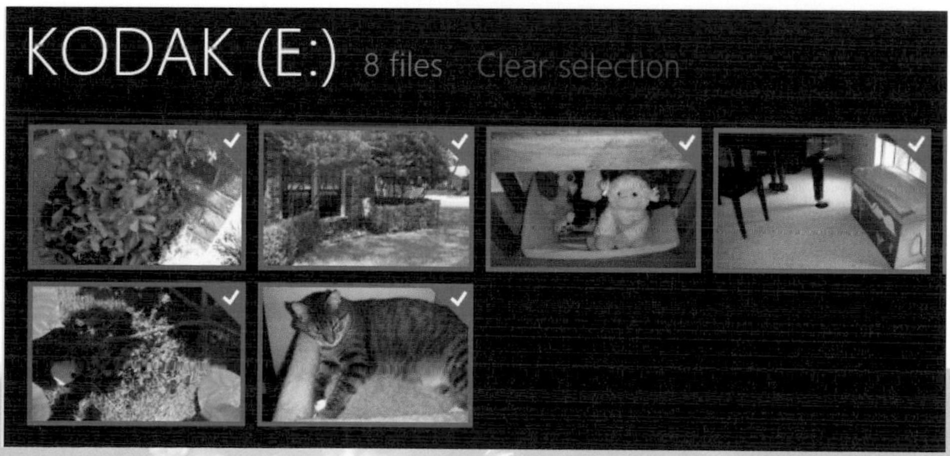

WHAT DOES THIS MEAN?

When you **import** photos, you copy them to your laptop.

6 Type a name for the folder these pictures will be imported to, and then click Import.

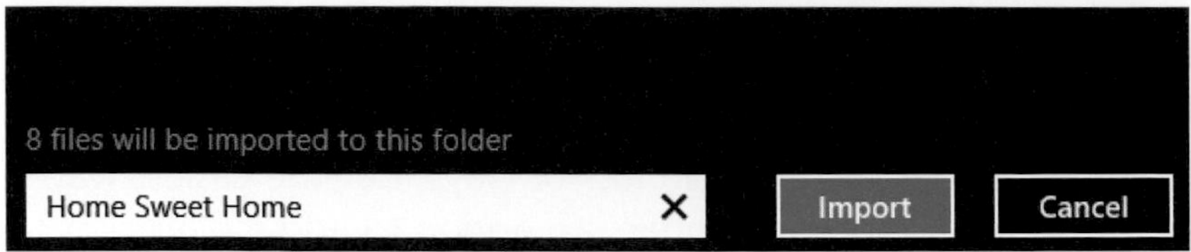

7 Click Open album (not shown) to view the photos.

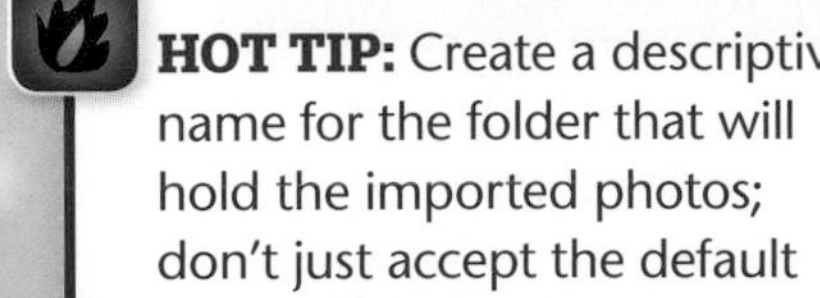

HOT TIP: Create a descriptive name for the folder that will hold the imported photos; don't just accept the default name offered.

ALERT: If you want to perform more complicated tasks, such as editing photos, grouping photos in folders, rotating photos, sharing photos and so on, you'll have to do that from the desktop using File Explorer, Paint and similar applications.

Play a slide show of photos

You can play a slide show of pictures in any folder. Once it starts to play, you can stop it in many ways. You can click Esc on the keyboard, right-click with a mouse, touch the screen, and more.

1. Open the Photos app from the Start screen.
2. Navigate to any folder that contains photos.
3. Right-click and choose Slide show. (Remember, on a tablet you can swipe up.)
4. Stop the show using any method desired.

HOT TIP: You can pause a slide show by tapping a key on the keyboard, and start it again with a right-click of the mouse. (You'll have to click Slide Show again.)

DID YOU KNOW?
You won't have any pictures available under SkyDrive, Facebook or Flickr until you click and log in with a compatible account.

Play a video

The Video app is very similar to the Music app. It contains a My Videos section, and offers access to the Store, where you can purchase movies and TV shows. If you have video, perhaps something you've purchased or something you've taken yourself with a video camera, copy them to the Videos library before starting here.

1. From the Start screen, open the Video app.
2. If you have video in your Video library, you'll see it under My Videos. (Scroll to the left side of the app to see this.)

3. Use the scroll bar, the scroll wheel on your mouse or flick with your finger to see the other video options, including options to purchase media.
4. To play a video in the Video app, click it one time. The video will play and controls will become available on the screen. If the controls disappear, move your mouse on the screen to show them.

SEE ALSO: If you don't know how to copy or move files, refer to Chapter 9, Learn desktop basics.

HOT TIP: As with other apps, you can use the default Settings charm to access the app's options.

8 Access and use available online stores

Introduction

Microsoft offers a 'Store', where you can obtain apps. There are many types of apps available, and they are arranged by category. You can search for both free and paid apps that relate to news, travel, productivity, games, health and fitness, and so on. If you worked through Chapter 7 you already know a little about the Store; that is where you obtained Skype, an app you use to video chat with other Skype users. It's important to understand that the Store offers only what are considered *Start screen apps*. The Store does not offer full-fledged desktop applications.

There are also stores that offer music and videos. If you worked through Chapter 7 you saw these. At these stores you can rent or buy a movie or television show, or sample or buy the latest album by your favourite artist.

Although these stores and the items in them are useful for all Windows 8 users, they are especially suitable for those with laptops and tablets. One of the best things about having a mobile device is that you can take your media with you! You can watch the movies on an aeroplane, play games while waiting for a bus, join meetings from a hotel room, make video calls to your grandkids, listen to audiobooks, and much, much more from wherever you are.

There are a few things to keep in mind before you start, though. You'll need a Microsoft account to access any store, so if you don't have one, you'll want to acquire one when prompted. You'll need to input credit information the first time you make a purchase from any store too. Finally, you'll need an internet connection, preferably wi-fi.

Explore the Store

There is a Store tile on the Start screen. This tile takes you to the default Store, where you can get free apps or buy them. If you aren't logged in with a Microsoft account, you'll be prompted to input one before you can enter.

1 From the Start screen, click or tap Store. Log in with a Microsoft account if prompted.

2 Scroll through the available categories and titles.

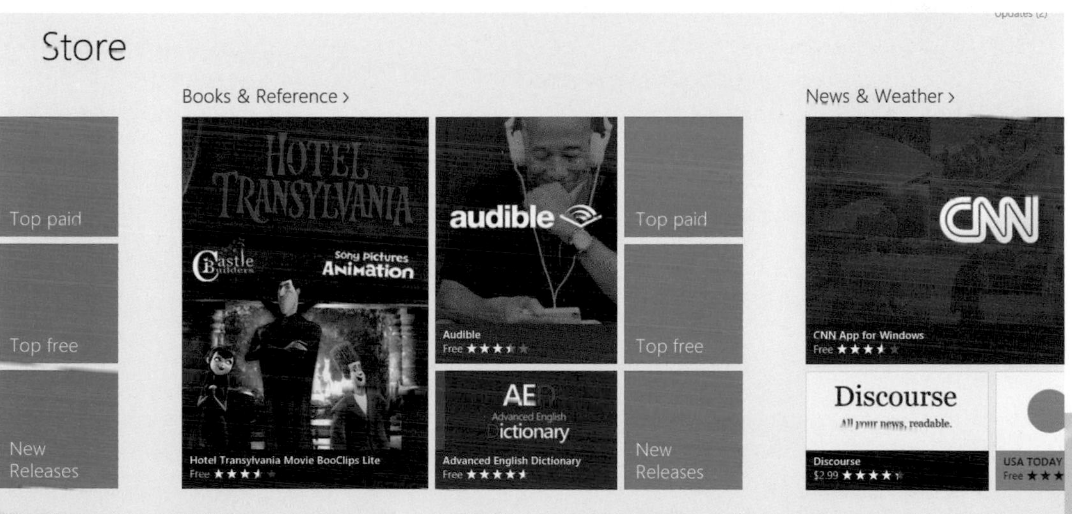

HOT TIP: The Spotlight category offers access to Top paid, Top free and New Releases.

3 Click or tap a category title that interests you, such as Games, Entertainment or News & Weather. We'll choose Books & Reference.

4 Note the options to filter what is shown. Filter and browse as desired. (Note the Back arrows.)

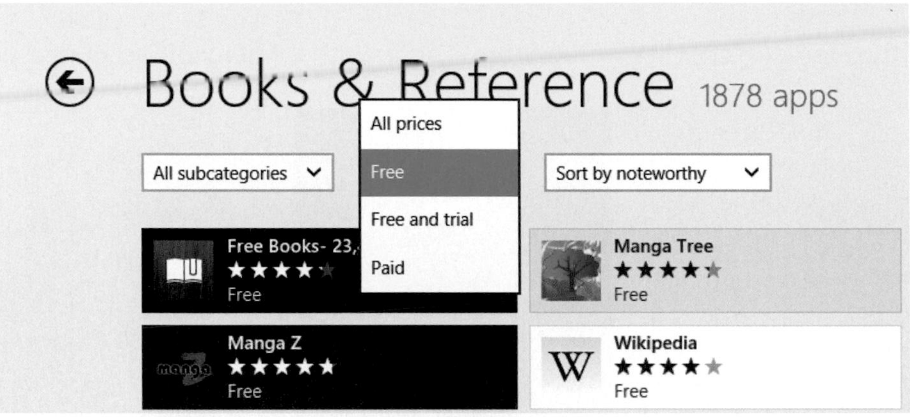

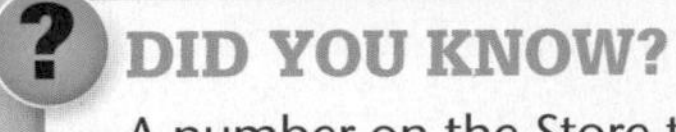

DID YOU KNOW?

A number on the Store tile means some of your apps have updates available.

DID YOU KNOW?

If you click or tap an app tile, its details page appears. From there you can buy or install an app, read reviews, get a description, and more.

Get a free app

There are thousands of free apps. Some, like Netflix and Audible, require you to be a member to access content. Others may include ads and offer an ad-free version for a price. Some free apps let you make in-app purchases to buy, for example, more farm animals, gaming 'lives', additional content and so on. Some free apps are simply awesome, and are just fine on their own.

1. From the Start screen, click or tap Store.
2. If necessary, click any back buttons to get to the starting page, and then, under Spotlight, click Top free.

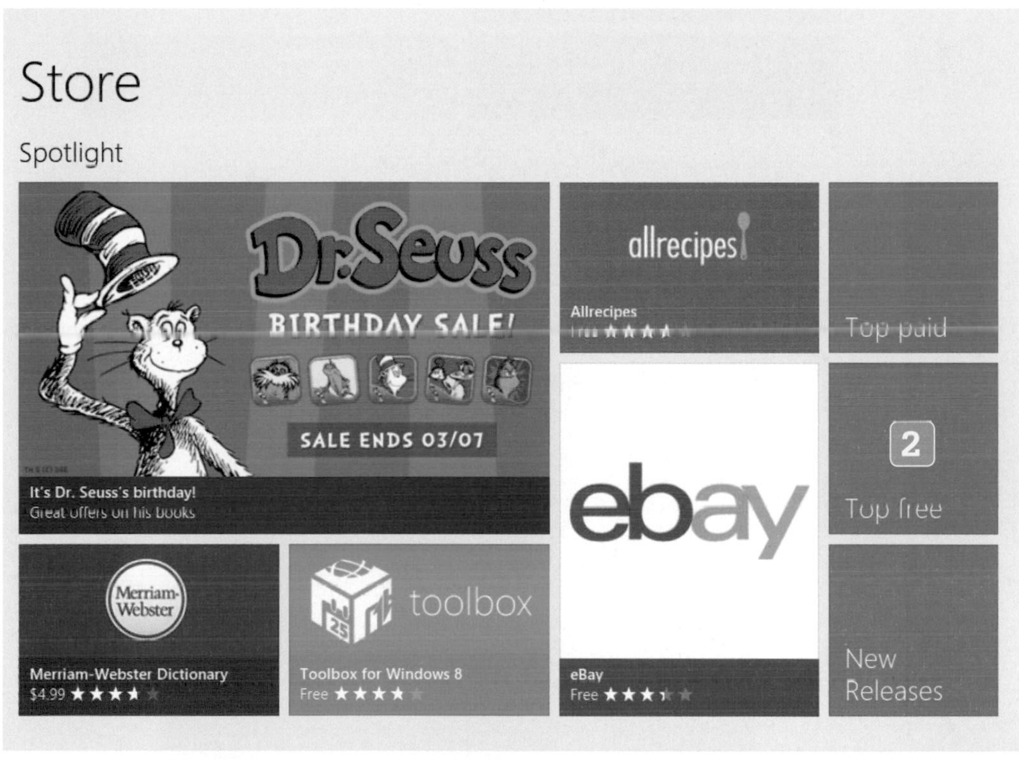

HOT TIP: Look for free apps that are provided by services you already use, like Netflix or Skype, for a better Windows 8 experience with those products.

3 Click any app that interests you. These are all very popular.

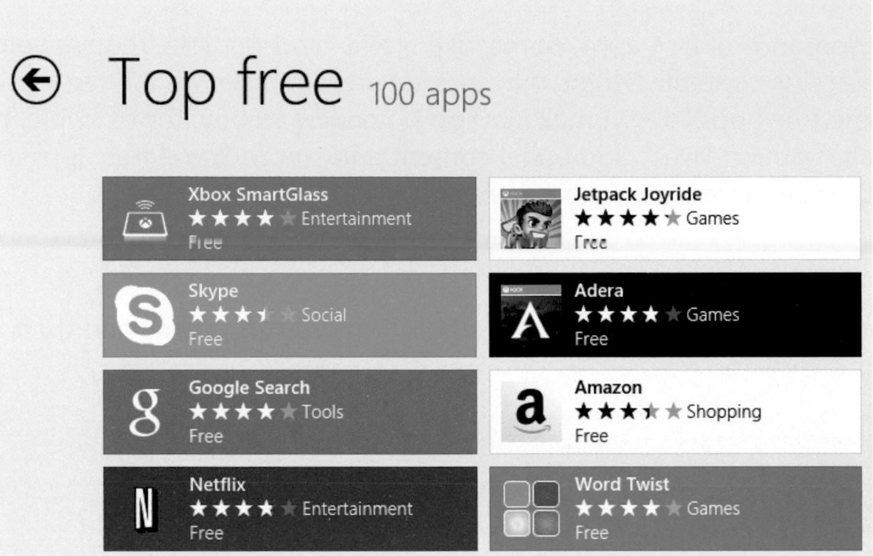

4 Click Install.

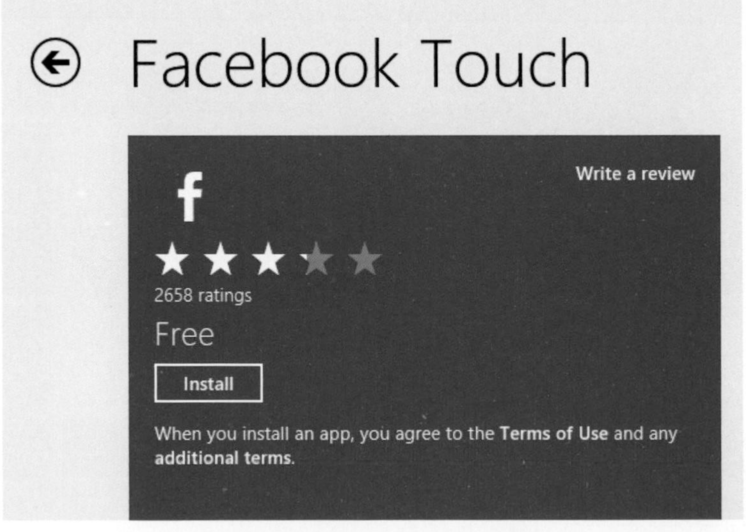

DID YOU KNOW?
You can read reviews and learn more about any app from its Details page.

HOT TIP: It's OK to try any free app; you can easily uninstall it if you don't like it.

Get app updates

The Store tile is a live tile. When you see a number on the tile it means updates for apps you own are available. It's best to update your apps when notified, because updates often fix problems with the app or add features.

1. From the Start screen, look at the Store tile.
2. If the Store tile has a number on it, click the tile.

3. In the top right corner of the Store interface, click Updates.

Updates (15)

4. Right-click to deselect any app update.
5. Click Install (not shown).

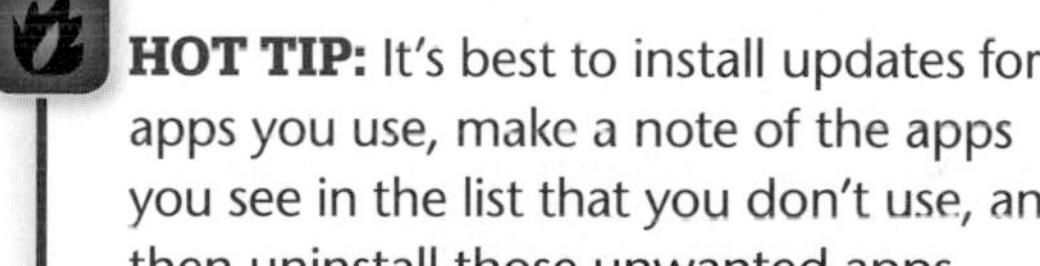

HOT TIP: It's best to install updates for apps you use, make a note of the apps you see in the list that you don't use, and then uninstall those unwanted apps.

DID YOU KNOW? You can continue to work or browse while the updates are installing.

ALERT: The Music & Video category of the default Store doesn't offer albums, movies and the like. It offers apps that have to do with music and video, such as YouTube Player, IHeart Radio, Play Guitar!, and so on. If you want to buy music and videos, you'll have to access the related Xbox store, detailed next.

Explore the Xbox Music Store

The Xbox Music Store offers a place to purchase music. You access it from the Music app.

1. From the Start screen, click or tap Music.
2. In the top right corner of the interface, if applicable, click Sign In. Input your Microsoft account credentials.

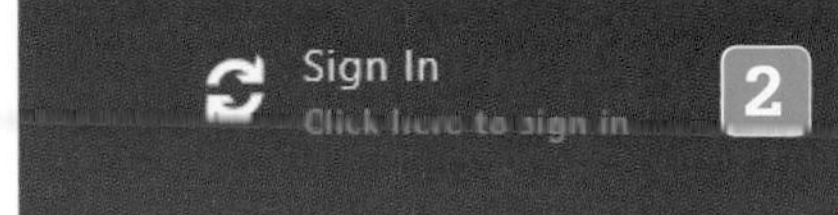

3. Scroll right and click All Music.

4. Choose a category on the left and select a song on the right.

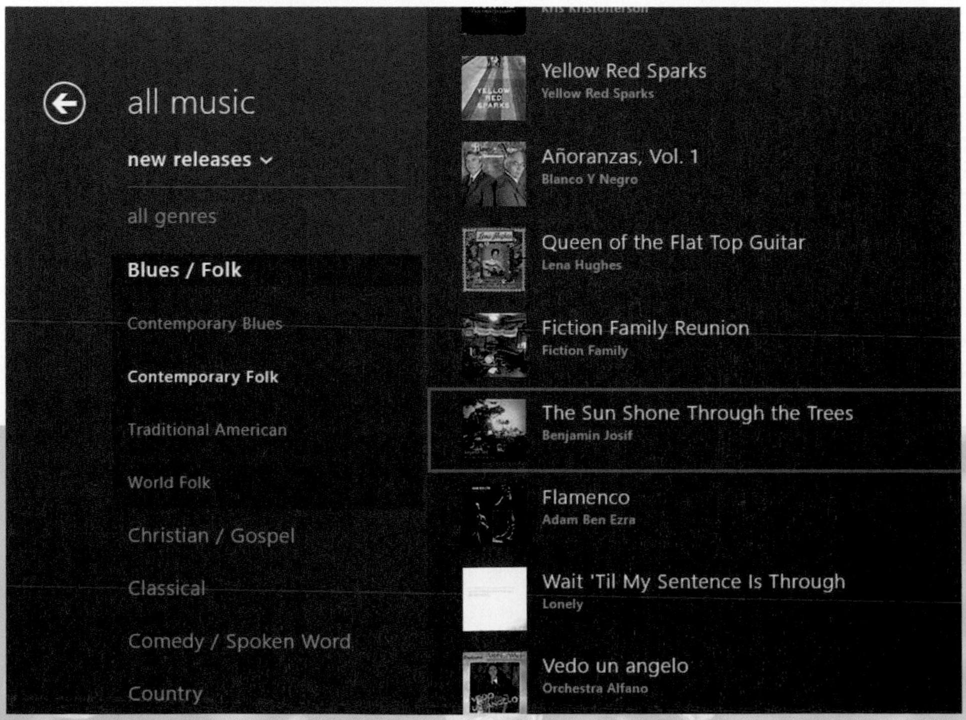

5 Note the options, including the option to buy the music.

6 Right-click while a song plays to view the controls.

HOT TIP: If you decide to make a purchase, follow the prompts provided to complete the transaction.

Explore the Xbox Video Store

The Xbox Video Store offers a place to purchase video media. You access it from the Video app.

1. From the Start screen, click or tap Video.
2. In the top right corner of the interface, if applicable, click Sign In. Input your Microsoft account credentials.
3. Scroll right to view the movies store and the television store.

4. Click either option and browse the titles. Click any title to learn more.

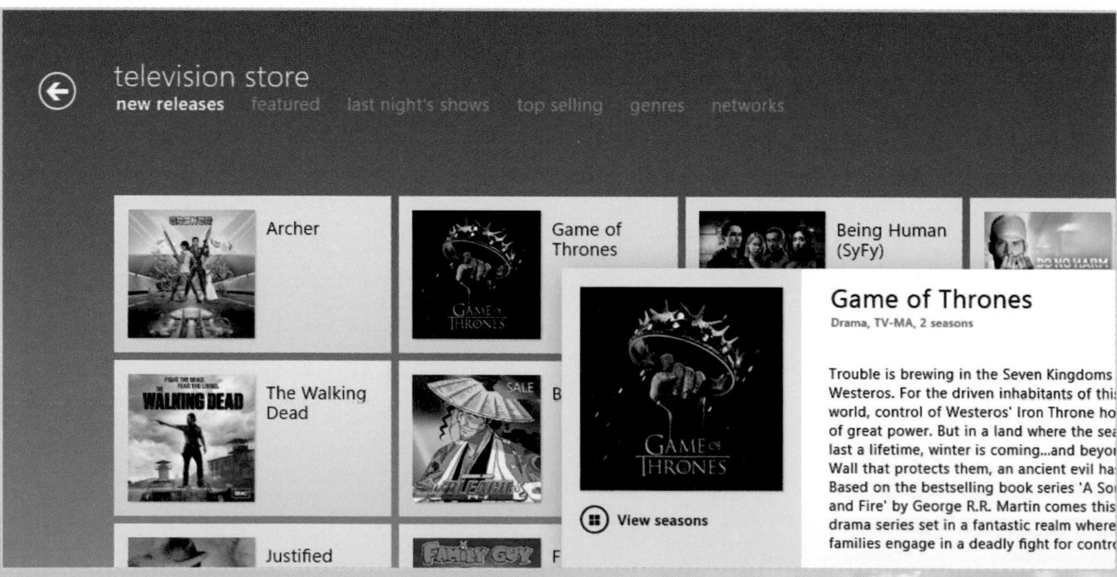

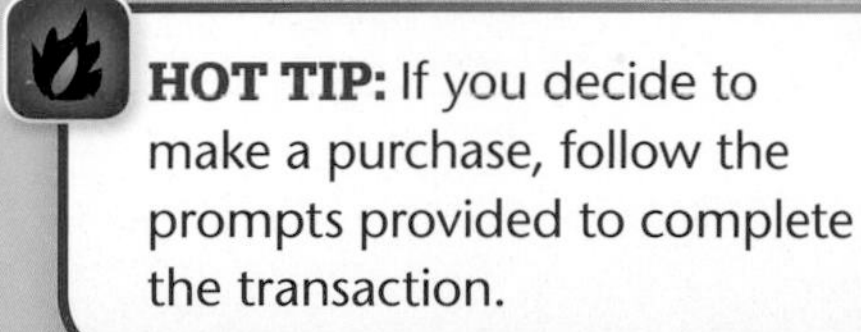

HOT TIP: If you decide to make a purchase, follow the prompts provided to complete the transaction.

5 If you want to make a purchase, you may have to select a season to view the purchasing options. If you select a movie, you can buy or rent it as applicable.

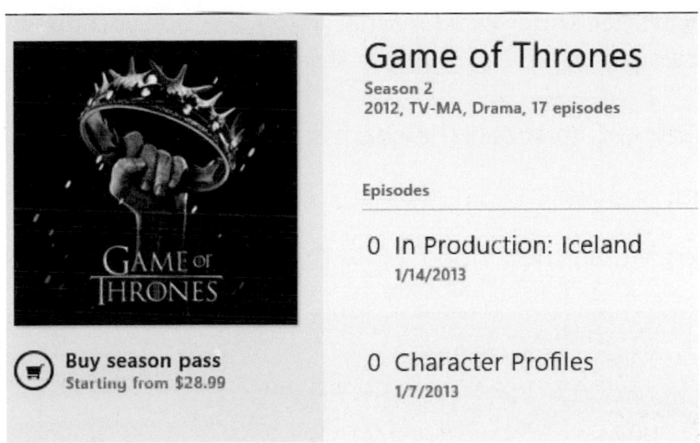

Search across stores

Sometimes you might not know exactly what you want but you have an idea. When this happens you can search across multiple stores easily.

1. Use Windows key + C to access the charms and click Search.
2. Type a keyword.
3. Click Store, then Music, then Video. Note the results for each. Video is shown here.

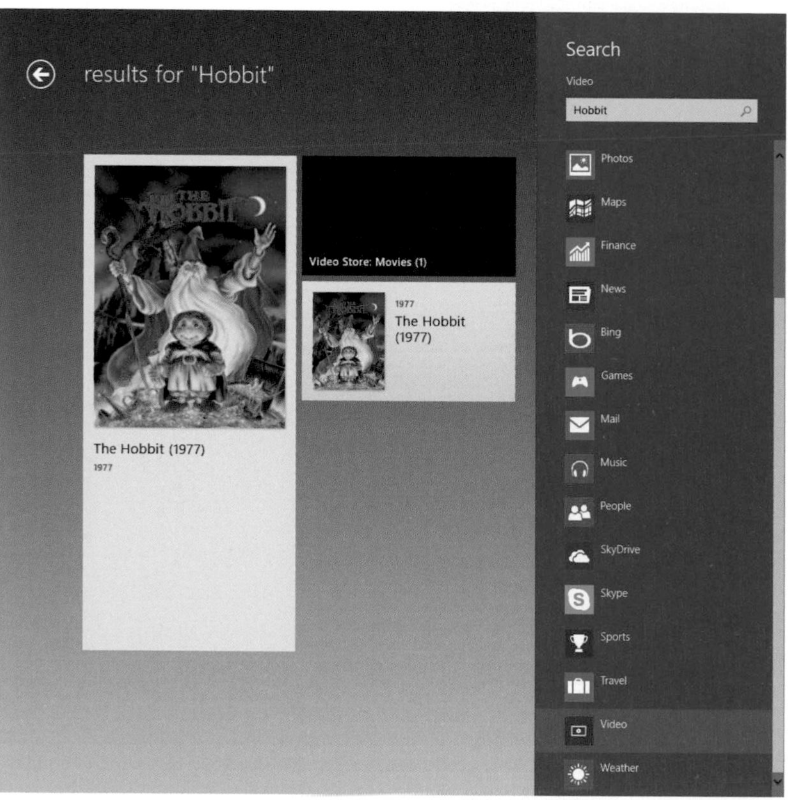

4. Click any result to see it in the applicable store.

DID YOU KNOW?

You can search across more than stores. You can type, say, Coffee in the Search window, and then click Maps to find coffee places near you, News to learn more about coffee, Finance to see the current price for coffee, and so on.

HOT TIP: When performing any search, use unique words like Hobbit, Coffee and the like to avoid extremely common words that could show up in multiple searches.

Remove or uninstall unwanted apps

After you've acquired a good amount of apps from the Store, you'll need to uninstall the ones you've decided you don't like or won't use. You do this from the Start screen. If you want to keep the app but don't want it on the Start screen, you can remove it.

1. Locate the app on the Start screen. (If you don't see it there, right-click and click All apps.)
2. Right-click the app to uninstall.
3. Click Uninstall.

4. If you like the app and want to keep it but do want to remove it from the Start screen, click Unpin from Start instead of Uninstall.

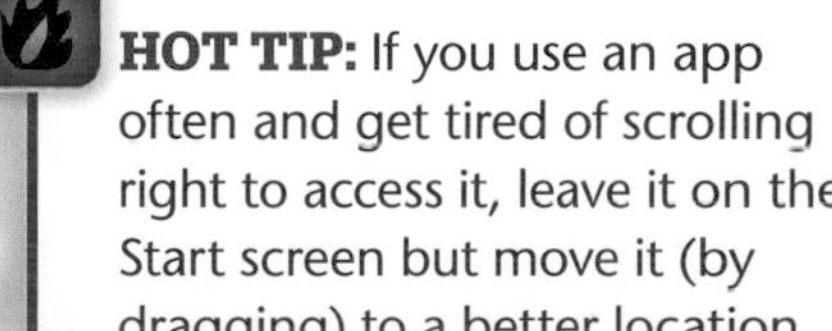

HOT TIP: If you use an app often and get tired of scrolling right to access it, leave it on the Start screen but move it (by dragging) to a better location.

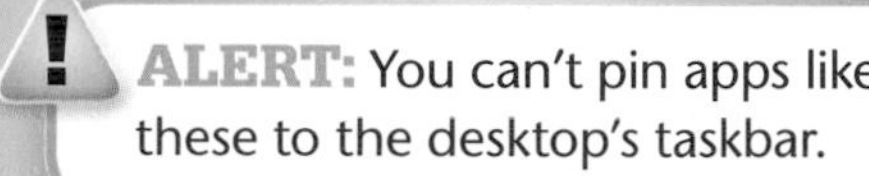

ALERT: You can't pin apps like these to the desktop's taskbar.

9 Learn desktop basics

Introduction

For the most part, just about everything you've learned so far in this book has had to do with the Start screen and Start screen apps. Now it's time to switch gears and talk about the desktop. The desktop is the traditional computing environment that has been around for decades. If you've used a computer before, you've experienced the desktop.

We need to spend a good amount of time talking about the desktop, because while apps do provide great functionality and can be used to easily *access* data, they generally can't help you *manage* data. Apps generally don't let you *edit* data either. You can't rotate a photo or copy music from a music CD from an existing app, for example.

In this chapter you'll learn the basics of the desktop. You'll learn how to personalise the desktop so you have access to the programs and data you use often. You'll learn how to use the taskbar and manage multiple open windows and applications. You'll create folders and use them to organise data files. In the next few chapters you'll learn even more, as we dive even deeper into the desktop.

Explore the desktop

No matter what kind of device you have, if it has Windows 8 installed on it, you have access to the desktop. You're probably more comfortable there than anywhere, and you'll need to be. You'll use the desktop often.

1. Use any method to access the Start screen. (You can tap the Windows key on the keyboard.)
2. From the Start screen, click or tap Desktop.
3. Note the Desktop features:
   - A The Recycle Bin.
   - B The taskbar.
   - C The Internet Explorer icon. IE is open here.
   - D The File Explorer icon (we've opened File Explorer here).
   - E The Notification area.
   - F Personal items.
   - G Open programs.
   - H Programs pinned to the taskbar.

ALERT: The Start button is no longer available on the taskbar, at least not when this book was published. If you'd like to access something a bit like it, press the Windows key + X key combination.

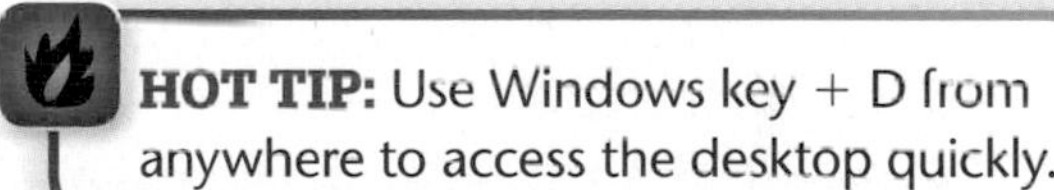

HOT TIP: Use Windows key + D from anywhere to access the desktop quickly.

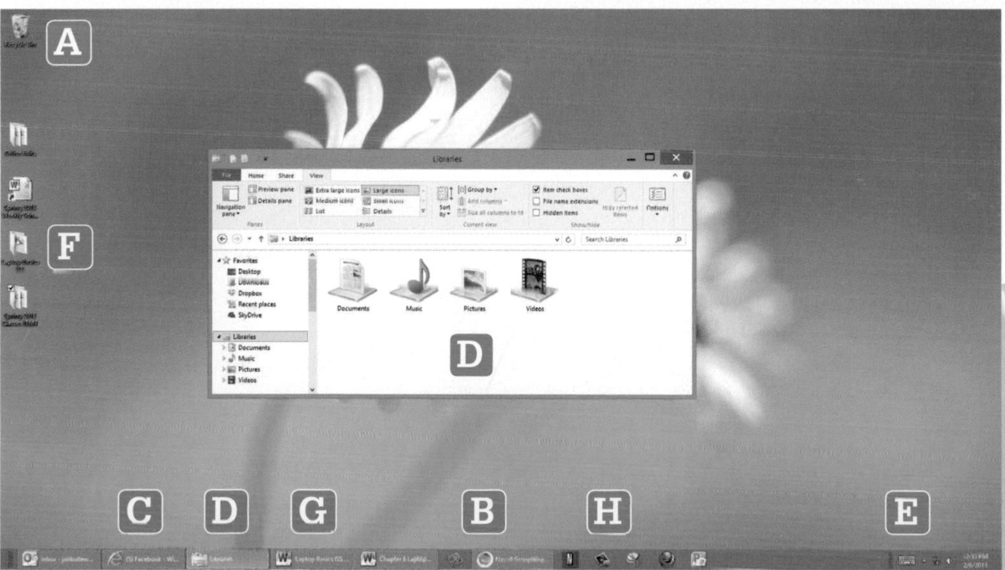

Choose which desktop icons appear

By default, the Recycle Bin is the only icon on the desktop. You can add icons for commonly used items from the Personalization options in Control Panel, though, and then you won't have to go looking for them when you need them!

1. Right-click an empty area of the desktop and click Personalize.
2. Click Change desktop icons.

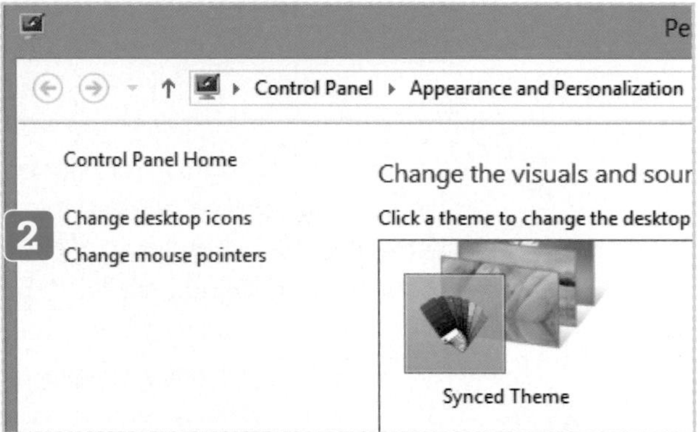

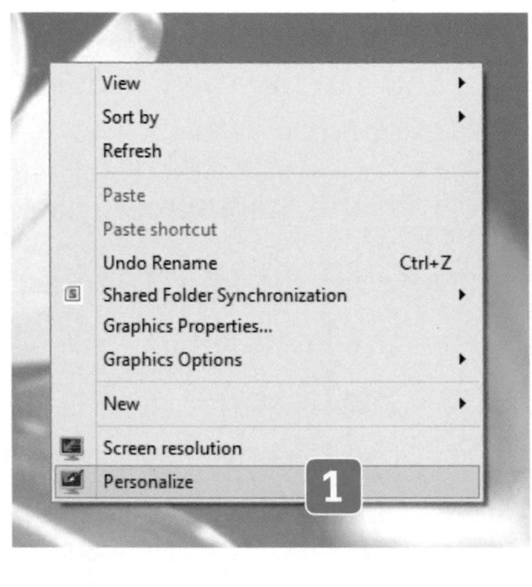

3. Place a check by the items you'd like to add to the desktop and click OK.

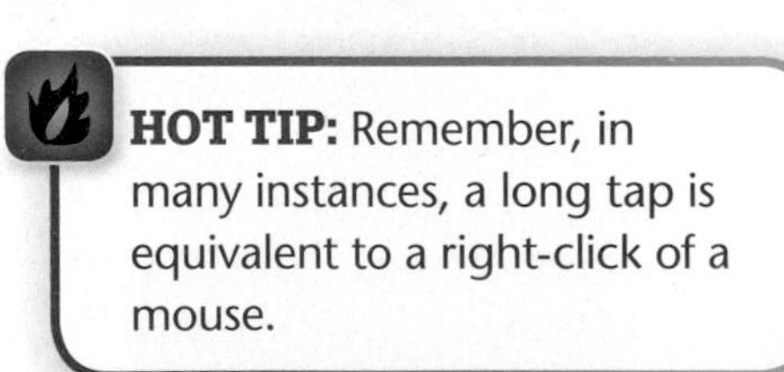

HOT TIP: Remember, in many instances, a long tap is equivalent to a right-click of a mouse.

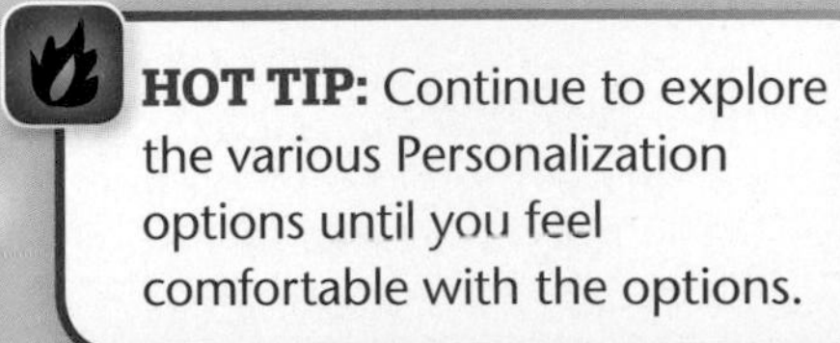

HOT TIP: Continue to explore the various Personalization options until you feel comfortable with the options.

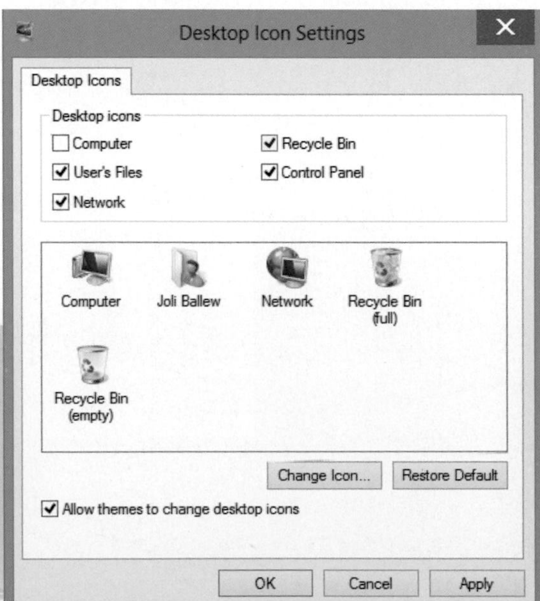

Make desktop icons easier to see

If the icons on the desktop are too small to see comfortably, you can change the size.

1. Right-click an empty area of the desktop and click Properties.
2. Click Display.
3. Choose Medium instead of Smaller.

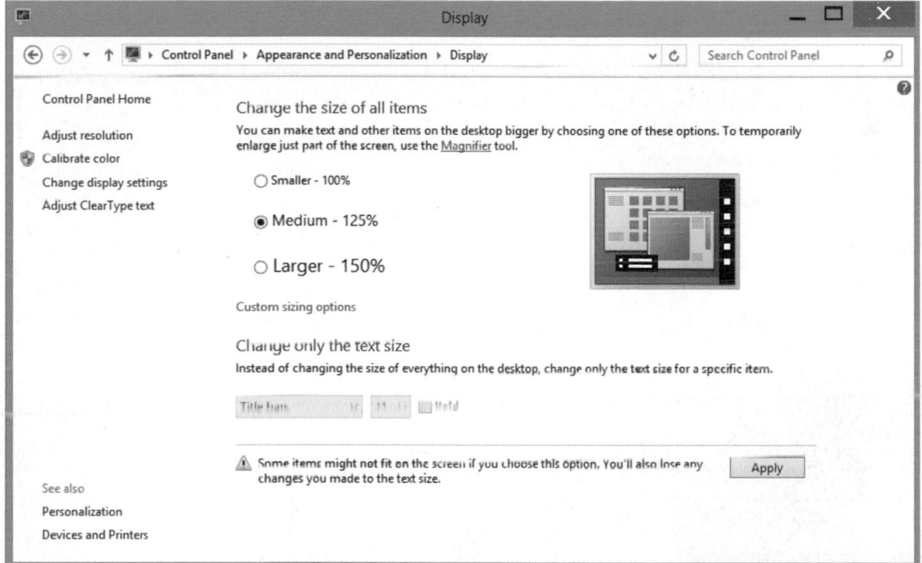

4. As prompted, log off and log back on:
   - Click the Windows key to return to the Start screen.
   - Click your user name.
   - Click Sign out.
   - Sign in again and the changes will be applied.

ALERT: If you have a small monitor, some items may not appear as expected on the screen. If this happens, consider changing the resolution instead of the display size (see Chapter 1).

DID YOU KNOW?
You can make very specific changes to the display by opting to change the text size of specific elements, like title bars.

Learn desktop techniques

The desktop has a few unique techniques for performing tasks, such as using a right-click to access a contextual menu, and dragging and dropping to move icons. You can also right-click while you drag, to see an option that asks if you want to move or copy whatever you're dragging. Right-clicking while you drag is always the safest option.

1. If you aren't on the desktop, use Windows key + D to get there.
2. Right-click (or tap and hold on a touch screen) to access various desktop options. Hover your mouse over the options to view them.

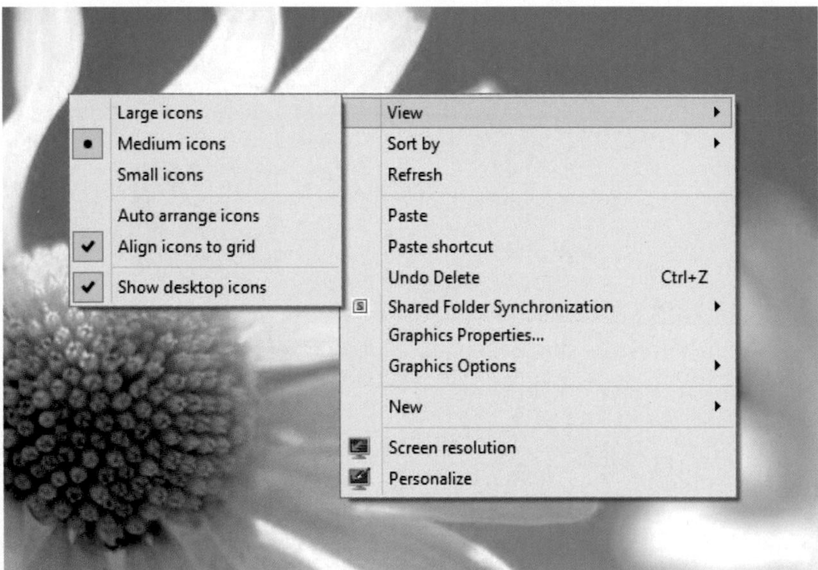

3. Click outside of these options to hide the contextual menu.
4. Left-click and drag the Recycle Bin to another area of the screen.
5. Drop it there.

DID YOU KNOW?
You can right-click an empty area of the desktop and click Personalize to change the desktop background, among other things.

ALERT: Some computer manufacturers add their own touches to what's available when you right-click on the desktop. You may not see any items that involve a graphics adapter, for instance, but you may see something else that isn't.

Explore the taskbar

The taskbar runs across the bottom of the desktop and holds icons for File Explorer and Internet Explorer, among others. You can click or tap the icon to open the item it represents. Additionally, you can personalise the taskbar by adding your own icons for programs, folders and so on that you use often. The taskbar also holds the Notification area.

1. Locate the taskbar.
2. Locate the Notification area.
3. Locate the Internet Explorer icon.
4. Locate the File Explorer icon.
5. Right-click an empty area of the taskbar to access Personalization options.

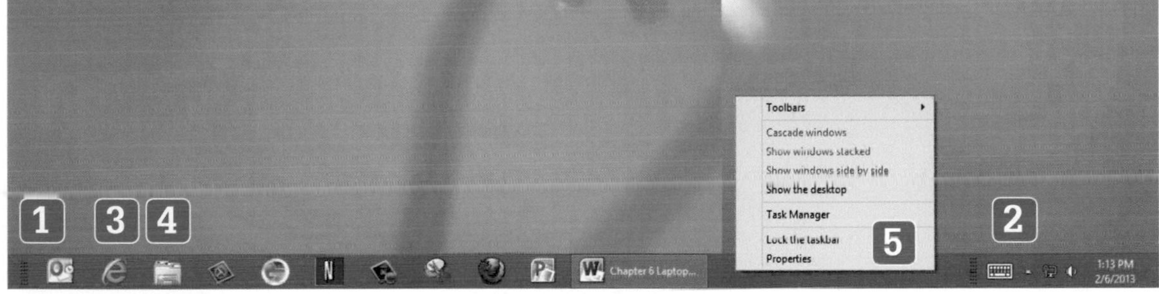

DID YOU KNOW?
You can drag the taskbar to another side of the screen – left, right or top – provided it is not locked (right-click the taskbar to find out).

HOT TIP: Right-click an empty area of the taskbar and choose Properties, then opt to hide the taskbar when you aren't using it. You can access it by moving your cursor to where it was before you hid it.

Add an item to the taskbar

Since there isn't a Start button, locating an item while you are on the desktop requires you tap the Windows key on the keyboard, type what you want to find on the Start screen, and click the result to open it. It's much easier to add items you use often to the taskbar. When you do, you won't have to leave the desktop to find what you need. This is called 'pinning' an item. You can only pin desktop applications though; you can't pin Start screen apps to the taskbar.

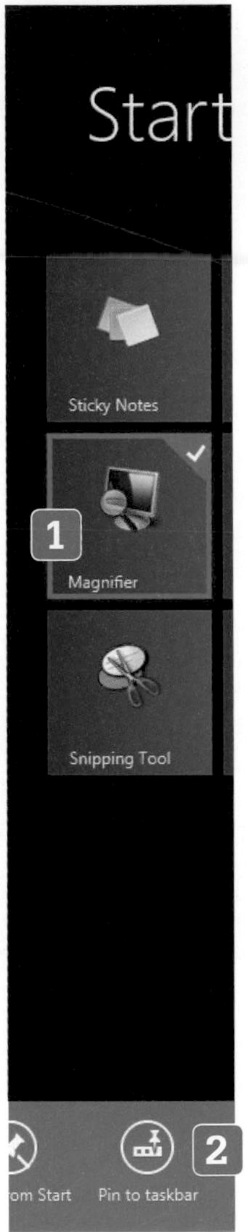

1. From the Start screen (or the All Apps screen) right-click an item you'd like to add to the taskbar.
2. Click Pin to taskbar. If you don't see this option, it can't be pinned.
3. Repeat as desired, and then note the new items that are pinned.

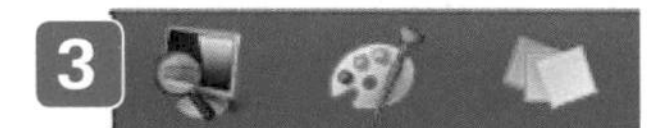

HOT TIP: As you get to know Windows 8 and learn which desktop apps you use most, pin them to the taskbar. You may want to pin Windows Media Player, Sticky Notes, Help and Support and others.

HOT TIP: Once an item is pinned to the taskbar, you only have to click or tap it one time to open the related application.

Make the taskbar easier to see

Our taskbar has been modified so that it is easier to see. You can do the same to yours if everything on it seems too small and is hard to see.

1 Right-click an empty area of the taskbar and click Properties.

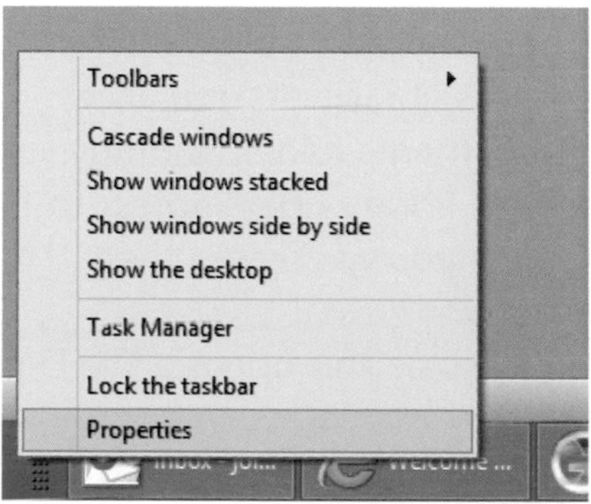

2 Deselect Use small taskbar buttons.

3 Next to Taskbar buttons choose anything other than Always combine, hide labels.

4 Click OK.

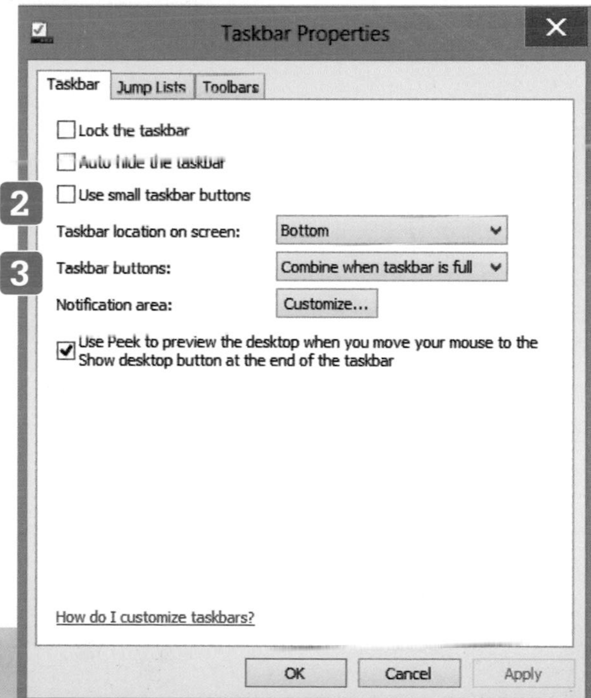

HOT TIP: If the icons on the desktop are too small to see, consider changing the screen resolution. See Chapter 1 to learn how.

Understand libraries in File Explorer

You store files in folders, and you access the folders in File Explorer. There are several default folders already created for you, including My Documents, My Pictures, My Videos and My Music, and they have Public folder counterparts. These folders are accessible in lots of ways, but one way is through Libraries. Libraries offer a place to access related data. The Documents library lets you access documents stored in the My Documents folder, the Public Documents folder, and any subfolders you've created in those folders. Likewise, the Pictures library offers access to the My Pictures and Public Pictures folders, and any subfolders you've created there. Let's explore these.

1. Click the folder icon on the taskbar. This opens a File Explorer window.
2. Click Libraries in the left pane.
3. Click any library icon in the resulting right pane to view its contents. Here, we've selected Pictures; Pictures becomes the selected item in the left pane. (Look at all of those subfolders!)
4. Continue to explore as time allows.

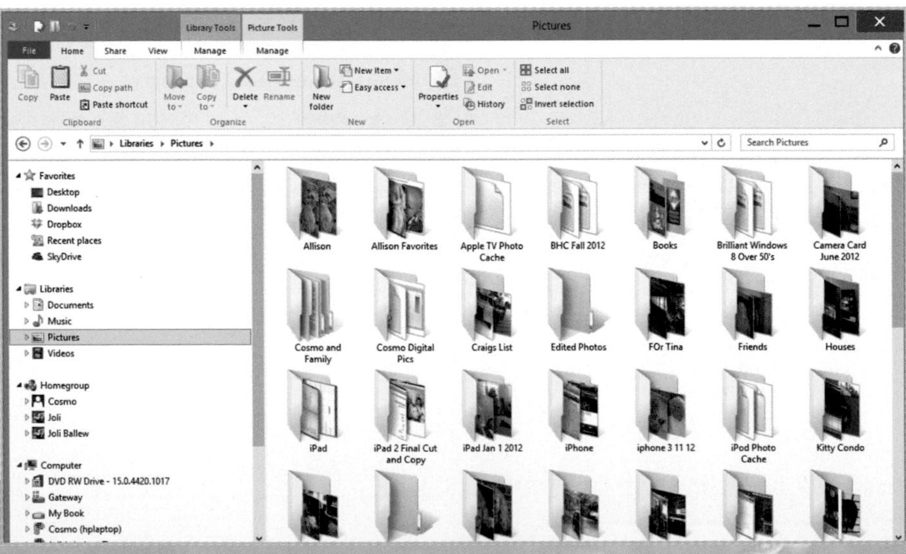

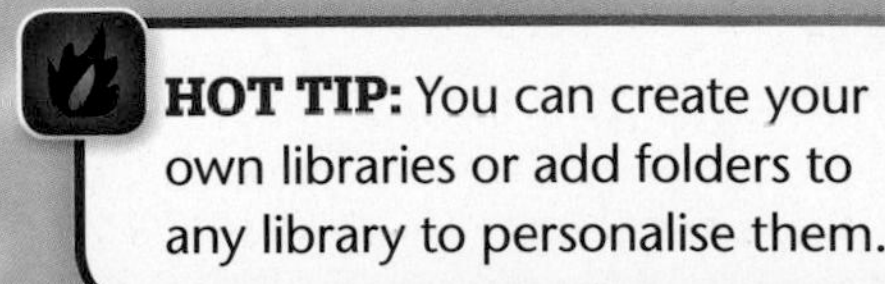

HOT TIP: You can create your own libraries or add folders to any library to personalise them.

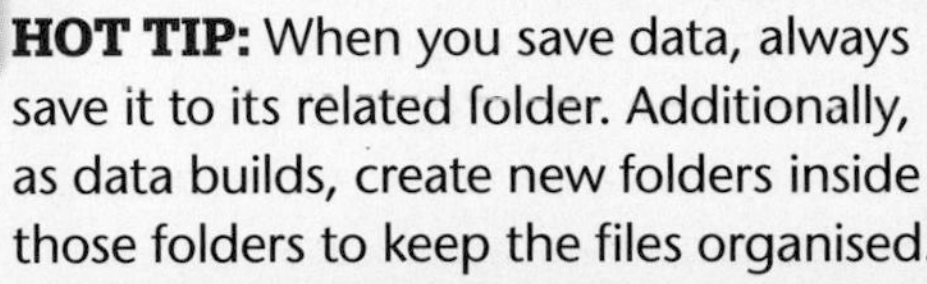

HOT TIP: When you save data, always save it to its related folder. Additionally, as data builds, create new folders inside those folders to keep the files organised.

Create a shortcut for a folder

If you know you'll use a folder often, you can create a shortcut for it on the desktop. This can be a 'parent' folder like My Pictures, or it can be any subfolder, a 'child' folder, therein.

1. Open File Explorer by clicking the folder icon on the taskbar.
2. Locate the folder to add a shortcut for it.
3. Right-click the folder and click Send to, then click Desktop (create shortcut).

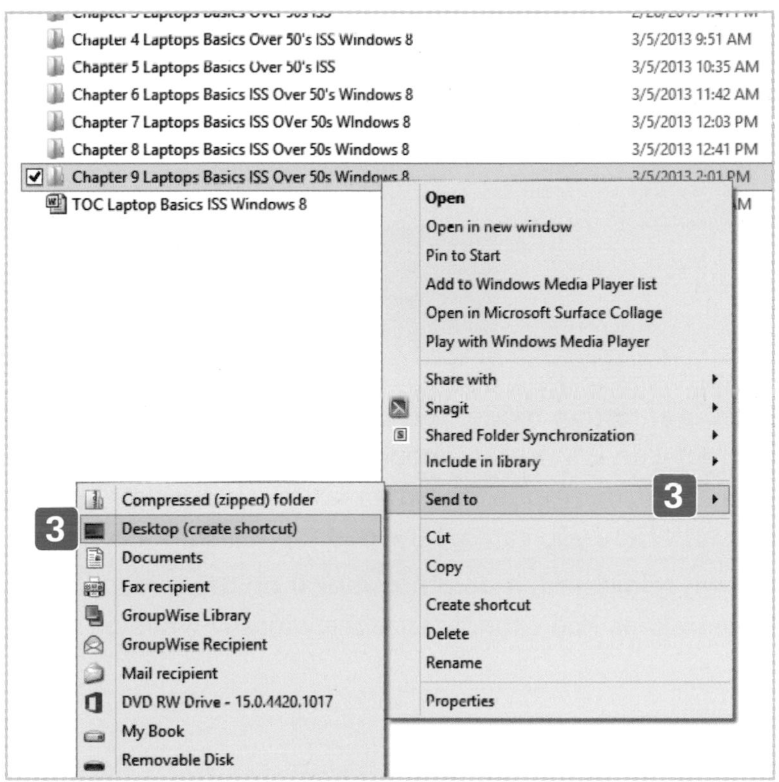

HOT TIP: Don't add so many things to the desktop (or the taskbar for that matter) that the area feels cluttered. It will take longer to find what you're looking for when this is the case.

DID YOU KNOW?

When you create a shortcut for something you're simply creating a pointer to it. You can delete a shortcut without deleting the actual data, since there is no data actually stored in a shortcut itself.

Open, close, resize the File Explorer window

A window can be minimised (on the taskbar), maximised (filling the entire desktop) or in restore mode (not maximised or minimised, but showing on the desktop). When in restore mode, you can drag from any corner or edge to resize it. (You can't do that when it is maximised because every corner is a hot corner!)

- A maximised window is as large as it can be and takes up the entire screen. You can maximise a window that is on the desktop by clicking the square in the top right corner. If the icon shows two squares, it's already maximised. (You can drag down from the middle of the title bar to change its size.)

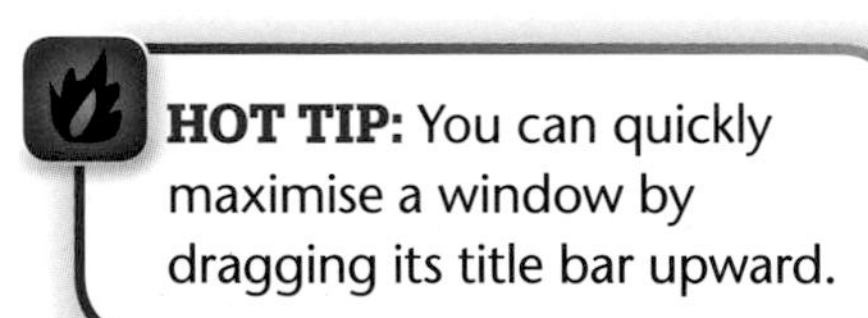

HOT TIP: You can quickly maximise a window by dragging its title bar upward.

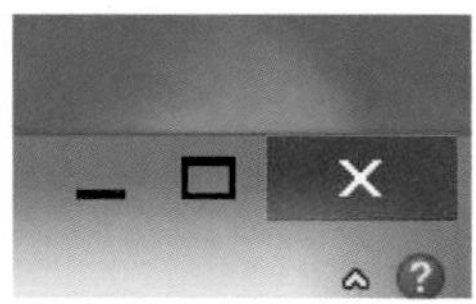

- When a window is in restore mode, you can resize the window by dragging from any corner or edge. An icon is in restore mode if there is a single square in the top right corner. You can access this mode from the maximised position by dragging from the title bar downward. Here you can see the desktop background behind the window.
- When a window is minimised, it does not appear on the screen, and instead is relegated to the taskbar. You cannot resize the window while on the taskbar.

DID YOU KNOW?
Hold down the Alt key and press the Tab key repeatedly to move through open windows on the Desktop. When you stop, the selected window will become the active window.

HOT TIP: To bring any window to the front of the others, click its title bar. This makes it the active window.

Change the view in a window

When you open most File Explorer windows, you will see additional folders inside them. You'll use these subfolders to organise the data you create and save, such as documents, pictures and songs. You can change the appearance of these folders so that you can more easily view them on your laptop or tablet.

1. Open File Explorer.
2. In the Navigation pane, click Pictures.
3. From the View tab, select a new layout. For Pictures, try Extra large icons.

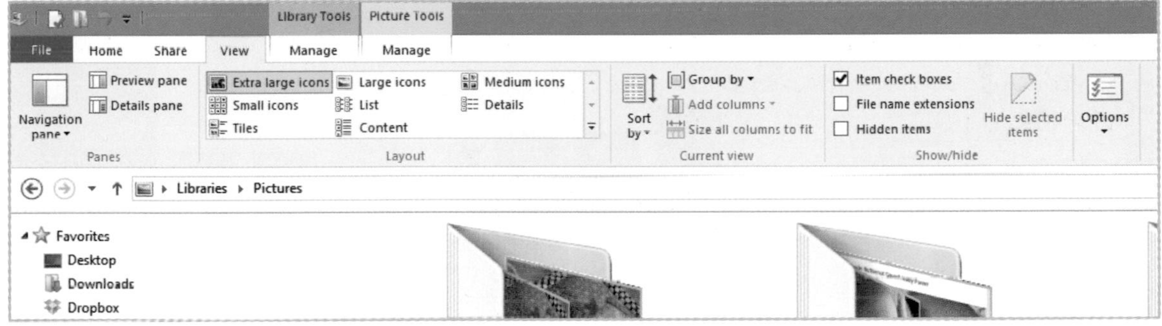

HOT TIP: To see information about the content in a folder such as the date it was last modified, its size or type, choose Details from the View pane.

DID YOU KNOW?
You can opt to show the Preview pane or Details pane in any File Explorer window. These options are also on the View tab.

Snap a window to the side of the desktop

When working on the desktop with multiple open windows, sometimes minimising, maximising and restoring or resizing isn't exactly what you want to do. Perhaps you want to make two windows share the screen equally; see what is behind the open windows; or minimise all of the open windows except one quickly. You can do this with Snap, Peek and Shake.

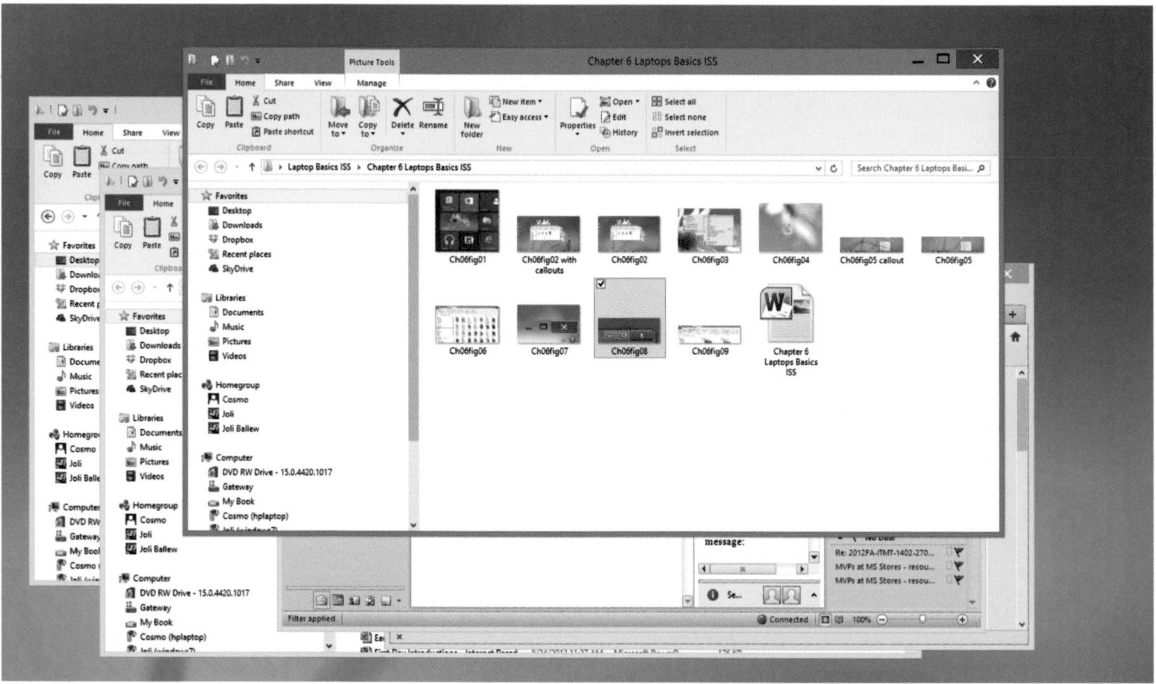

- **Snap** – To position two open windows so that each takes up half of the screen, using their title bars, drag one quickly to the left and the other quickly to the right. Each will 'snap' into place.

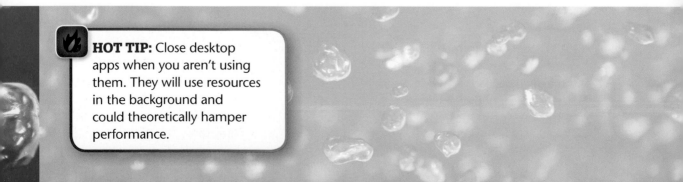

HOT TIP: Close desktop apps when you aren't using them. They will use resources in the background and could theoretically hamper performance.

- **Peek** – To view what's on the desktop, position your mouse in the bottom right corner of the desktop. The windows will become transparent and you can see behind them.
- **Shake** – To minimise all but one window, click, hold, and quickly move your mouse left and right on the window to keep. This 'shaking' motion will make the others fall to the taskbar.

If you have an app open, you can position the app to take up a third of the screen by dragging it in from the left side. Position your mouse in the top left corner, drag downward to find the app to position, and drag inward. It will snap into place.

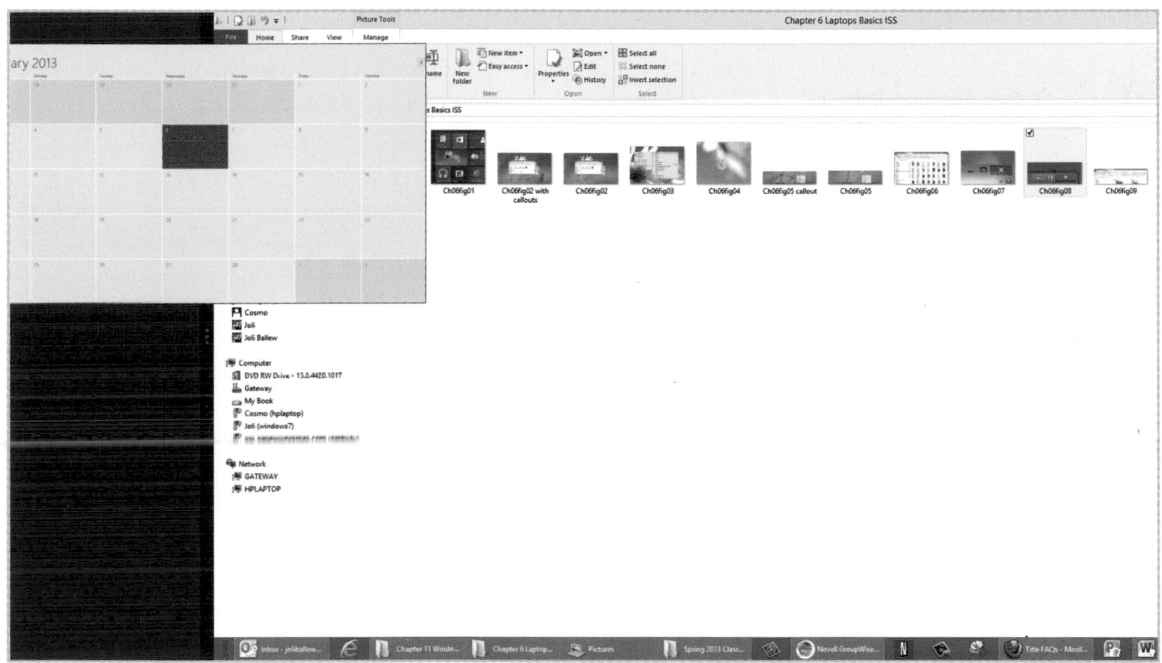

DID YOU KNOW?

You can cause two Start screen apps to share a single screen by dragging one inward from the left side of the screen. Touch users, use your finger.

Create a folder or subfolder

The default folders and subfolders will suit your needs for a while, but soon you'll need to create your own subfolders to manage your data and keep it organised. You could create subfolders inside My Pictures named Grandchildren, Pets, Holidays and Friends, and then move related photos into them, for example. Likewise, you could create subfolders inside My Documents named Taxes, Health and Letters.

1. On the desktop, from the taskbar, open File Explorer.
2. In the Navigation pane, select the folder to hold the new folder you'll create. (We've chosen My Videos.)
3. From the Home tab, click New folder.

? DID YOU KNOW? You can right-click the desktop or inside any folder, point to New, and then click Folder to create a subfolder.

! ALERT: If you can't type a name for the folder or if you'd like to rename it, click the folder and from the Home tab, click Rename. (You can also right-click the folder to rename it.)

4 Name the folder and press Enter on the keyboard.

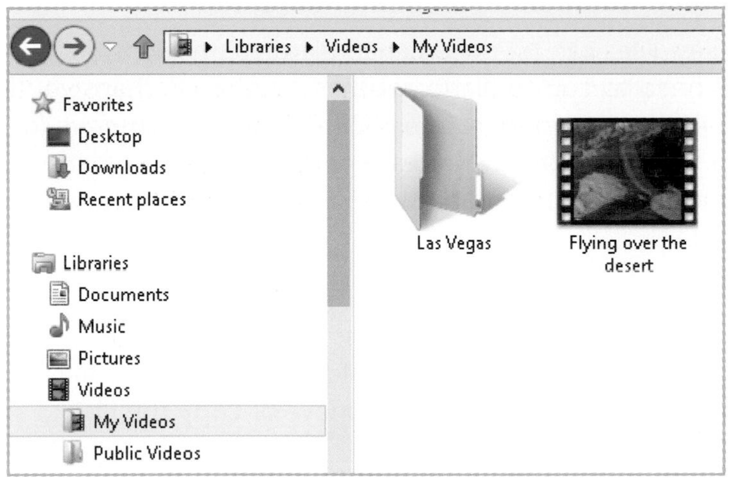

DID YOU KNOW?
You can drag the folder to another area of the desktop or even to another area of the hard drive to move it there. (To make sure you're moving and not copying though, right-click while you do it.)

HOT TIP: Create a folder to hold data related to a hobby, tax information, work or family.

Move a folder or file

Folders contain files. Files can be documents, pictures, music, videos and more. Sometimes you'll need to copy a file to another location. Perhaps you want to copy files to an external drive, memory card or USB thumb or flash drive for the purpose of backing them up. In most other instances though, moving is a better option, such as when you create a subfolder to organise data in a parent folder and want to propagate the folder with data.

1 In File Explorer, locate a file to copy or move; click it one time to select it.

2 If the subfolder is available in the open folder, right-click the file and drag it there. Let go. You can then choose whether to move or copy the file.

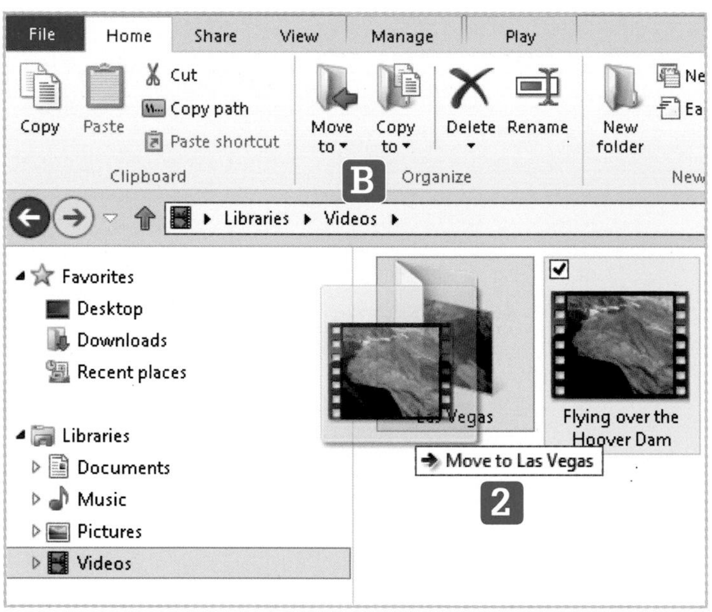

? DID YOU KNOW?

When you copy something, an exact duplicate is made. The original copy of the data remains where it is and a copy of it is placed somewhere else. For the most part, this is not what you want to do when organising data. When organising data, you generally want to move the data.

3 If the subfolder is not readily available:

A Click the file one time to select it.

B From the Home tab, click either Move to or Copy to.

C Choose the desired location from the list. If you don't see it, click Choose location.

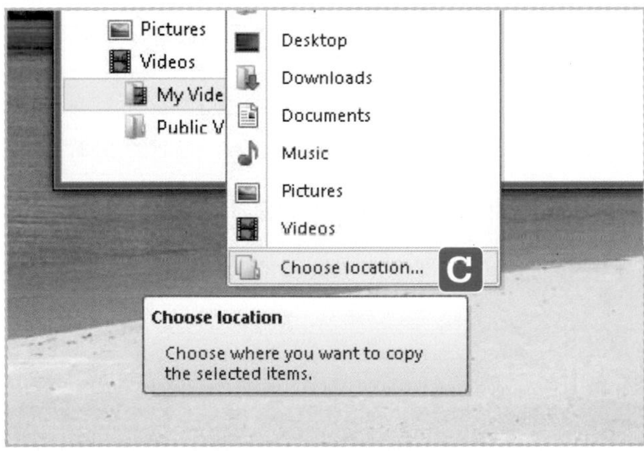

HOT TIP: Hold down the Ctrl key to select non-contiguous files or the Shift key to select contiguous ones. Then, you can perform tasks on multiple files at once.

Search for a file or other item

After you create data, like a Notepad document, you save it to your hard drive. When you're ready to use the file again, you have to locate it and open it. There are several ways to locate a saved file. If you know the document is in the My Documents folder, you can open File Explorer and click Documents. Then you can double-click the file to open it. However, if you aren't sure where the file is, you can search for it from the Start screen. Here, we'll search for a video.

1. Click the Windows key on the keyboard to return to the Start screen.
2. Start typing the name of the file or a unique word in the file.
3. Click Files in the Search pane.
4. Click the desired result.

DID YOU KNOW?

You can search for a word *in a file*, such as a word in a document or presentation slide. You don't have to search using a word in the file name. The word will need to be unique though, so that the results don't offer too many files to browse through.

HOT TIP: If you have to search for files often, it may be because your file system isn't organised very well. Consider spending some time creating subfolders and moving data into them to be better organised.

Back up a folder to an external drive

One way to back up your data is to copy it to an external drive. You can copy data to a DVD drive, a USB drive, a network drive or a larger external backup drive (among others). You copy the folder to the external drive the same way you'd copy a folder to another area of your hard drive – you use the Copy command from the Home tab of any File Explorer window.

1. Using File Explorer, select the data to copy.
2. From the Home tab, click Copy to.
3. Click Choose Location.
4. Click Copy.

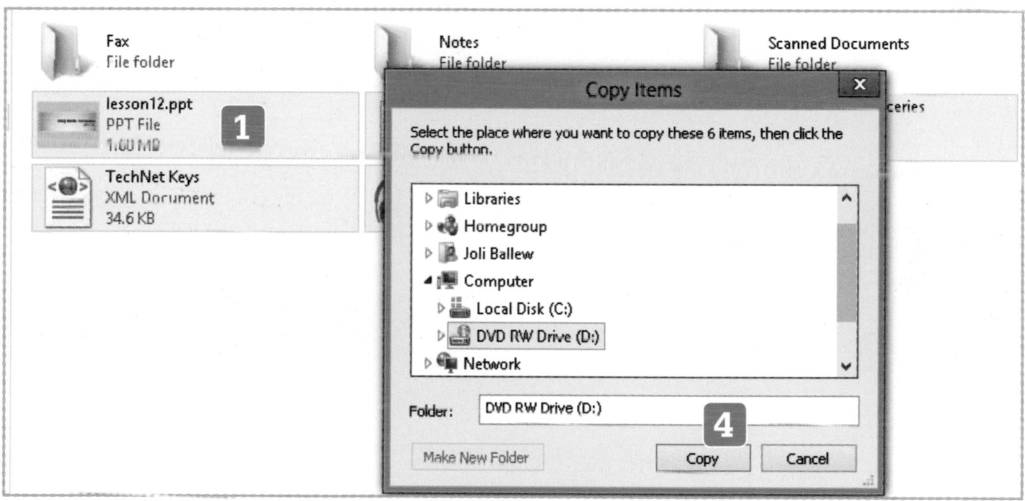

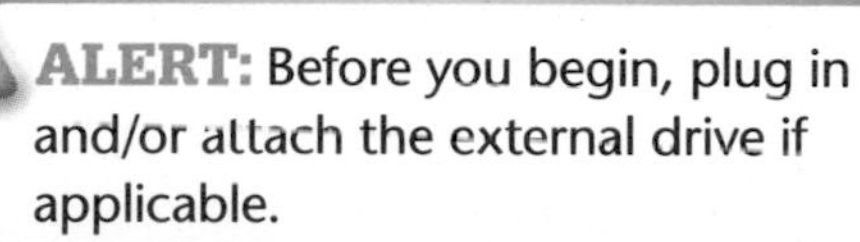

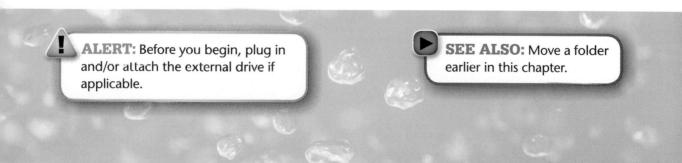

ALERT: Before you begin, plug in and/or attach the external drive if applicable.

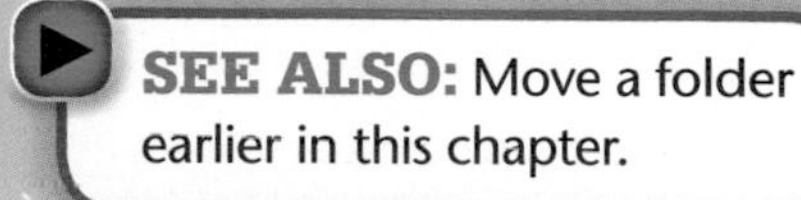

SEE ALSO: Move a folder earlier in this chapter.

10 Use the Internet Explorer Desktop app

Introduction

You use Internet Explorer to access the internet and browse web sites. Windows 8 comes with two versions of this application. You learned about the Internet Explorer *Start screen app* in Chapter 4; in this chapter, you'll learn about the Internet Explorer *Desktop app*.

If you recall, the IE Start screen app (the IE app) provides limited functionality, but is streamlined to offer a clean and efficient web browsing experience. You should use this version when you want to visit your favourite websites and do some basic web surfing, especially if you have a small screen, such as you find on tablet computers and smaller laptops. The *IE Desktop app* is the fully functional version of IE that you may already be familiar with. It offers what the IE Start screen app offers and much, much, more, including the ability to save a list of favourites, use the familiar tabbed browsing features, and enable the Favorites bar, among other things. You may prefer this version on larger laptops, so at the end of this chapter we'll show you how to make it the default web browser, should you prefer.

Explore the Internet Explorer Desktop app

If you've used a Windows-based computer before, you've likely used the traditional version of Internet Explorer. You open this from the desktop, specifically by clicking the big blue E on the taskbar. Microsoft has made a few changes from previous versions though; the Menu bar is hidden, the 'Do not track' feature is enabled, and performance is improved, among other things.

1. If you are on the Start screen, click or tap the Desktop tile or use the Windows + D keyboard shortcut to get to the desktop.
2. Tap the Internet Explorer icon on the taskbar.

3. To go to a website you want to visit, type the name of the website in the window at the top of the page. This is called the Address bar. Press Enter on the keyboard.
4. Explore these features:
   - A Tabs – Click any tab to access the related web page.
   - B Home – Click to access your configured Home page(s).
   - C Add to Favorites – Click to view favourites or to add a web page as a favourite.
   - D Tools – Click to access all of the available settings.
   - E Web content – To read the information offered on the web page.

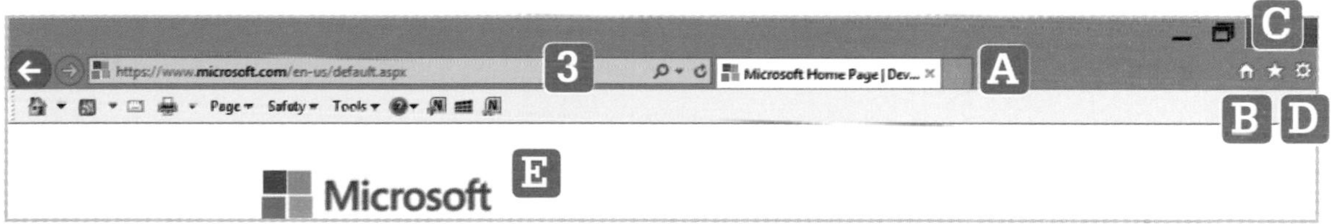

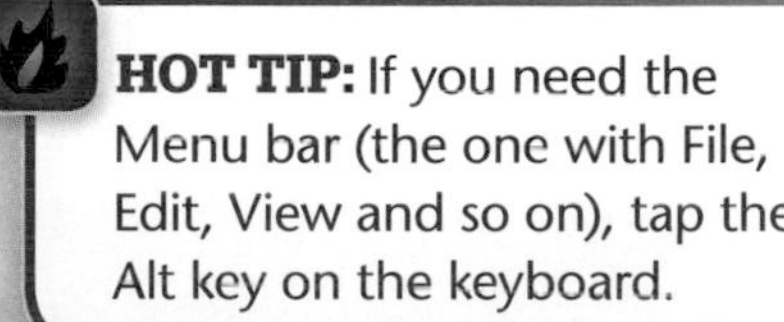

HOT TIP: If you need the Menu bar (the one with File, Edit, View and so on), tap the Alt key on the keyboard.

HOT TIP: Right-click just above the area where you type the website name to enable hidden toolbars.

Use tabs

You can open more than one website at a time in the Internet Explorer Desktop app. To do this, click the tab that appears to the right of the open web page. Then type the name of the website you'd like to visit.

1. Open Internet Explorer.
2. Click an empty tab.
3. Type the name of the website you'd like to visit in the address bar.
4. Press Enter on the keyboard.

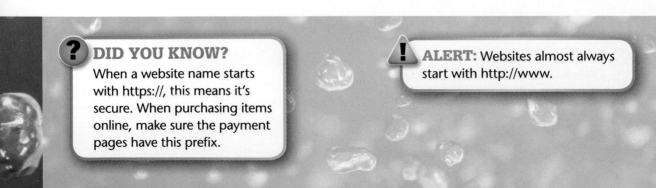

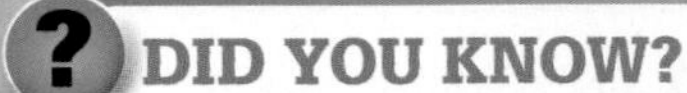

DID YOU KNOW?
When a website name starts with https://, this means it's secure. When purchasing items online, make sure the payment pages have this prefix.

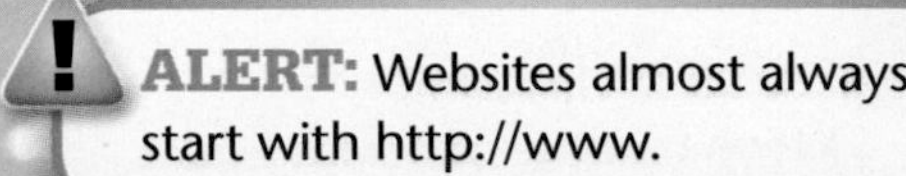

ALERT: Websites almost always start with http://www.

Mark a favourite

Favourites are websites you save links to for accessing more easily at a later time. The favourites you save appear in the Favorites Center. You can also save favourites to the Favorites bar, an optional toolbar you can enable in IE.

1. Go to the web page you want to configure as a favourite.
2. Click the Add to Favorites icon. (It's the star.)
3. Click Add to favorites. (To add the website to the Favorites bar, click the arrow beside the Add to favorites option.)

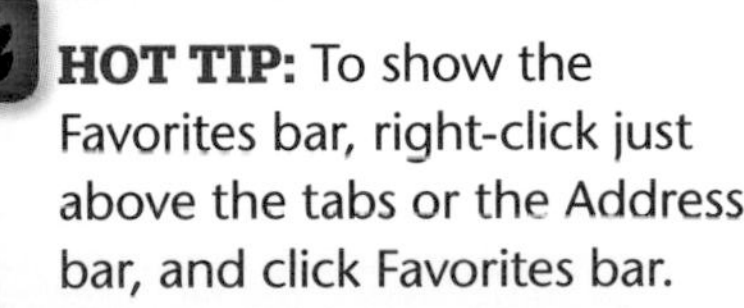

HOT TIP: To show the Favorites bar, right-click just above the tabs or the Address bar, and click Favorites bar.

HOT TIP: You can organise your favourites in your personal Favourites folder. To get started, click the arrow next to Add to favorites in the Favorites Center.

Set a home page

You can select a single web page or multiple web pages to be displayed each time you open the Internet Explorer Desktop app. In fact, there are three options for configuring home pages:

- Use this webpage as your only home page – Select this option if you only want a single web page, the one you have open and selected, to serve as your home page.
- Add this webpage to your home pages tabs – Select this option if you want the page you have open and selected to be added to the other home pages you've already configured.
- Use the current tab set as your home page – Select this option if you've opened multiple tabs and you want all of them to be home pages.

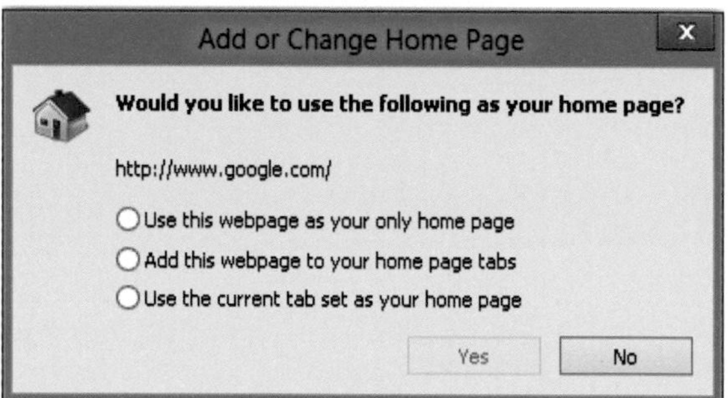

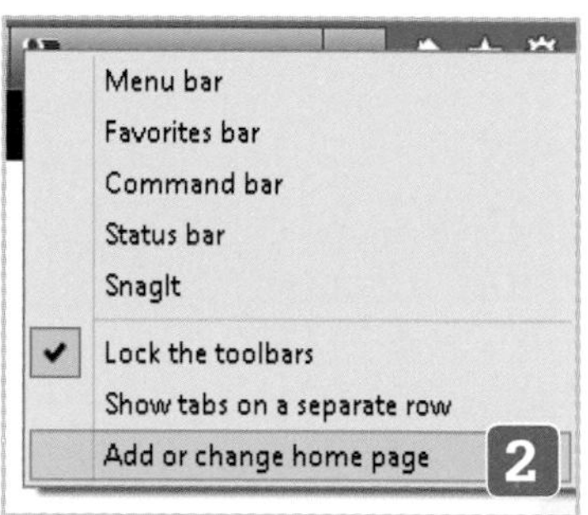

1. Use the Address bar to locate a web page (and use the empty Tab button to repeat to open additional web pages).
2. Right-click the Home icon and click Add or change home page. (Note you have additional choices, including showing various toolbars.)
3. Make a selection using the information provided regarding each option.
4. Click Yes.

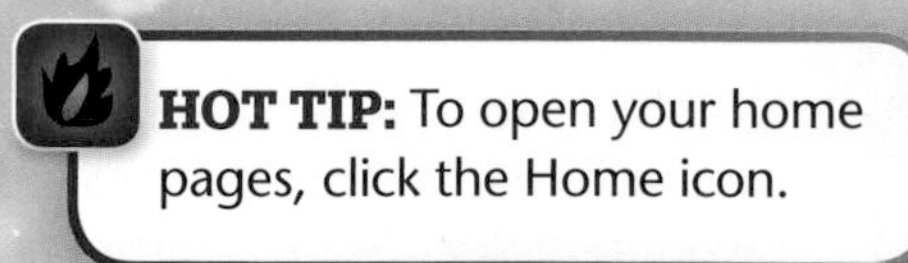

HOT TIP: To open your home pages, click the Home icon.

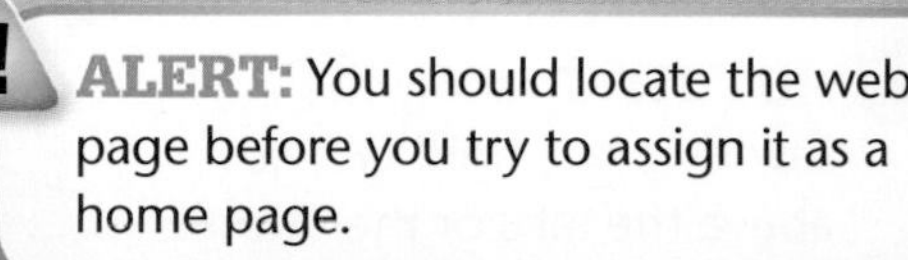

ALERT: You should locate the web page before you try to assign it as a home page.

Zoom in or out

If you have trouble reading what's on a web page because the text is too small, use the Page Zoom feature. Page Zoom preserves the fundamental design of the web page you're viewing. This means that Page Zoom intelligently zooms in on the entire page, which maintains the page's integrity, layout and look.

1. Open the Internet Explorer Desktop app and browse to a web page.
2. If you have a physical keyboard, use the Ctrl + = and the Ctrl + – combinations to zoom in and out.
3. If you have a touch screen, pinch in and out with two or more fingers to zoom in and out.
4. If you prefer to use a mouse or track pad, right-click the area above the tabs and Address bar and place a check by Status bar and then click the arrow on the right end of the Status bar to zoom to a specific amount.

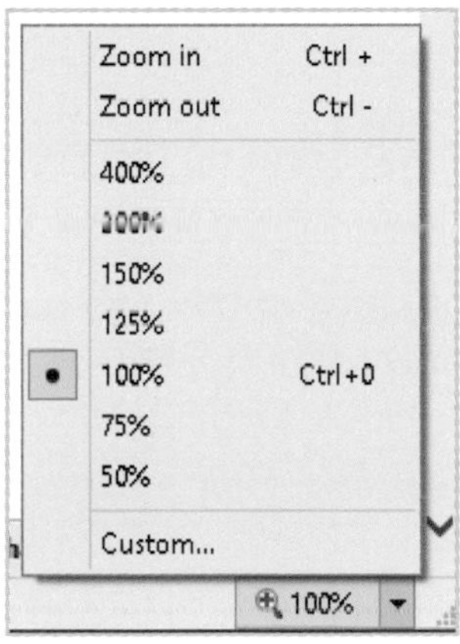

DID YOU KNOW?
The term browse is used to describe both locating a file on your hard drive and locating something on the internet.

DID YOU KNOW?
On a laptop it's easiest to zoom with Ctrl + = and Ctrl + – .

Print a web page

You can print a web page in several ways. When you do though, remember that the pictures and ads will be printed too, so you may want to copy the text and paste it in a WordPad document first.

1. The Print icon is available from the Command bar. To show the Command bar, right click just above the tabs and Address bar and place a check by it. The Command bar and the Print option is shown here.

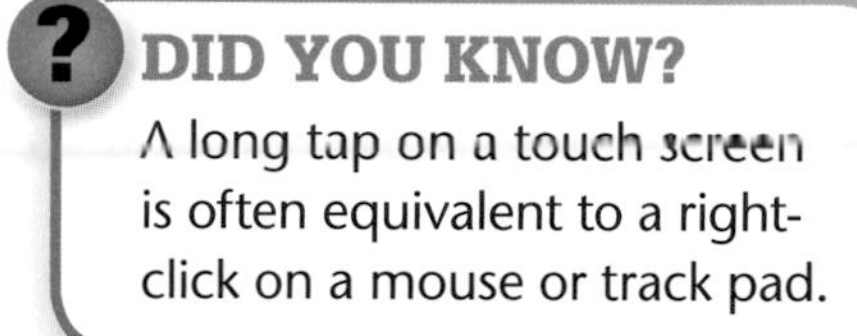

DID YOU KNOW?

A long tap on a touch screen is often equivalent to a right-click on a mouse or track pad.

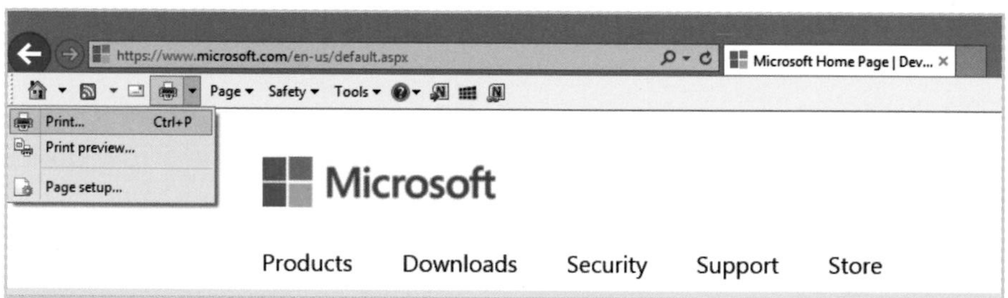

2. The key combination Ctrl + P will bring up the Print dialog box.

3. You can right-click on an empty area of the web page and click Print from the resulting contextual menu.

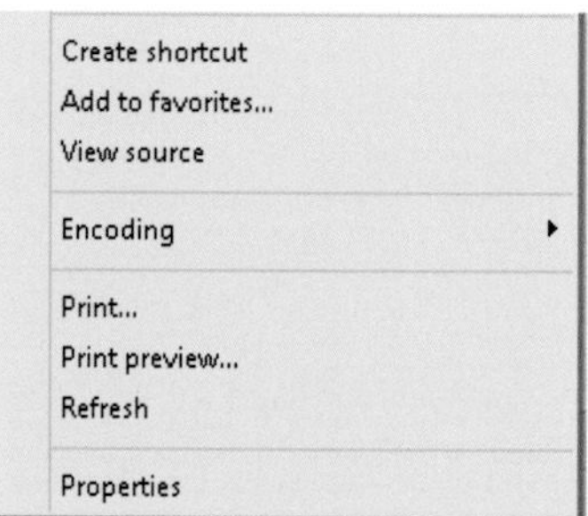

WHAT DOES THIS MEAN?

There are three menu options under the Print icon:

Print: Clicking Print opens the Print dialog box where you can configure the page range, select a printer, change page orientation, change print order and choose a paper type. Additional options include print quality, output bins and more. Of course, the choices depend on what your printer offers. If your printer can print only at 300 × 300 dots per inch, you can't configure it to print at a higher quality.

Print Preview: Clicking Print preview opens a window where you can see before you print what the printout will actually look like. You can switch between portrait and landscape views, access the Page Setup dialog box, and more.

Page Setup: Clicking Page Setup opens the Page Setup dialog box. Here you can select a paper size, source, and create headers and footers. You can also change orientation and margins, all of which is dependent on what features your printer supports.

Clear history

If you don't want people (who have access to your computer) to be able to snoop around on your laptop and find out what websites you've been visiting, you'll need to delete your 'browsing history'. Deleting your browsing history lets you remove the information stored on your computer related to your internet activities.

1. Open the Internet Explorer desktop app.
2. Click the Alt key on the keyboard if you do not see the menu shown here.

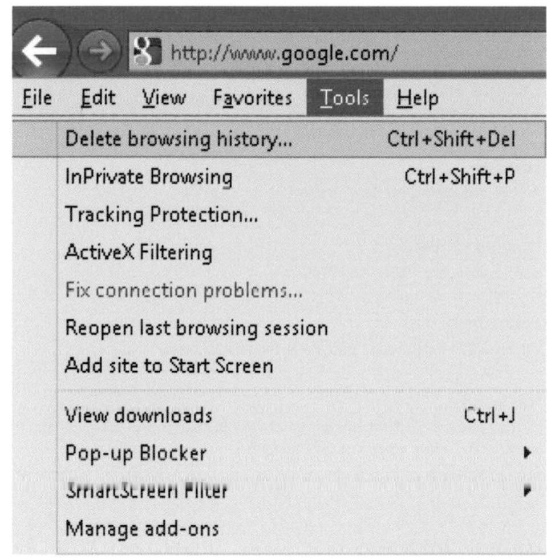

WHAT DOES THIS MEAN?

Temporary Internet Files: Files that have been downloaded and saved in your Temporary Internet Files folder. A snooper could go through these files to see what you've been doing online.

Cookies: Small text files that include data that identifies your preferences when you visit particular websites. Cookies are what allow you to visit, say, www.amazon.com and be greeted with 'Hello <your name>. We have recommendations for you!' Cookies help a site offer you a personalised web experience.

History: The list of websites you've visited and any web addresses you've typed. Anyone with access to your laptop can look at your History list to see where you've been.

Form data: Information that's been saved using Internet Explorer's autocomplete form data functionality. If you don't want forms to be filled out automatically by you or someone else who has access to your computer and user account, delete this.

Passwords: Passwords that were saved using Internet Explorer autocomplete password prompts.

InPrivate Blocking data: Data that was saved by InPrivate Blocking to detect where websites may be automatically sharing details about your visit.

3 Click Tools.

4 Click Delete browsing history.

5 Select what to delete, and click Delete. (You may want to keep Preserve Favorites and website data selected.)

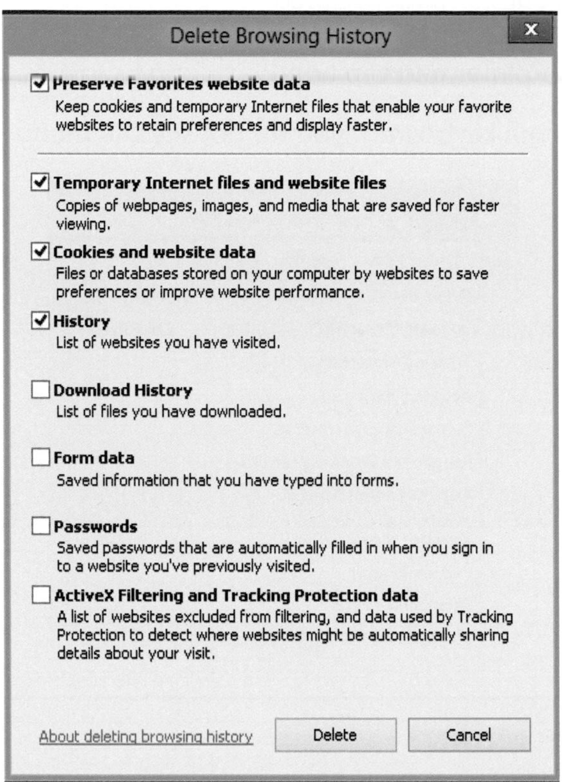

Delete Browsing History
Preserve Favorites website data
Keep cookies and temporary Internet files that enable your favorite websites to retain preferences and display faster.
Temporary Internet files and website files
Copies of webpages, images, and media that are saved for faster viewing.
Cookies and website data
Files or databases stored on your computer by websites to save preferences or improve website performance.
History
List of websites you have visited.
Download History
List of files you have downloaded.
Form data
Saved information that you have typed into forms.
Passwords
Saved passwords that are automatically filled in when you sign in to a website you've previously visited.
ActiveX Filtering and Tracking Protection data
A list of websites excluded from filtering, and data used by Tracking Protection to detect where websites might be automatically sharing details about your visit.
About deleting browsing history
Delete
Cancel

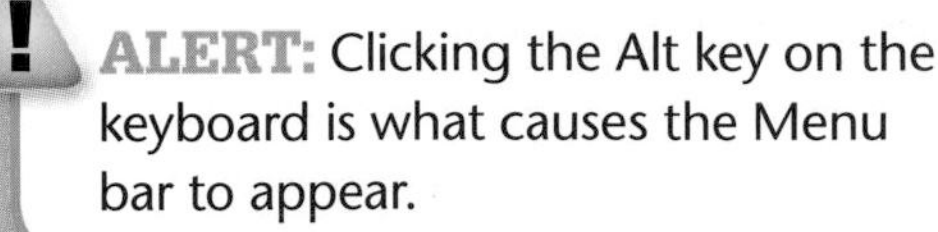

ALERT: Clicking the Alt key on the keyboard is what causes the Menu bar to appear.

DID YOU KNOW?
You can also click the Tools icon, Internet Options, and from the General tab, opt to delete your browsing history.

Stay safe on the internet

Although you can rely somewhat on anti-virus software, pop-up blockers, secure websites and such to keep you safe while surfing the internet, staying secure when online has more to do with common sense. When you're online, make sure you follow the guidelines listed below.

1. If you are connecting to a public network, make sure you select Public when prompted by Windows 8.
2. Always keep your computers updated with Windows Updates.
3. Limit the amount of confidential information you store on the internet.
4. When making credit card purchases or travel reservations, or when logging on to a service like Twitter, always make sure the website address starts with https:// and use a secure site.

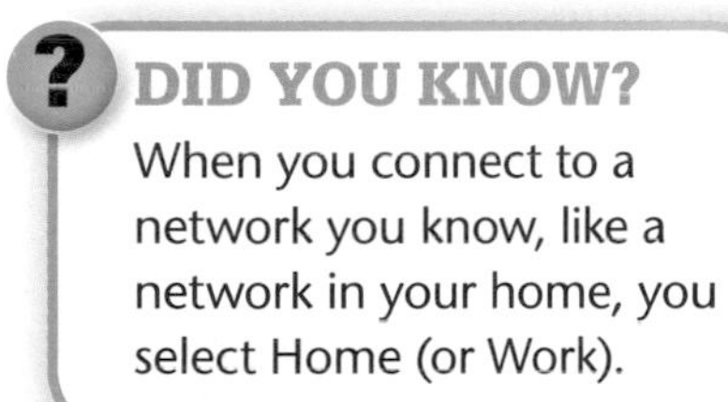

DID YOU KNOW?
When you connect to a network you know, like a network in your home, you select Home (or Work).

5. Always sign out of any secure website you enter.

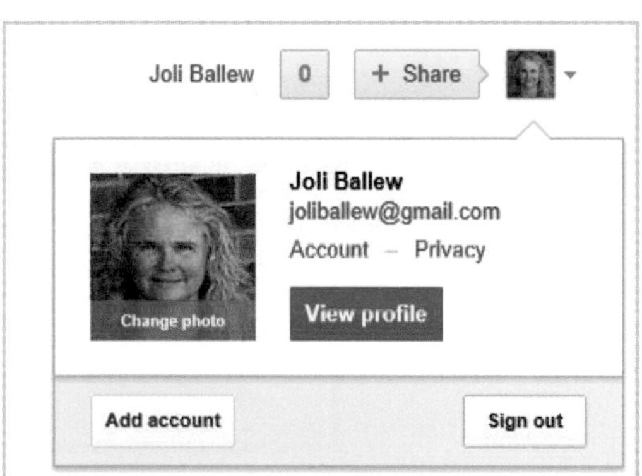

ALERT: Windows 8 comes with Windows Defender, which works hard to keep you and your computer safe. However, you may still want to consider a third-party anti-virus solution.

ALERT: Don't put your address and phone number on Facebook or other social networking sites.

Configure the Internet Explorer Desktop app as the default

If you'd prefer that the Internet Explorer Desktop app opens when you click a link in an email, message, document and so on, instead of the simpler IE app, you can configure this in Internet Explorer's settings. Doing so will make the Desktop app the default.

1. Open Internet Explorer on the desktop.
2. Click the Tools icon, then Internet Options.
3. Click the Programs tab.
4. Click the arrow beside Let Internet Explorer decide.
5. Click Always in Internet Explorer in the desktop.
6. Click OK.

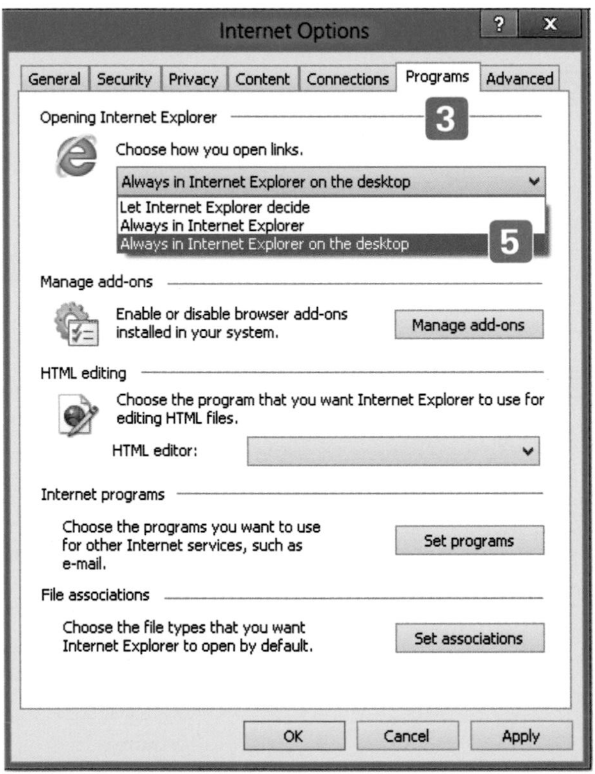

HOT TIP: While you have the Internet Options dialog box open, explore the other options available. From the General tab, for instance, you can configure IE to start each time with tabs from the last session (instead of your configured Home page(s)).

DID YOU KNOW?

If you make the change outlined here, when you click the IE app tile on the Start screen, the IE desktop app will open.

Configure Internet Explorer accessibility options

One of the reasons you may choose to use IE for all internet browsing is that it offers accessibility options. These options include the ability to assign your own colour, font, and font size to all of the web pages you encounter. If you have problems viewing most web pages, you may want to give it a try.

1. Open the Internet Explorer Desktop app.
2. Click the Alt key, click Tools and click Internet Options.
3. From the General tab, click Accessibility.

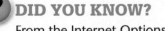

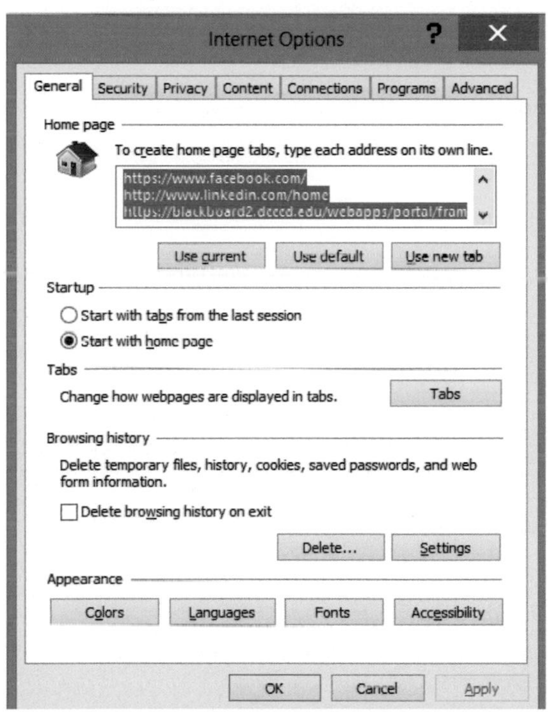

DID YOU KNOW?

From the Internet Options dialog box you can click the Content tab and enable Family Safety. This will help protect children from disagreeable web material.

4. Choose what to configure.
5. Click OK.
6. To assign your own choices:
   - A From the General tab, click the related option. We'll choose Colors.
   - B Deselect Use Windows colors.
   - C Click any item and choose a colour. Repeat as desired.
   - D Click OK.
7. Click OK to close the Internet Options dialog box.

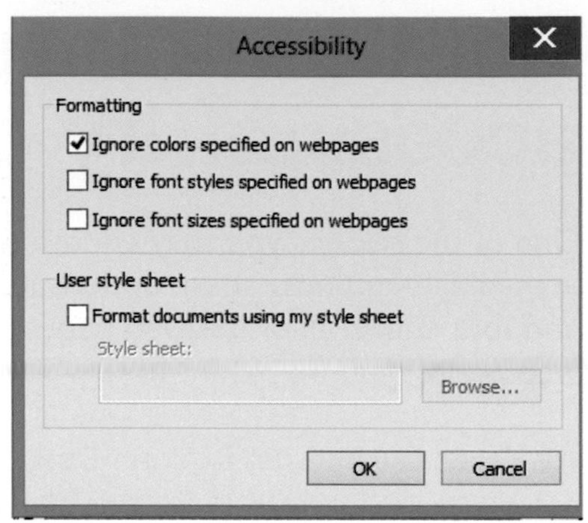

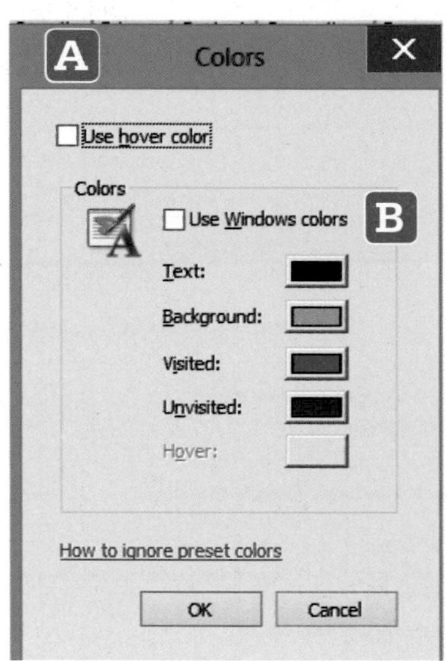

? DID YOU KNOW?

From the General tab of the Internet Options dialog box you can configure IE to open the web pages you used during your last browsing session.

11 Explore desktop apps

Introduction

Desktop applications are those programs that open on the desktop. The desktop is the traditional computing environment, and desktop applications are 'normal' programs. If you've ever used Windows XP, Windows ME, Windows Vista, Windows 7, or virtually any other version of Windows, you've used the desktop and desktop applications.

The desktop applications are much different from the Start screen apps you've learned about in this book. Desktop applications open in a window that you can minimise, maximise and resize easily, and generally offer menus including File, Edit, Home, Insert and so on. Unlike the Start screen apps, you don't have to right-click, flick up, or perform any other task to make menus and such appear.

Desktop applications aren't available from the Store, but you can download them from the internet or buy them on CDs and DVDs. You may have some already, perhaps Adobe Photoshop Elements or Mozilla Firefox, or applications that came with printers, cameras or scanners. Beyond applications you obtain, desktop applications can be Windows Accessories too, like the Calculator, WordPad, the Snipping Tool and Paint. Desktop applications virtually always offer more features than any Start screen app that is deemed similar (if there is one).

In this chapter you'll learn how to locate the desktop apps from the Start screen, and how to use a few of them. After that, any time an application opens on the desktop, you'll understand how to use it and why it's a desktop app.

Search for applications from the Start screen

The Start screen is the key to accessing everything and anything on your laptop. The Start screen offers access to all applications, programs, accessories and features, including the desktop applications (desktop apps). If there isn't a tile on the Start screen for the program you want to open, you can find it in the All Apps screen instead. The easiest way to find an application is to search for it (versus scrolling through the available tiles).

1. Access the Start screen. You can press the Windows key to get there.
2. Scroll through what's shown. Try to note a pattern between these:
   - A Start screen apps.
   - B Desktop apps.

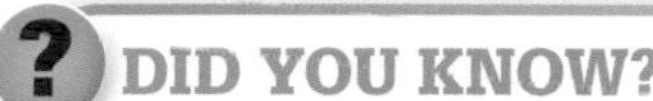

DID YOU KNOW?

Press the Windows key on the keyboard and, from there, you can search for whatever you want to find.

3 Right-click an empty area of the screen and click All apps.

4 Scroll right and look for additional desktop apps. A few are shown here.

WHAT DOES THIS MEAN?

The **desktop** is the traditional computing environment and offers the taskbar, the Recycle Bin, the Notification area and so on.

Write a letter with WordPad

Word processing programs guide you through the process necessary to create complex documents such as invoices, resumés, calendars, publications and so on. If you only need to create and print simple documents like grocery or to-do lists, or need to put together a weekly newsletter that you send via email, there's no reason to purchase a large office suite like Microsoft Office (and learn how to use it). Windows 8 comes with WordPad.

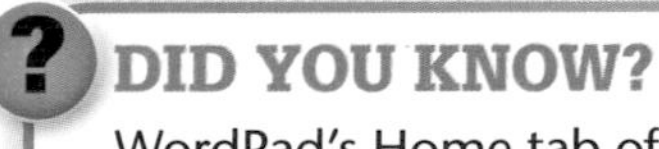

DID YOU KNOW?
WordPad's Home tab offers options for setting the font, font style, font size and more.

1. At the Start screen, type WordPad, and then click WordPad.

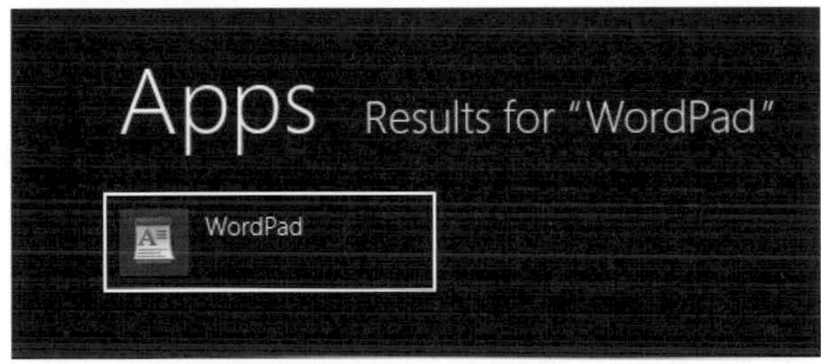

2. Click once inside WordPad, and start typing.

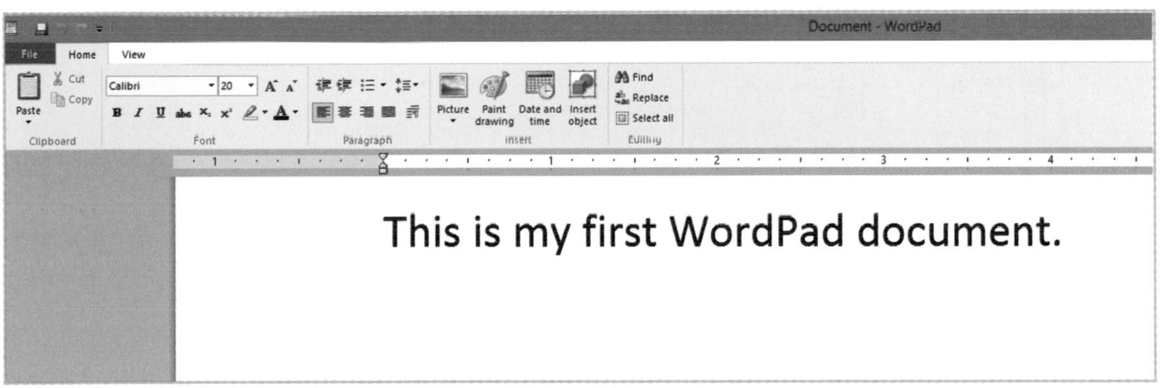

ALERT: WordPad has two tabs: Home and View. Each tab groups related tools. You'll see similar tabs and tab groups in other programs. If time allows, explore these tabs to see what is available there.

ALERT: If you close WordPad before saving the file, your work will be lost!

Save a letter with WordPad

If you want to save a letter, document or similar item you've written in WordPad so you can work with it later, you click the File tab and then click Save as. This will allow you to name the file and save it to your hard drive. The next time you want to view the file, at the Start screen type the file name and click Files to find it.

1. With WordPad open and a few words typed, click File.
2. Point to Save as, and click Rich Text document (this is a common file format and is compatible with other applications).

HOT TIP: You can access the Documents library (and thus your documents) from File Explorer. Click the folder icon on the desktop's taskbar to get started.

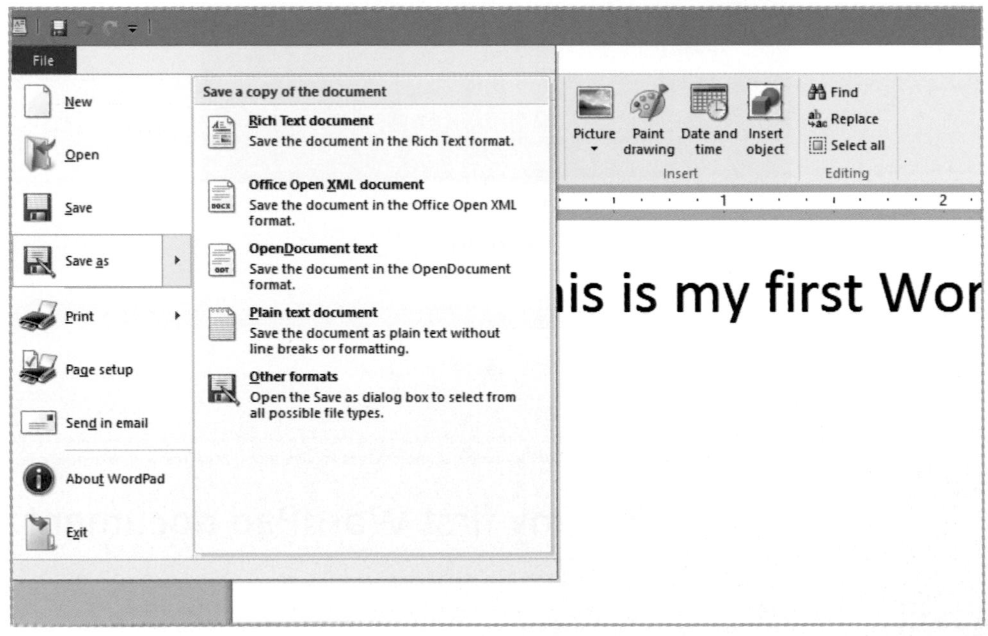

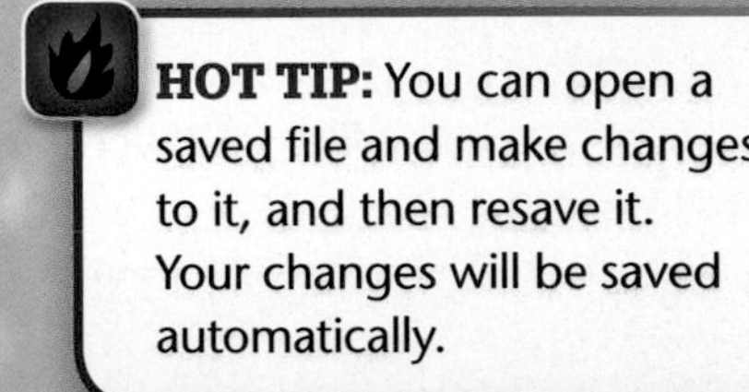

HOT TIP: You can open a saved file and make changes to it, and then resave it. Your changes will be saved automatically.

3 Type a unique name for the file. Notice that the default folder for saving a document is Documents library.

4 Click Save.

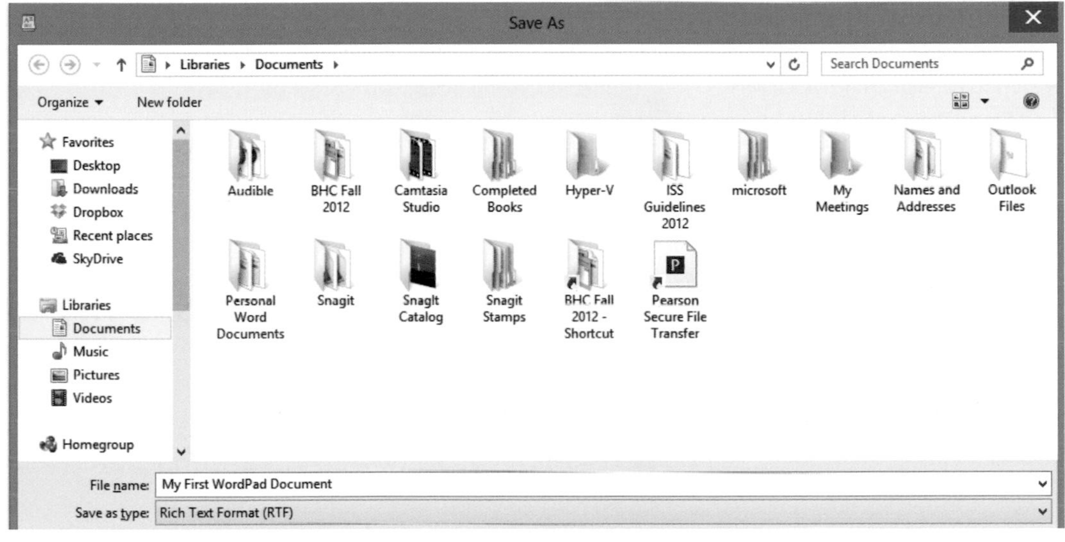

HOT TIP: You can change the folder a file is saved to by selecting another one from the left pane of the Save As window. This is called the Navigation pane. You could choose Desktop if you want the file to be saved directly to the desktop, for instance.

Print a letter with WordPad

Sometimes you'll need to print a letter so you can mail it, print a grocery list to take on a shopping trip, or print a recipe so you can use it in the kitchen. You can access the Print command from WordPad's File menu.

1. With the document open in WordPad, click File.
2. Click Print in the left pane. Note the additional options in the right pane.
3. Select a printer.
4. Increase the number of copies if desired; click Print.

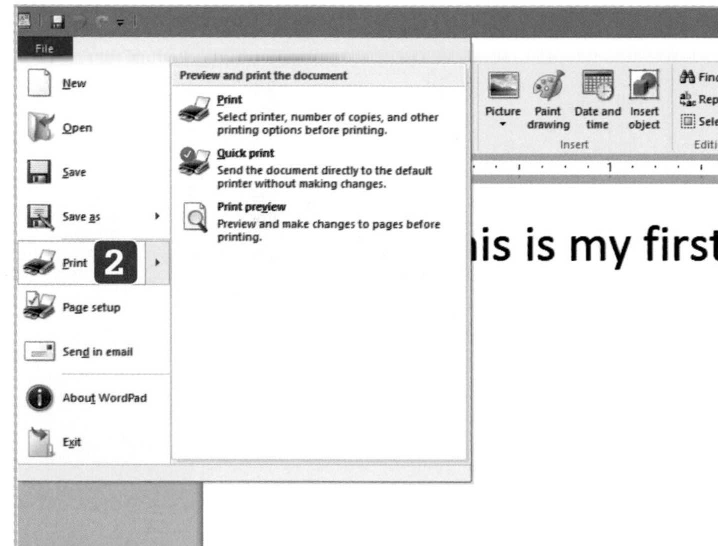

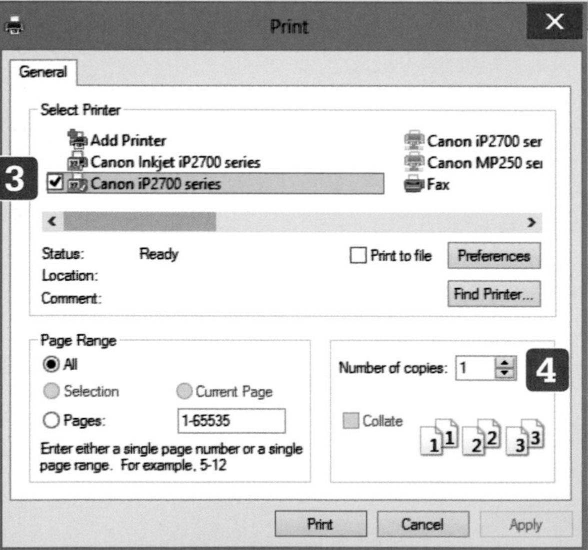

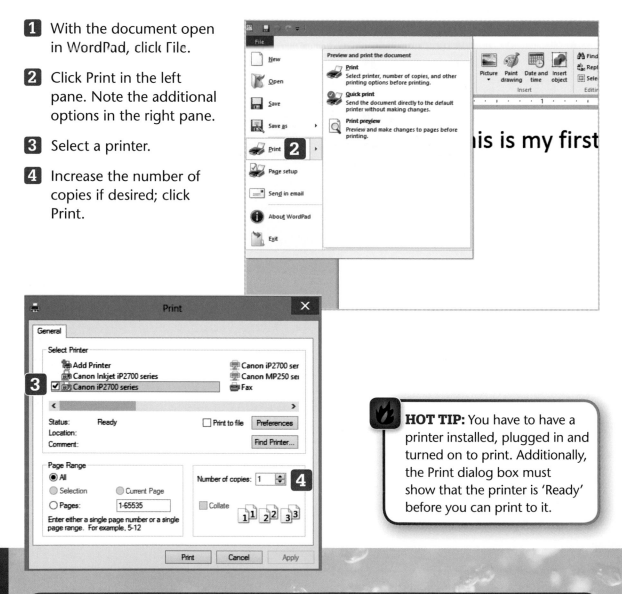

HOT TIP: You have to have a printer installed, plugged in and turned on to print. Additionally, the Print dialog box must show that the printer is 'Ready' before you can print to it.

WHAT DOES THIS MEAN?

Printer Preferences: Lets you select the page orientation, print order and the type of paper you'll be printing on, among other features.

Page Range: Lets you select what pages to print.

Use the calculator

You've probably used a calculator before, and using the Windows 8 calculator is not much different from a hand held one, except that you input numbers with a mouse click, keyboard, a number pad, or your finger on a touch screen. There are four calculators available and Standard is the default. Calculator is available from the All Apps screen.

1. At the Start screen, type Calc and click Calculator.

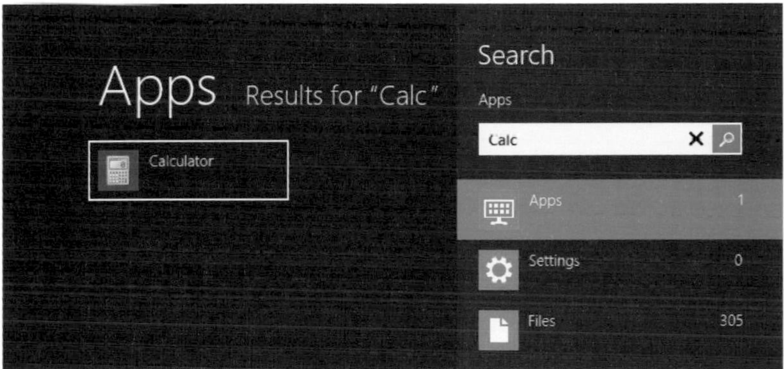

2. Input numbers and operations using any applicable method.
3. Click the View menu to see other calculator options. This is the Scientific calculator. Note the other options.
4. Close Calculator by clicking the X in the top right corner of it.

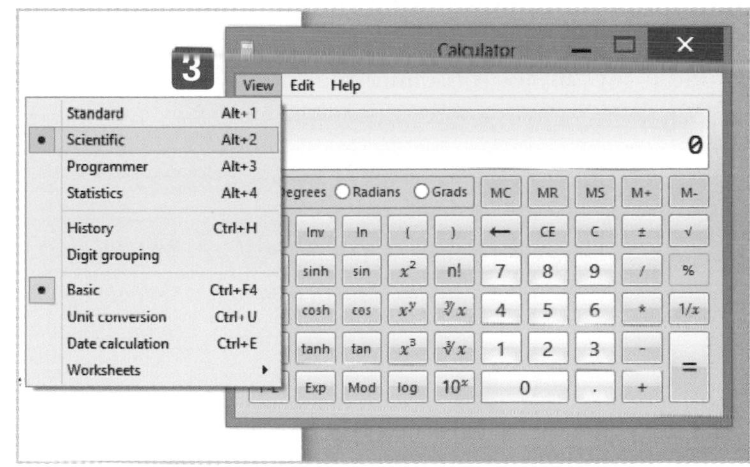

HOT TIP: If you have trouble using the mouse to click the numbers on the calculator, use the numbers on your keyboard.

HOT TIP: Explore each menu option and the available features there. Make sure to look at View>Worksheets>Mortgage, to see how worksheets function.

Use the Snipping Tool

Sometimes you'll see something on your screen you want to take a virtual snapshot of to keep or share. It may be a recipe or an article about a place you'd like to visit, for instance. It might be an error message you think your granddaughter can resolve. It doesn't matter what it is; you can capture anything that appears on your laptop's screen with the Snipping Tool. Once captured, you can save it, edit it and/or send it to an email recipient.

1. From the Start screen, type Snip.
2. In the results, click Snipping Tool.
3. Click New.
4. Drag your mouse across any part of the screen. When you let go of the mouse, the snip will appear in the Snipping Tool window. Here, I've captured the page I'm currently writing!
5. Explore each menu: File, Edit, Tools and Help, and the options on the toolbar. Refer to the next section for more information.

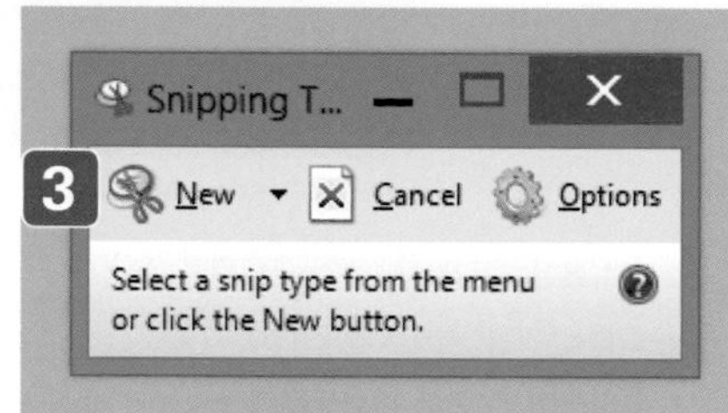

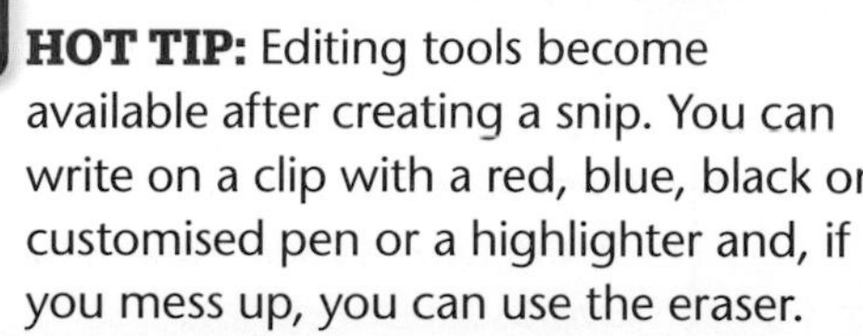

HOT TIP: Editing tools become available after creating a snip. You can write on a clip with a red, blue, black or customised pen or a highlighter and, if you mess up, you can use the eraser.

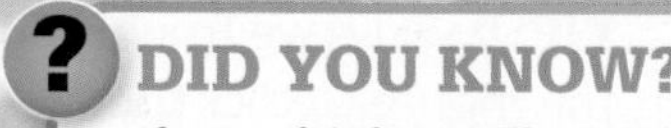

DID YOU KNOW?
If you think you'll use the Snipping Tool often, pin it to the taskbar. This is explained at the end of the chapter.

Email a snip

You can use the Snipping Tool to take a snapshot of your screen as detailed in the previous section. You can even write on it with a 'pen'. You can also email that snip if you'd like to share it with someone.

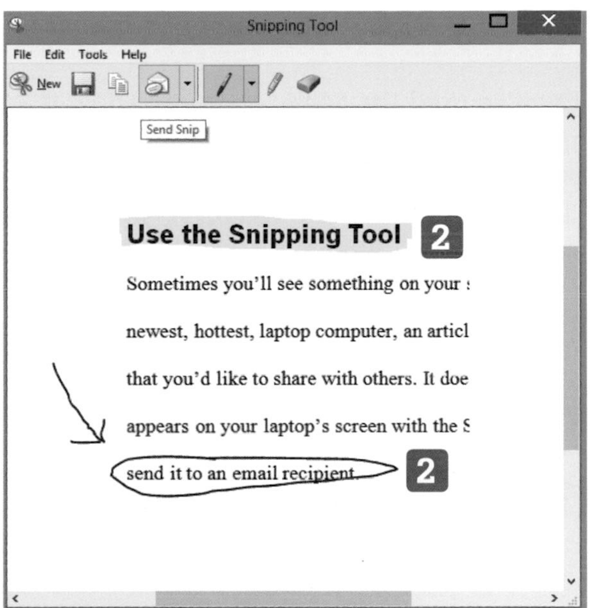

1. Take a shot of your screen with the Snipping Tool.
2. If desired, use the pen, highlighter and other tools to write on the image.
3. Click File, and click Send To.
4. Click Email Recipient.

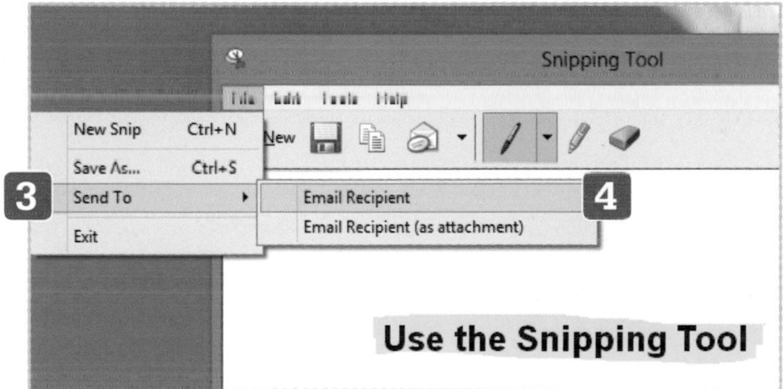

5. Insert the recipients' names, change the subject if desired, type a message if desired, and click Send.

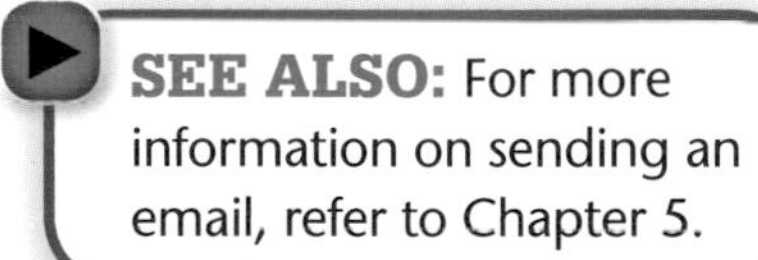

SEE ALSO: For more information on sending an email, refer to Chapter 5.

ALERT: If you select Email Recipient, this will insert the snip inside an email. Note that you can also send the snip as an attachment.

DID YOU KNOW?

If you need more editing tools than the Snipping Tool provides, press Print Screen on your keyboard, open Paint (a desktop application), and click Paste. The capture will appear there and you can use Paint to finalise the screen shot.

Play a song in Windows Media Player

If you've used the Music app, you know it doesn't offer very many features; for the most part it's just for playing music and buying music from the Store and nothing much else. If you want to do something with music that the Music app can't provide (like create your own music CD), you do so with Windows Media Player. The best way to get to know Media Player is to play a song.

1. From the Start screen, type Media Player. Click Windows Media Player in the results. If prompted, opt to use the default options.

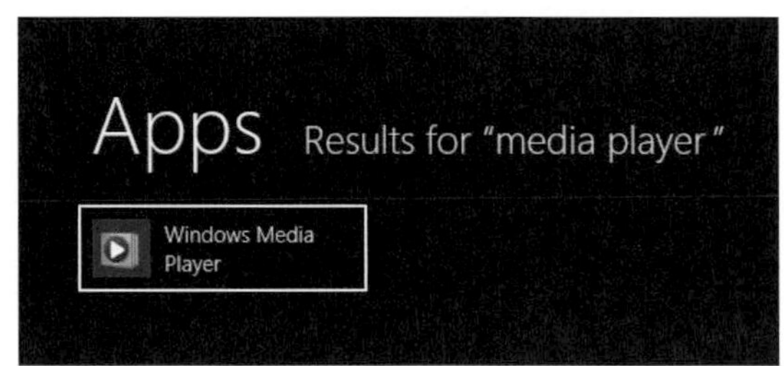

2. Click Music in the Navigation pane. (Note you can also click Artist, Album or Genre to locate a song.)

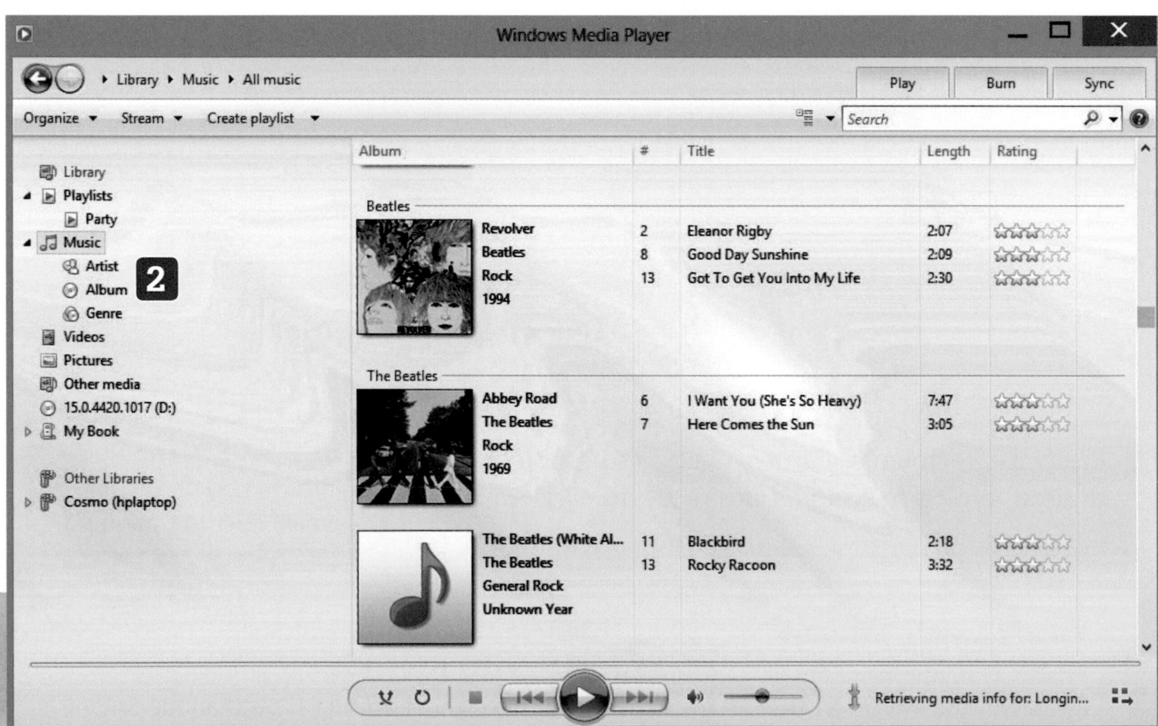

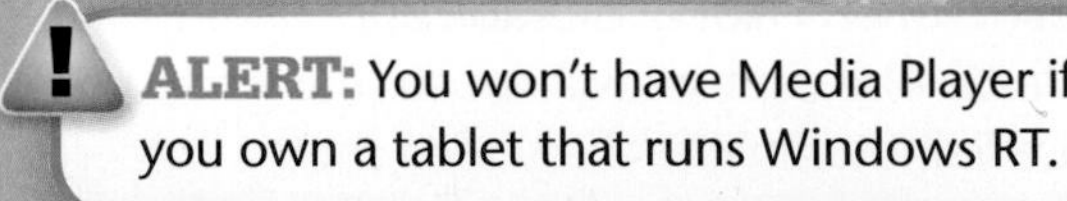

ALERT: You won't have Media Player if you own a tablet that runs Windows RT.

3. Double-click any song in the right pane to play it.

4. Use these media controls located at the bottom of the Media Player interface:
   - A Shuffle – To let Windows Media Player choose what order to play the selected songs.
   - B Repeat – To play the current song again.
   - C Stop – To stop playback.
   - D Previous – To play the previous song in the list, on the album, and so on.
   - E Play/Pause – To play and pause the song (and playlist).
   - F Next – To play the next song in the list, on the album, and so on.
   - G Mute – To quickly mute the song.
   - H Volume – To change the volume of the song.

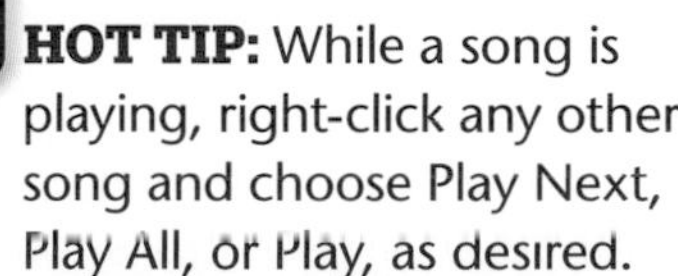

HOT TIP: While a song is playing, right-click any other song and choose Play Next, Play All, or Play, as desired.

DID YOU KNOW?

Media Player has Back and Forward buttons you can use to its interface.

Copy music from a CD you own

You can use Windows Media Player to copy the music on the CDs you own to your laptop. This is called 'ripping'. To rip means to copy in media-speak. Once music is on your laptop, you can listen to it in the Music app and in Media Player, burn compilations of music to other CDs, and sync the music to a portable music player.

1. Insert the CD to copy into the CD drive.
2. Deselect any songs you do not want to copy to your computer.
3. In Windows Media Player, click the Rip CD button.

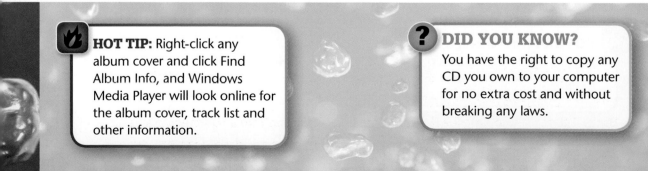

HOT TIP: Right-click any album cover and click Find Album Info, and Windows Media Player will look online for the album cover, track list and other information.

DID YOU KNOW?
You have the right to copy any CD you own to your computer for no extra cost and without breaking any laws.

Create your own music CD

Although you can take your laptop with you, it's unwieldy if you just want to listen to music. There are two additional ways to take music with you when you are on the road or on the go. You can copy the music to a portable device (MP3 player or phone, for example) or you can create your own CDs, choosing the songs to copy and placing them on the CD in the desired order. Here you'll learn how to create a music CD. (To copy songs to a portable player, use the Sync tab instead of the Burn tab.)

1. Open Media Player.
2. Insert a blank CD and click the Burn tab.
3. Click any song or album to add and drag it to the List pane, shown here. You can drag any song to move it to a new position in the Burn list.
4. When you've added the songs you want, click Start burn.

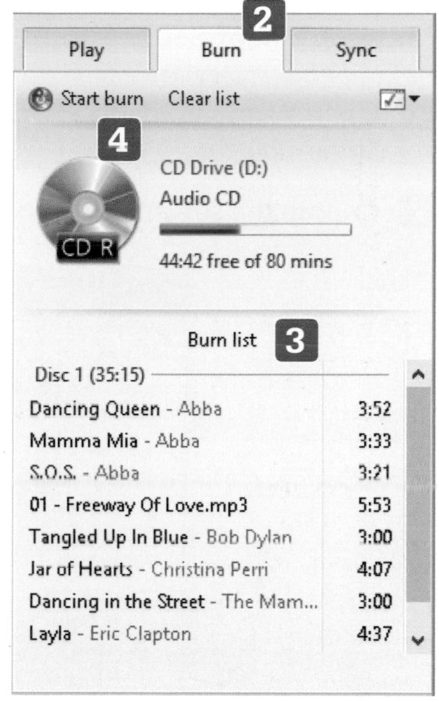

ALERT: If you have a tablet you may not have a CD drive. If this is the case you'll have to consider some sort of workaround, like network sharing. If you have Windows RT, even some workarounds (like sharing media and so forth) won't work.

HOT TIP: Click the arrow beside Organize, and click Options to change the settings configured by default, including whether or not to use 'volume leveling' when burning CDs or if you want to burn the CD without any gaps between tracks.

DID YOU KNOW?
Look at the slider in the List pane to see how much room is left on the CD. A typical CD can hold about 80 minutes of music.

WHAT DOES THIS MEAN?
Burn: A term used to describe the process of copying music from a computer to a CD.

Access media on networked devices

If you have a network at home, you can share the media on your laptop with other computers that are members of it. Likewise, you can share media from networked computers and access that media from your laptop. Sharing allows you to keep only one copy of media (music, videos, pictures) on one computer, while sharing it with other computers, laptops, some tablet computers, various media extenders, and Microsoft's Xbox 360.

1 Open Windows Media Player and click the Stream button.

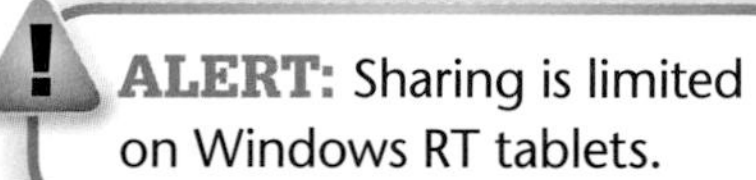

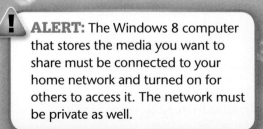

ALERT: Sharing is limited on Windows RT tablets.

2 Choose the streaming options you desire.

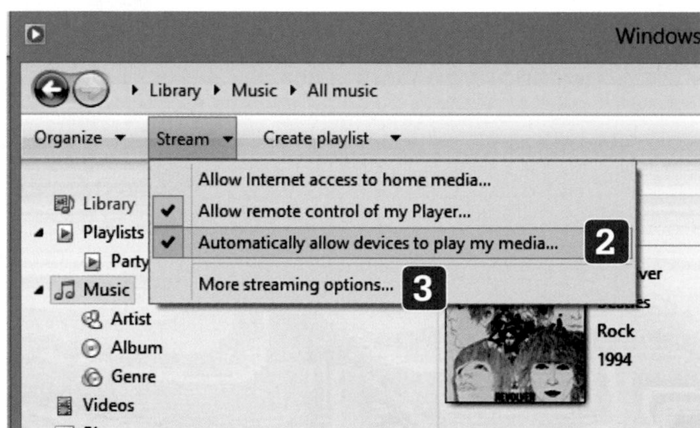

3 To see additional options, click the Stream button again and choose More streaming options.

4 Configure options as desired and click OK when finished.

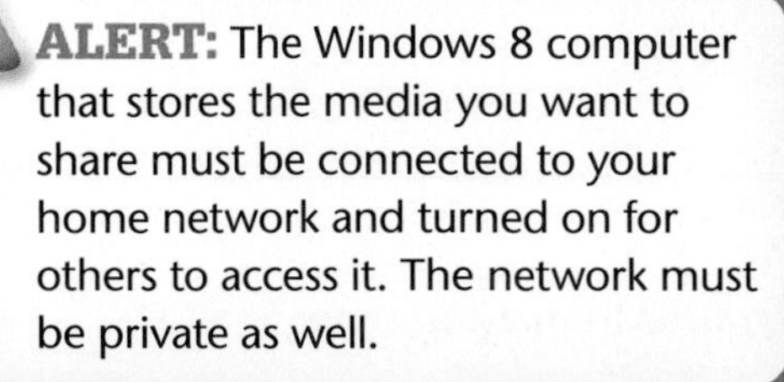

ALERT: The Windows 8 computer that stores the media you want to share must be connected to your home network and turned on for others to access it. The network must be private as well.

HOT TIP: You must repeat this task on other Windows computers on your network in order for streaming to work effectively.

Explore Paint

If you've explored the Photos app, you know it doesn't offer too many features beyond looking at photos and uploading photos from external devices. You can't edit photos, for instance, and you can't rotate them either (at least not at the time this book was published). Here are a few things you can do in Paint that you can't do in the Photos app.

1. Click Select and drag the cursor to select an area. Then, you can crop it.

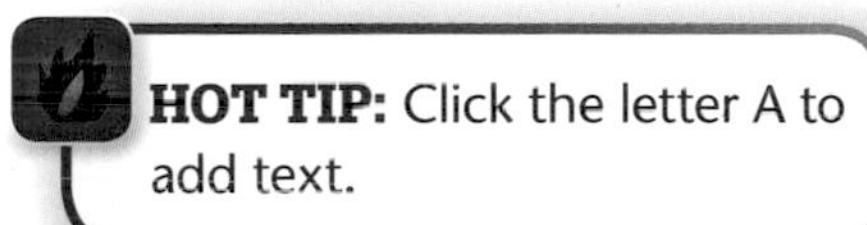

HOT TIP: Click the letter A to add text.

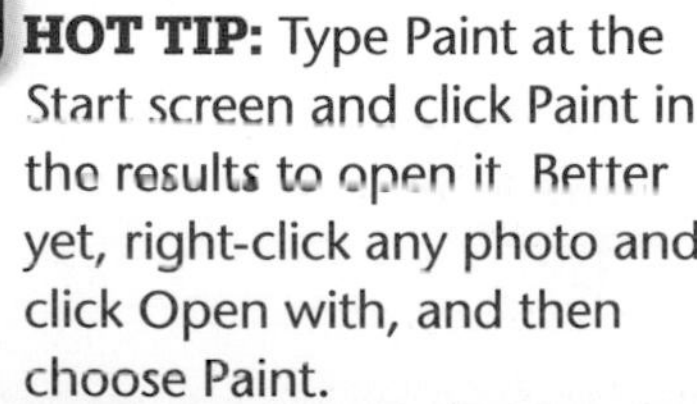

HOT TIP: Type Paint at the Start screen and click Paint in the results to open it. Better yet, right-click any photo and click Open with, and then choose Paint.

DID YOU KNOW?
There are better tools for photo editing than Paint, but Paint is a great tool for creating Lost Pet and Help Wanted signs.

2 Use the Rotate options to rotate a photo.

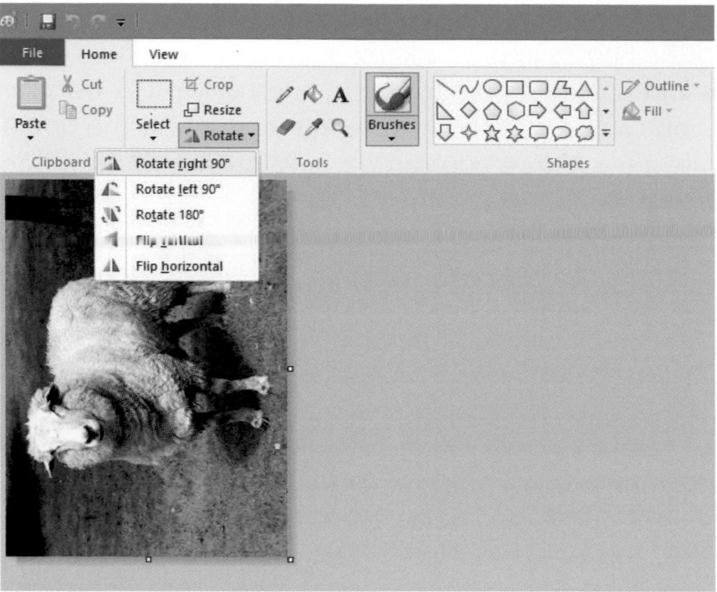

3 Use the Brushes option to draw on the photo.

4 Click File, New, and then use the Shapes options to draw shapes on the photo. Use the icon that looks like a paint can to fill the shapes with colour.

5 Use the Eraser to remove parts of a photo.

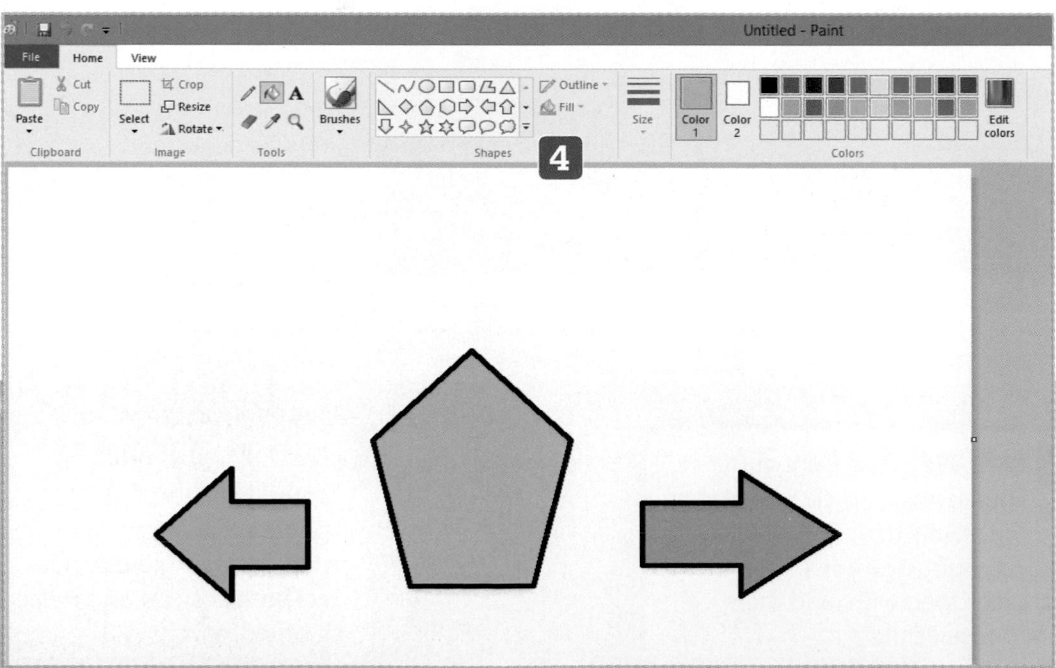

Find other desktop apps

There are many more desktop apps available than have been introduced here. All are available from the All Apps screen, or you can simply start typing at the Start screen to locate them. Here are a few to try before moving on.

- **Math Input Panel** – Write an equation with your finger, stylus or pen and this application will type it for you. You can then copy and paste the equation anywhere that accepts text.
- **Sticky Notes** – Create your own digital Post-It Notes.
- **Control Panel** – To personalise all aspects of your laptop or tablet.

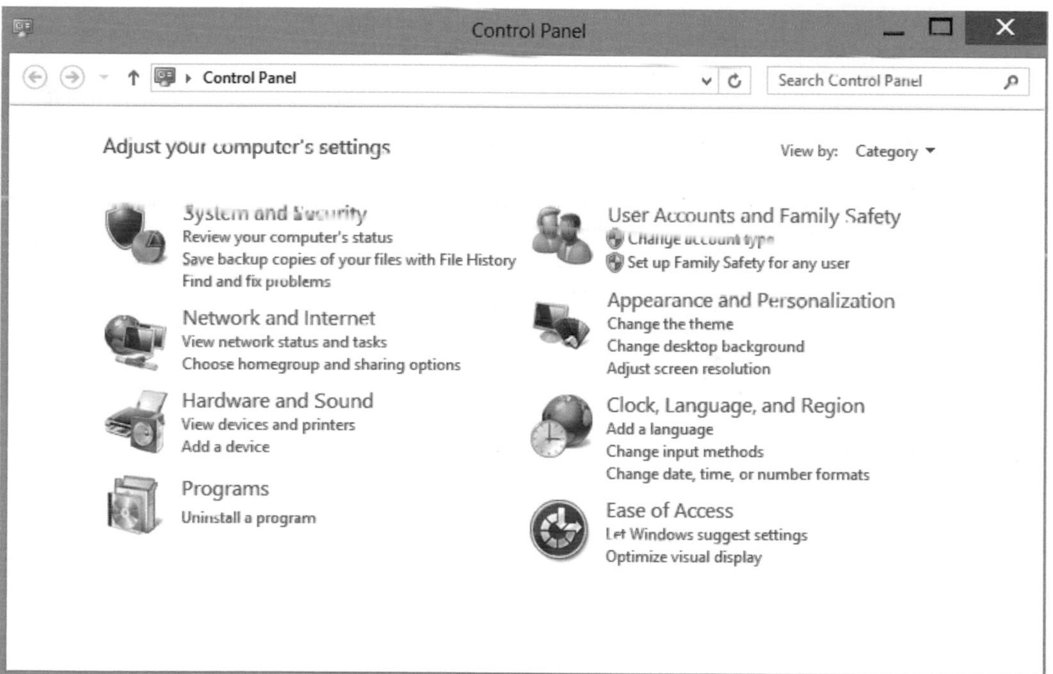

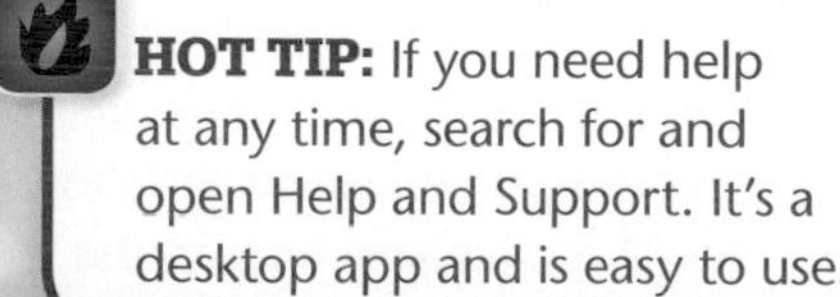

HOT TIP: If you need help at any time, search for and open Help and Support. It's a desktop app and is easy to use.

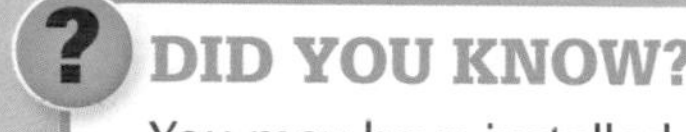

DID YOU KNOW?

You may have installed a few desktop apps yourself; iTunes and Photoshop are both desktop applications.

Pin your favourite desktop apps to the taskbar

If there is a desktop app you use often, and you don't want to have to access the Start screen to find it each time you need it, you can pin a shortcut to the taskbar for easy access.

1. Locate the app's tile on the Start screen or the All Apps screen.
2. Right-click the tile.
3. Click Pin to taskbar.

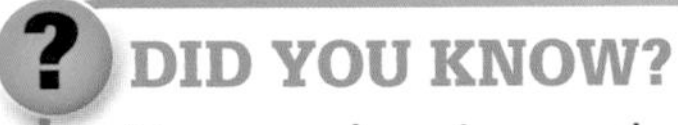

DID YOU KNOW?
You can also pin any desktop app's tile to the Start screen if it isn't already there.

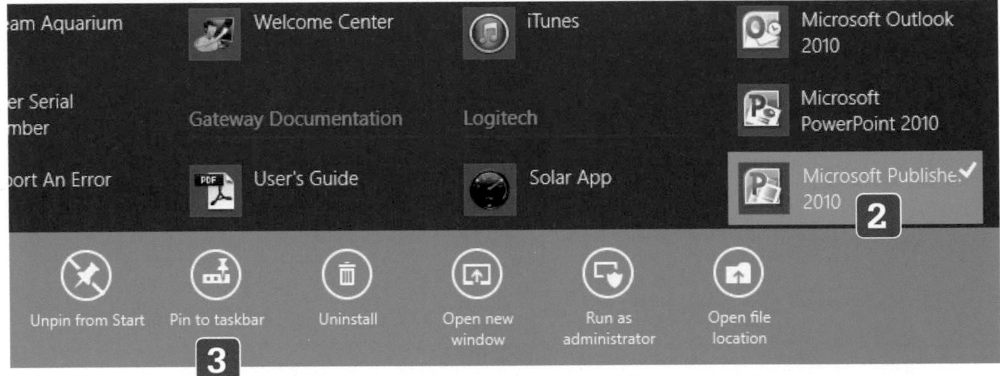

4. Return to the desktop to see the item on the taskbar.

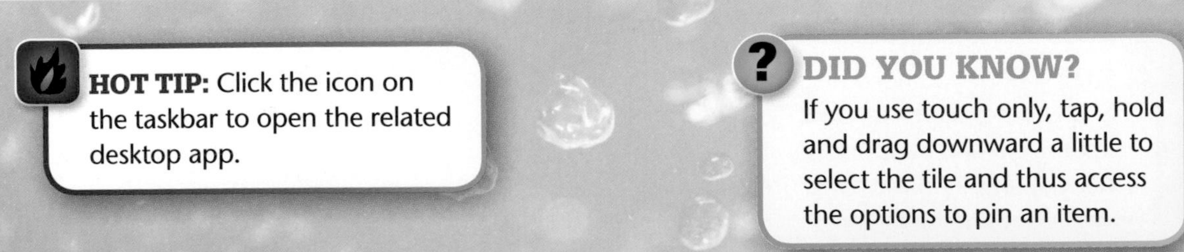

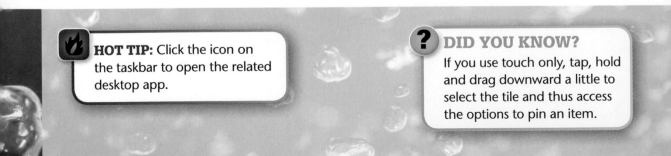

HOT TIP: Click the icon on the taskbar to open the related desktop app.

DID YOU KNOW?
If you use touch only, tap, hold and drag downward a little to select the tile and thus access the options to pin an item.

12 Configure network sharing

Introduction

Networks let you share your personal data, printers and media with other people you trust. Likewise, other people can share data with you. Often this minimises the amount of data you have to keep because everyone can share data when it's appropriate to do so (such as the case with most pictures, videos and music). It also minimises how much hardware you must purchase and maintain (for instance, when you share a single printer among multiple users). There are many ways to share.

If you have more than one computer at home and if those computers share the same internet connection, you already have a basic network in place. You can share data from your laptop to your other computer (and back again) using a homegroup. This is very easy to do.

If you have more than one computer at home and aren't sure if you have a network or not (but you know you have some networking hardware that provides an internet connection and looks like it can be used to connect multiple computers), you can connect your laptop to that hardware to create a network. You can then create a homegroup or use some other sharing option (like Public folder or personal folder sharing).

If you don't have any networking hardware at home but you do have some sort of internet connection, you can save your data to your SkyDrive account and share your data over the internet.

Enable Network Discovery

In order for your laptop to be able to discover available networks and join them (and ultimately share data with computers on that network), Network Discovery must be enabled. Verify that this is the case before continuing.

1. From the Start screen type Network. Click Network in the results.
2. If you see the prompt here that states: 'Network discovery is turned off', click it.
3. Click Turn on network discovery and file sharing.

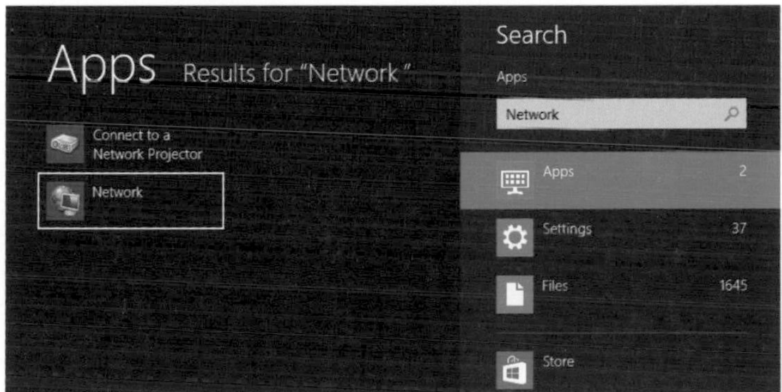

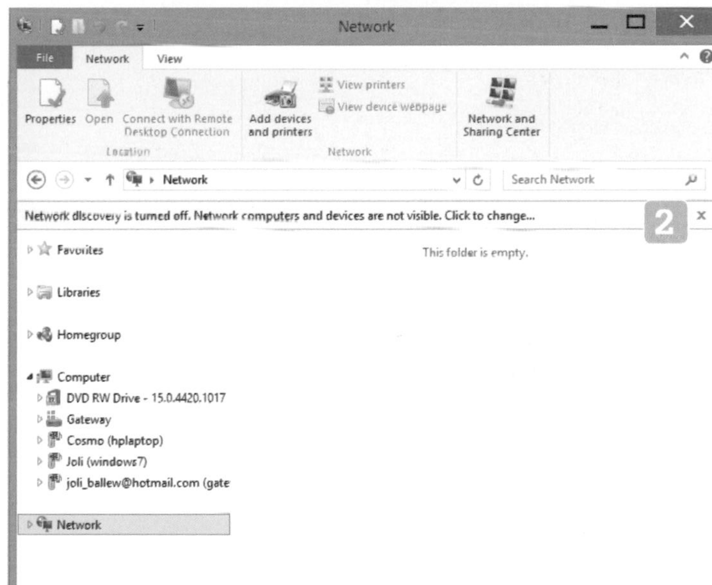

ALERT: If at any time you are prompted about the type of network you want to create or join, choose Private or Home or Work (as applicable) and opt to share data (versus not sharing it).

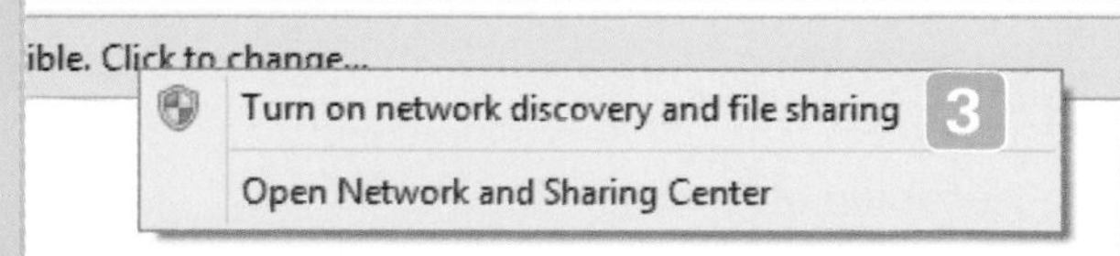

DID YOU KNOW?
Airplane mode should remain disabled until you are actually on an aeroplane. Enabling Airplane mode will disrupt network functionality.

Connect to your existing network

If you have a network already in place or if you have a single computer and some networking hardware, specifically a device that lets you connect to the internet, you can create and/or join a network.

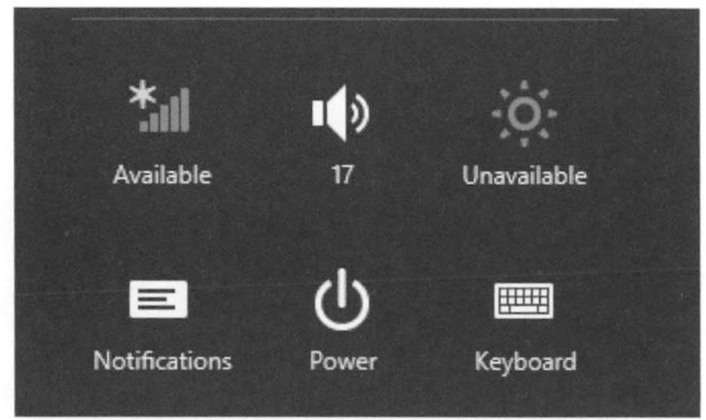

1. If you have a wireless router or similar hardware available:
   - From your laptop, use Windows key + C to access the charms.
   - Click Settings.
   - Click the network icon that shows networks are available.
   - Type the password and if prompted choose to allow sharing.
   - If prompted, choose Private, Home or Work for the network type.

2. If you have a wired router or similar hardware available:
   - Connect your laptop to the device using an Ethernet cable.
   - If prompted, opt to make the network Private, Home or Work and to enable sharing.

ALERT: To connect to a wireless network, the wireless feature must be enabled on your laptop.

ALERT: If you have connected to your home network but can't access the internet, you may need to change your sharing options. If this is the case, refer to the next page, Change or set network sharing status.

Change or set network sharing status

In order to get the most from your network you need to enable sharing when you connect to it. If you didn't or if you think there is a problem, check to see what type of sharing setting you configured.

1. Use Windows key + C to access the charms and click Settings.
2. Click the network icon.
3. Right-click the network you are connected to and click Turn sharing on or off.
4. Choose Yes, turn on sharing and connect to devices.

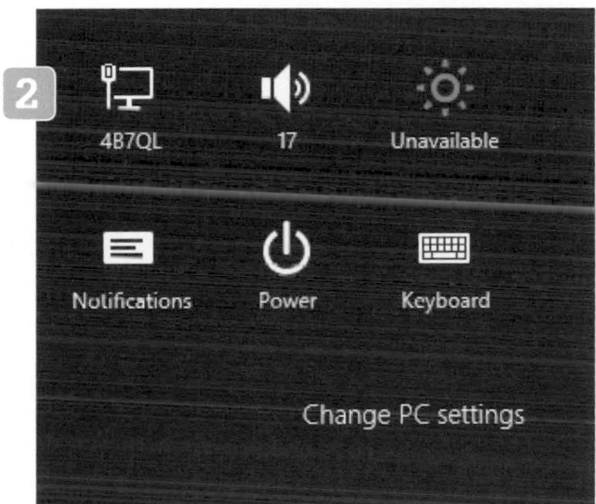

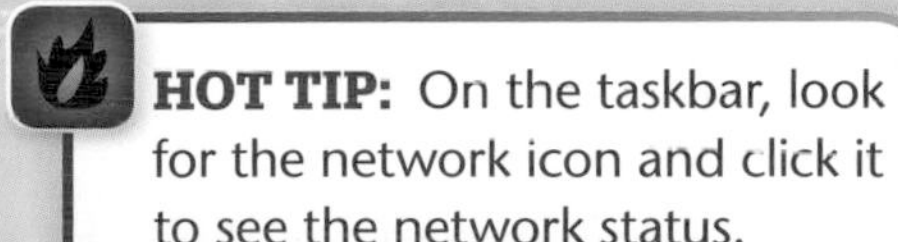

HOT TIP: On the taskbar, look for the network icon and click it to see the network status.

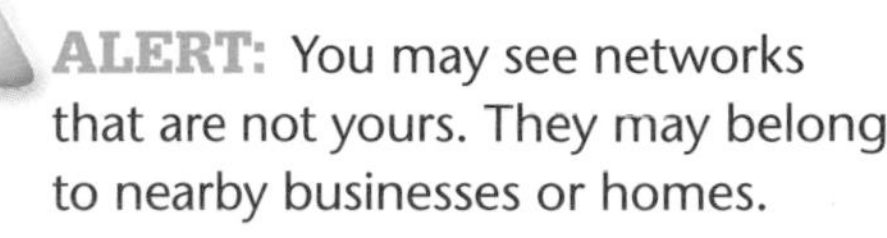

ALERT: You may see networks that are not yours. They may belong to nearby businesses or homes.

Create or join a homegroup

You can share data, printers, media and so on in many ways using various techniques; likewise, there are lots of options for accessing the items and data shared by others. Using a homegroup facilitates sharing the most easily. If you know that a homegroup is available, you will probably want to join it. If you don't see a homegroup you can create one. Since laptops are generally used to join homegroups instead of creating them, you may want to start by creating a homegroup on your main desktop computer.

1 At the desktop, right-click the Network icon on the taskbar; click Open Network and Sharing Center.

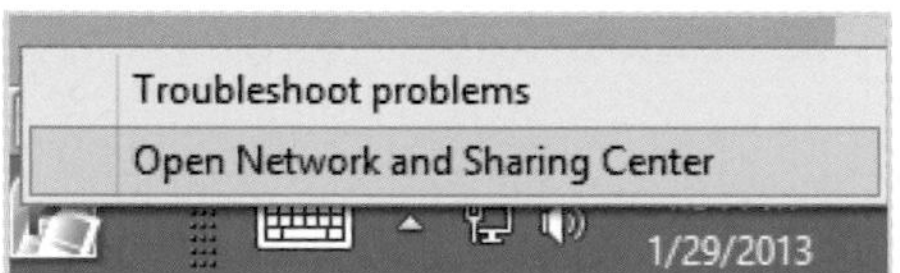

2 If a homegroup exists on the network already, you'll see Available to join. Click this. (If not you can opt to create a homegroup instead.)

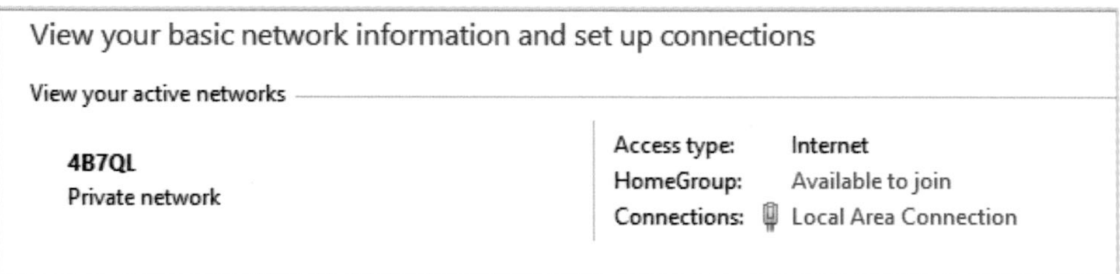

3 Click Join Now (or another prompt as applicable).

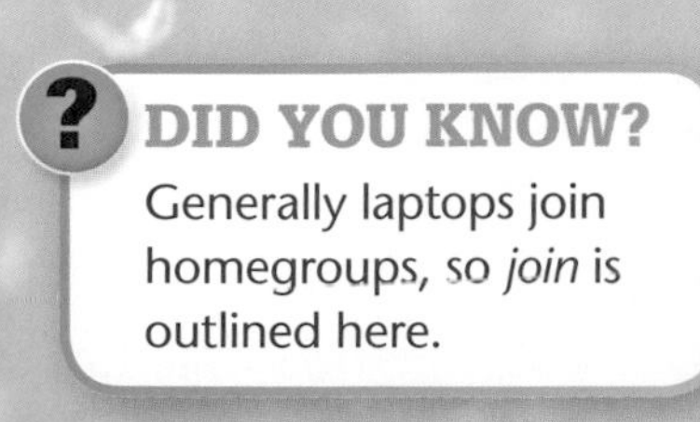

DID YOU KNOW?

Generally laptops join homegroups, so *join* is outlined here.

4 Proceed through the wizard by clicking Next and choosing what to share.

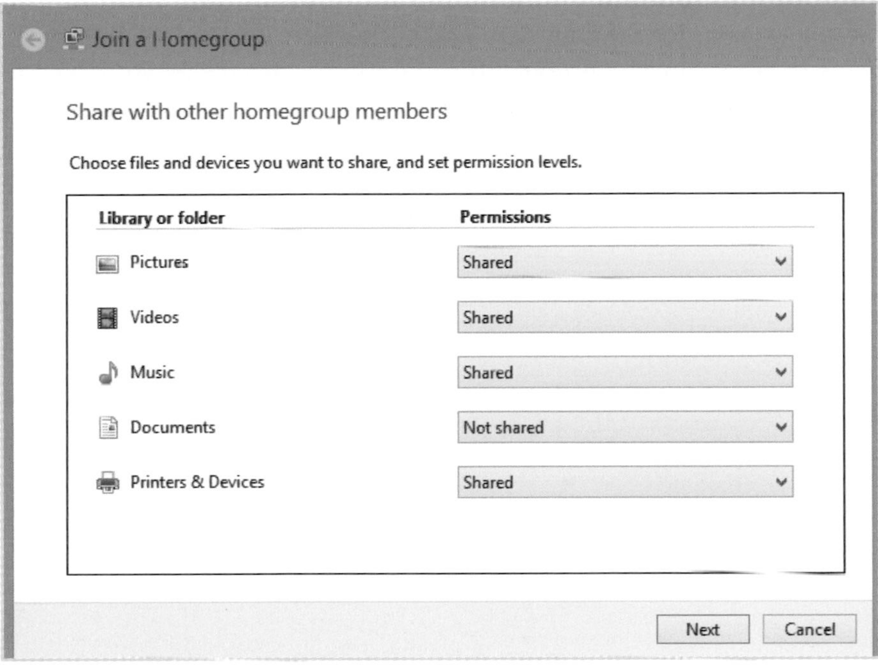

5 Type the existing homegroup password. You can find the password on another network computer (just search for homegroup).

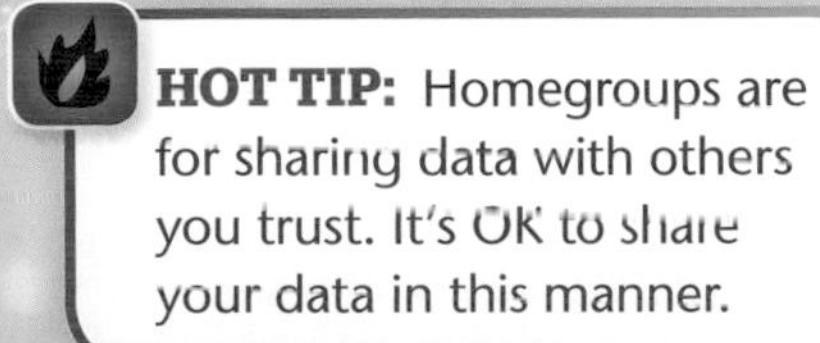

HOT TIP: Homegroups are for sharing data with others you trust. It's OK to share your data in this manner.

Create a new user

You created your user account when you first turned on your new Windows 8 laptop. Your user account is what defines your personal folders as well as your settings for desktop background, screen saver and other items. If you share the computer with someone else, perhaps a grandchild, they should have their own user account too. When you create additional users in this manner they are 'standard' users and have fewer permissions and rights than the administrator (which is likely you). This is good!

1. Click the Settings charm. (Use Windows + C to access the charms.)
2. Click Change PC settings.
3. If applicable, click Users in the left pane. Then, select Add a user in the right pane.
4. Work through the process to add a new user. It's the same process you worked through when you set up Windows 8.

ALERT: You must be logged on with an administrator account to create a new user.

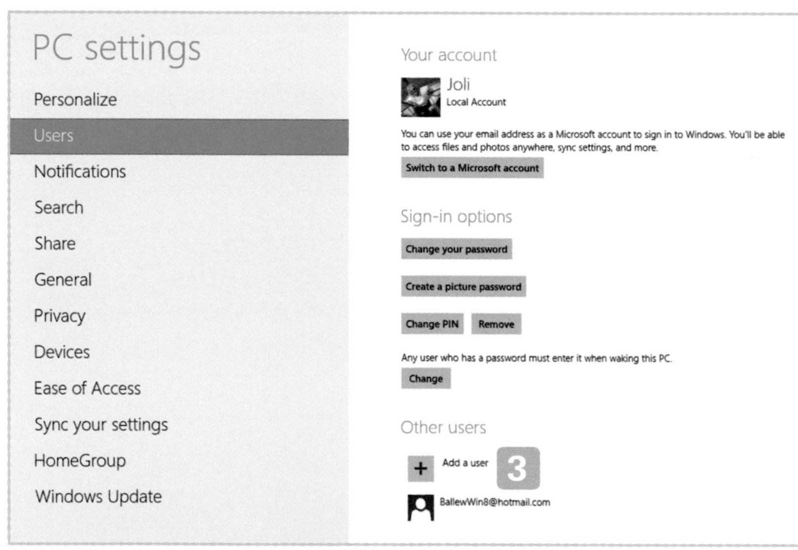

DID YOU KNOW?
You can apply parental controls to standard accounts to limit when the user can access the computer, what types of games they can plan, and more.

ALERT: All accounts should have a password applied to them. You can apply passwords in Control Panel. Click User Accounts and Family Safety, and then User Accounts. Select the account to apply a password to.

Share with the Public folder

Windows 8 comes with Public folders you can use to share data easily with others on your network or others who share your computer. The Public folders are located on your local disk, generally C:, under Users.

1. From the desktop, open File Explorer. (Click the folder icon on the taskbar.)
2. Click Computer in the left pane, double-click the disk that contains your data, and double-click Users.
3. Double-click the Public folder.

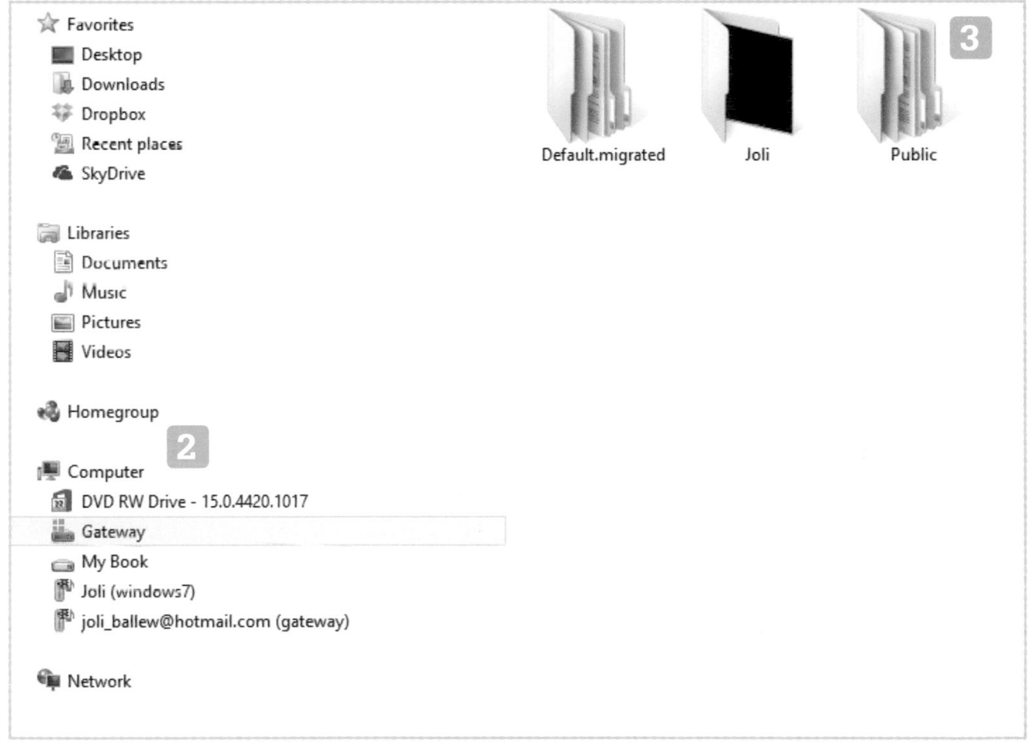

HOT TIP: Create a shortcut for the Public folder on the desktop so it's easy to access.

4 Now, save, move or copy data to these folders as desired.

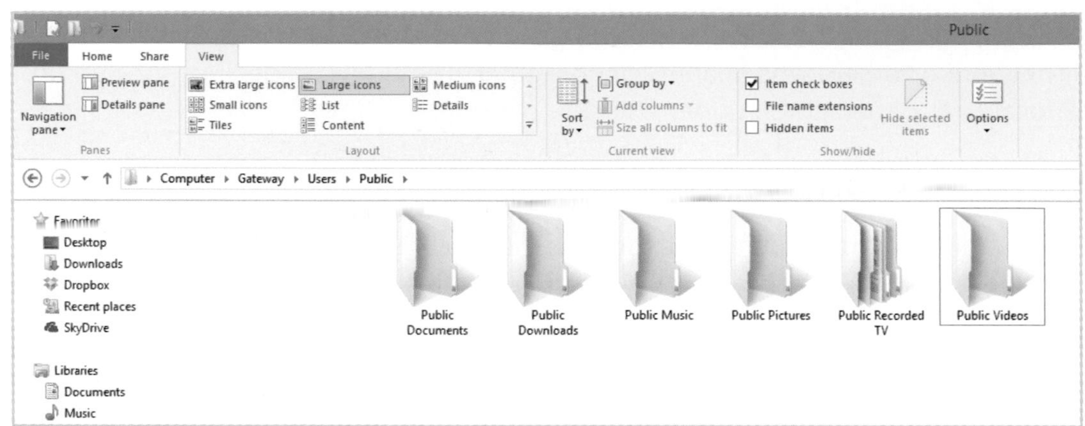

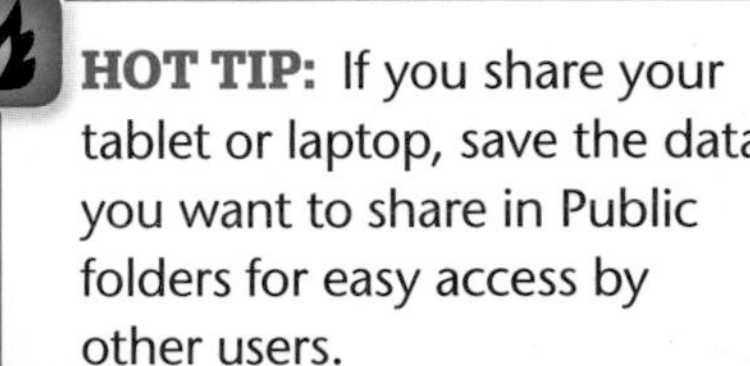

HOT TIP: If you share your tablet or laptop, save the data you want to share in Public folders for easy access by other users.

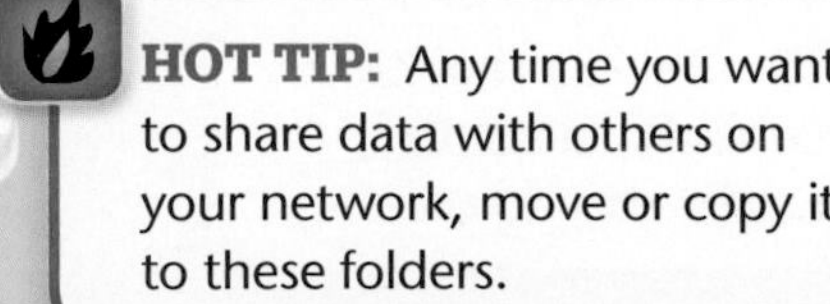

HOT TIP: Any time you want to share data with others on your network, move or copy it to these folders.

Share a personal folder

Sometimes you won't want to save, move or copy data into Public folders. Instead, you'll want to share data directly from a personal folder.

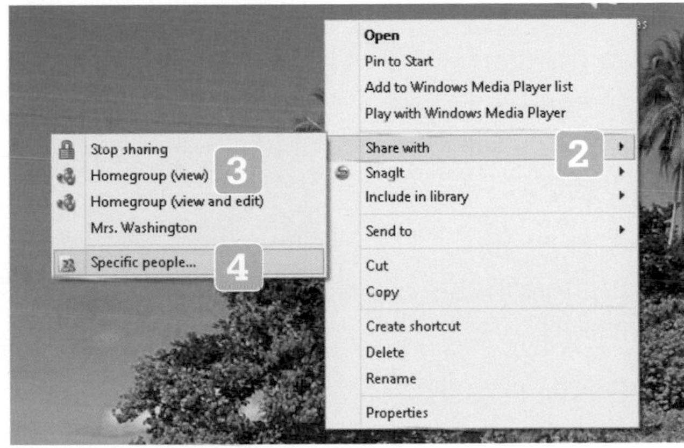

1. From File Explorer or the desktop, locate the folder to share.
2. Right-click the folder, and click Share with.
3. If you want to share with your homegroup or another user, select the appropriate option from the list. Follow any prompts to complete the process.
4. If you want to share with specific people who are not in a homegroup, choose Specific people, then:
   - Click the arrow and choose with whom to share. (Everyone is an option.)
   - Click Add.
   - Click the arrow to set the permissions for the user.
   - Click Share.

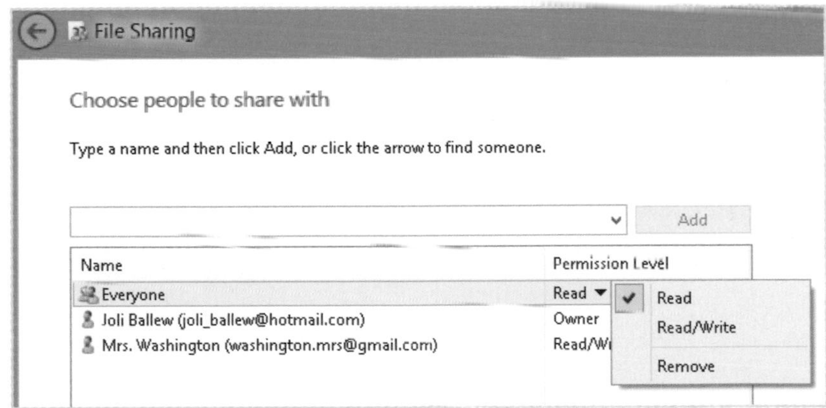

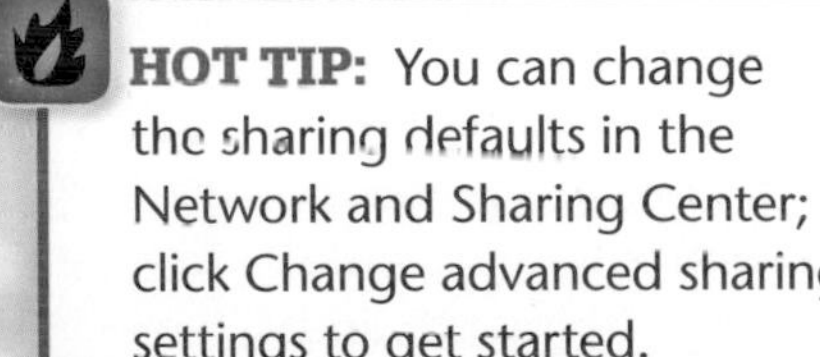

HOT TIP: You can change the sharing defaults in the Network and Sharing Center; click Change advanced sharing settings to get started.

HOT TIP: Create and then share a folder on the Desktop to share data like gardening ideas, a child's homework, recipes and travel ideas.

Share a printer

If you have a network, you have other computers in your home. If you have other computers, you may have a printer attached to one of them. You should share that printer so you can access it from your laptop. Here is how to do this on Windows 8.

1. At the Start screen type Share printers. Click Settings.
2. Click Share printers in the results.
3. Enable Printers and devices.

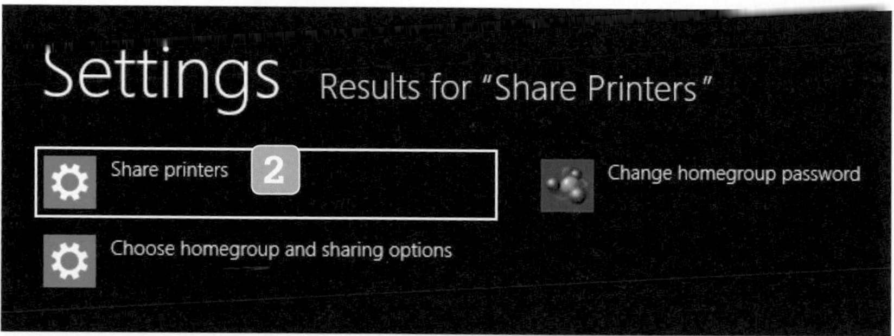

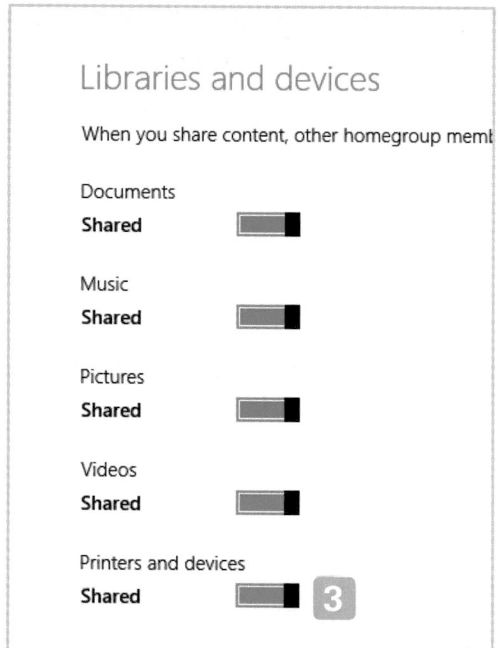

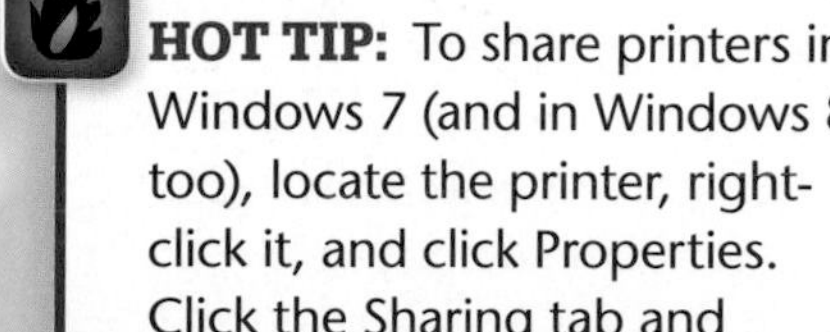

HOT TIP: To share printers in Windows 7 (and in Windows 8 too), locate the printer, right-click it, and click Properties. Click the Sharing tab and choose how to share.

DID YOU KNOW?
The first time you access the shared printer from your laptop, you may be prompted to install the driver for it. This is OK and you should do it.

Copy data from another computer

You can access shared data only when you are connected to the network it is shared on. Thus, while sharing may work in many instances, if you're going to be away from your network you'll want to copy necessary data so you will have it with you. There are many ways to do this. We prefer to set up two windows, one that has the data to copy and the other that contains the place to copy it to, and then drag data to copy it.

1. Use File Explorer on your laptop to open a window to hold the files you want to copy.

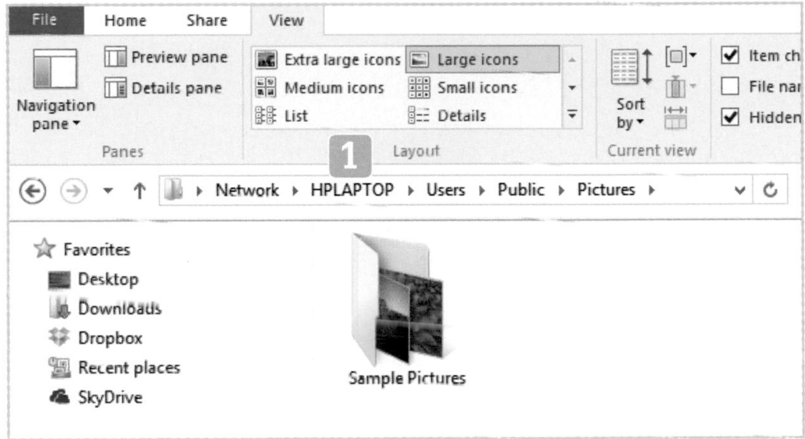

2. Right-click the File Explorer icon and click File Explorer to open a second File Explorer window.
3. Use this second File Explorer window to locate the data you want to copy. You'll have to click Network in the Navigation pane to browse to and locate the data.

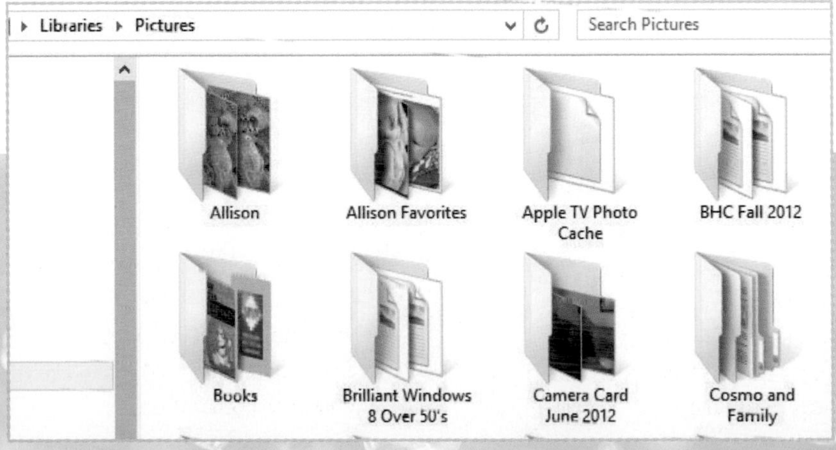

4 Hold down the Ctrl key and select the items in this second window to copy.

5 Right-click and drag the data from the second File Explorer window to the first.

6 Let go and choose Copy here.

DID YOU KNOW?

There are a lot of rules to learn if you want to drag and drop data using a left-click, and the rules are hard to remember. With a left-click you aren't prompted to move or copy when you let go of the mouse; in fact, one or the other will happen automatically based on the circumstances. However, when you drag and drop with a right-click you are always prompted to move or copy the data, and you have to make a choice before anything happens. This is much safer and easier than guessing.

ALERT: What you see when you perform this task and what is shown here will differ greatly!

Switch from a local account to a Microsoft account

When you first set up your laptop or tablet, you were prompted to create an account. In fact, you were strongly encouraged to create and use a Microsoft account (instead of a local account). If you didn't create a Microsoft account, you'll have to make the change now to share data on SkyDrive as detailed next.

1. Access the Windows 8 charms. You can flick in from the right on a touch screen or use the Windows key + C key combination with a keyboard.
2. Click Settings.
3. Click Change PC settings.
4. Tap or click Users.

ALERT: You won't be able to use SkyDrive, Calendar, Store and lots of other apps unless you are signed on with a Microsoft account.

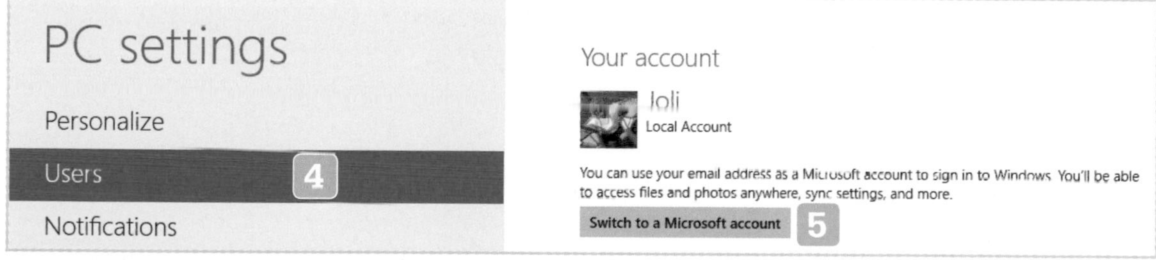
PC settings
Personalize
Users
4
Notifications
Your account
Joli
Local Account
You can use your email address as a Microsoft account to sign in to Windows. You'll be able to access files and photos anywhere, sync settings, and more.
Switch to a Microsoft account
5

5. Tap or click Switch to a Microsoft account. (If you see Switch to a Local account instead, you're already using a Microsoft account.)
6. Enter your existing Microsoft account, one you recently obtained, or your favourite email address. You can also get a new email address from this screen.
7. Complete the process as instructed.

Sign in with a Microsoft account
Joli Ballew
joli_ballew@hotmail.com
You're almost done changing your account. Next time you sign in to Windows, use your Microsoft account and password.

Upload data to SkyDrive

SkyDrive is a place where you can store your personal files on the internet. Microsoft has set aside some space for you already, and it is free. When you store data on these internet 'servers', you are able to access that data from any internet-connected computer, laptop or tablet. You may even be able to access the files from your mobile phone.

1. At the Start screen, click SkyDrive. If it isn't there, type SkyDrive to find it.
2. If prompted, sign in with your Microsoft account.
3. Right-click an empty area of the screen and click Upload.
4. Locate a file to upload and click it once.
5. Repeat as desired.
6. Click Add to SkyDrive.

ALERT: You can't use SkyDrive unless you sign in with a Microsoft account.

HOT TIP: Data you store in SkyDrive is protected by a password, among other things.

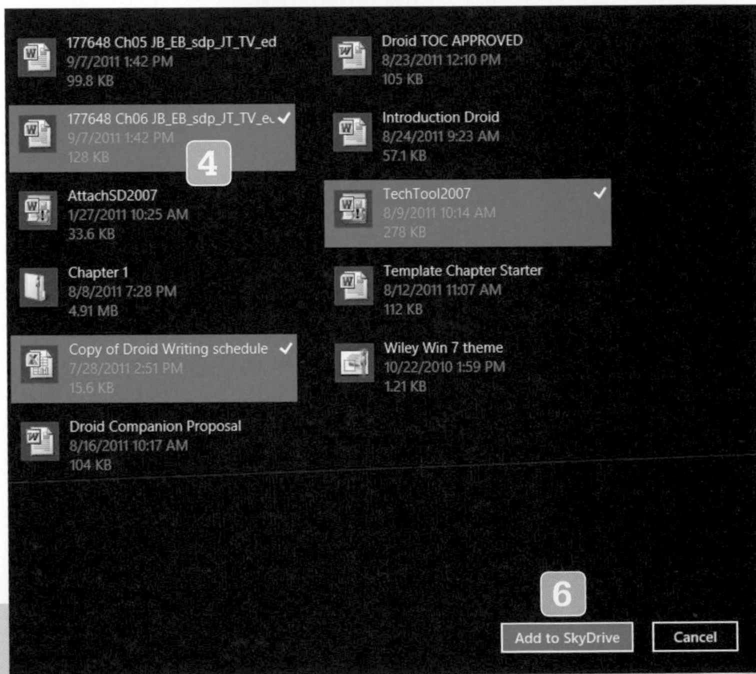

DID YOU KNOW?

You can right-click an empty area of SkyDrive and opt to create a new folder there. This will enable you to better organise your data.

Access data from SkyDrive

Once data is stored in your SkyDrive area, you can access it from virtually anywhere. To access it from a Windows 8 computer, click the SkyDrive tile on the Start screen. To access data from any other device, browse to www.skydrive.live.com. In case you want to access your files from somewhere other than your Windows 8 laptop, we focus on the latter option here.

1. Open you web browser and navigate to www.skydrive.live.com.
2. Note your folders and browse to the location of the file to access.

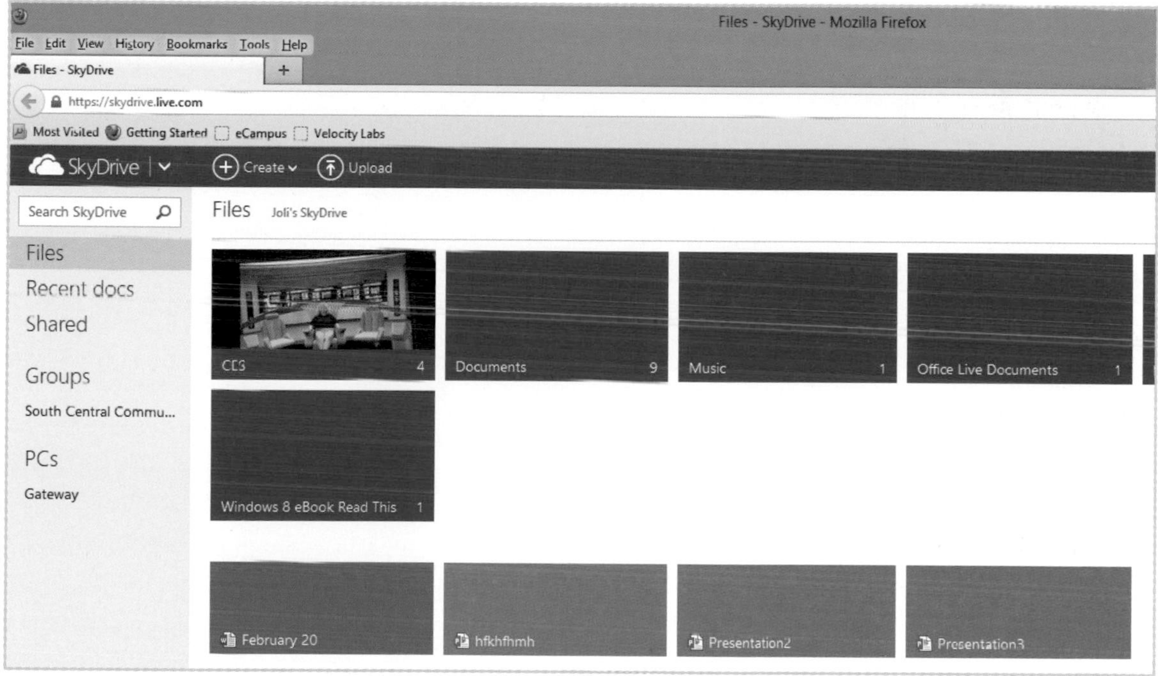

3 Open the desired file. (This is a music file.)

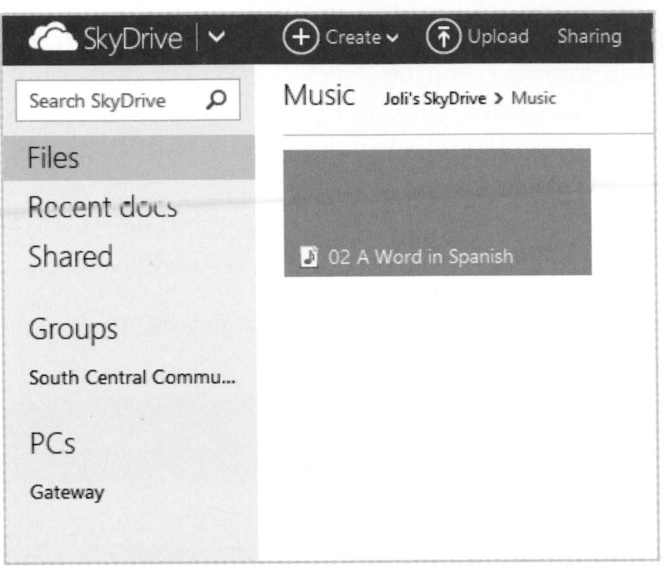

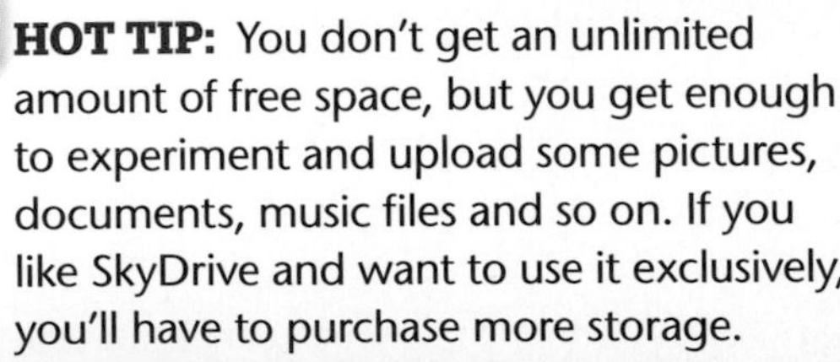

HOT TIP: You don't get an unlimited amount of free space, but you get enough to experiment and upload some pictures, documents, music files and so on. If you like SkyDrive and want to use it exclusively, you'll have to purchase more storage.

DID YOU KNOW?

You can use any web browser to access SkyDrive, it doesn't have to be Internet Explorer.

13 Enable and use accessibility options

Introduction

If you have any type of disability that makes it difficult for you to use your laptop or tablet computer, you can enable the accessibility options available in Windows 8. Even if you don't have a disability, these options can still prove useful. Perhaps you have a difficult time reading what is on the screen, have trouble hearing the sounds your computer makes, or have difficulty typing for long periods of time. The Ease of Access options can offer assistance.

Here are a few examples of what you might enable: if you wear reading glasses, you can make the text larger on the screen; if you are completely blind, you can let Windows read the text on the screen to you. If you are deaf, you can enable text captions where applicable. If you have trouble using the mouse or the keyboard you can enable various options to make this easier too. You can also speak to Windows 8 using commands, such as 'Open Recycle Bin' or 'Close Internet Explorer' by enabling and training the Speech Recognition feature.

Let Windows suggest Ease of Access settings

The easiest way to find out how Windows 8 can help you use your computer more effectively is to let Windows 8 suggest the settings that are right for you. This happens on the desktop.

1. At the Start screen type Ease of Access. Click Settings.
2. Click Let Windows suggest Ease of Access settings.

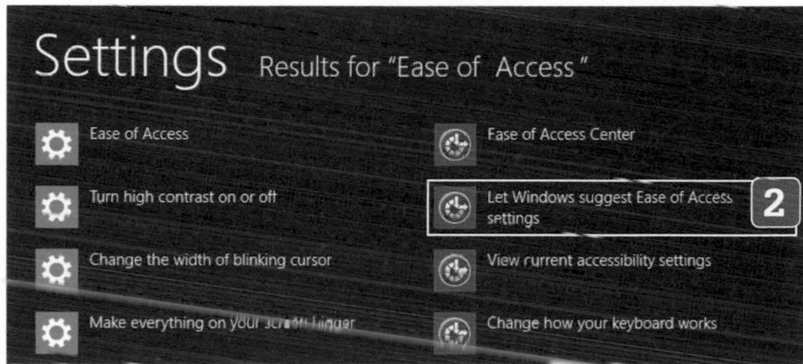

3. Work through the wizard provided. The first screen asks about eyesight. Click Next as you move through the pages.

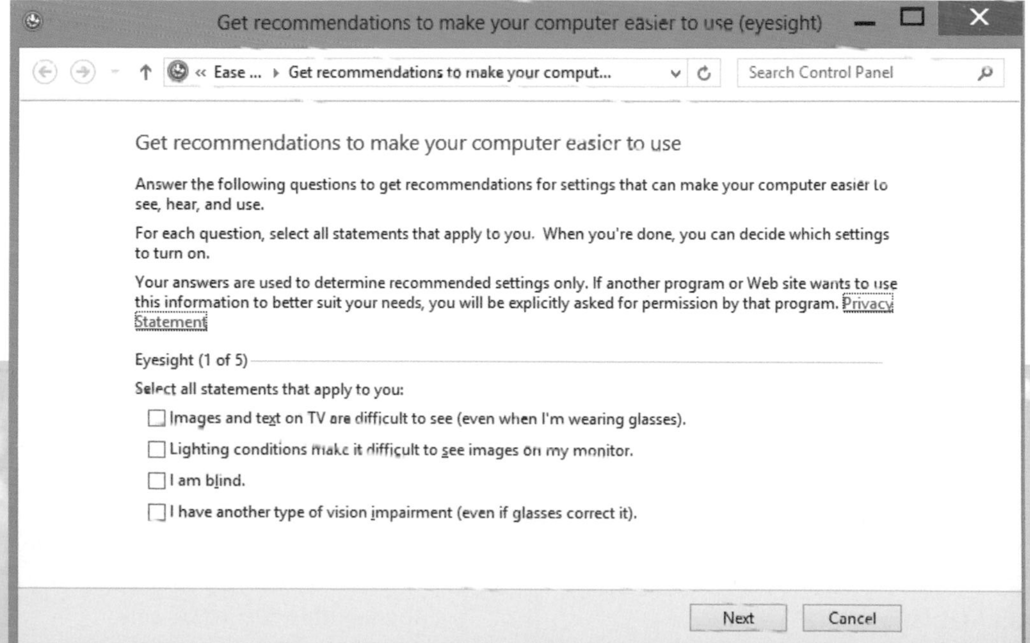

4. Review the recommended settings. Note that you can enable the settings to use (disable ones you don't).

5. Click Apply to apply the changes right away (we suggest you read the entire chapter first, though).

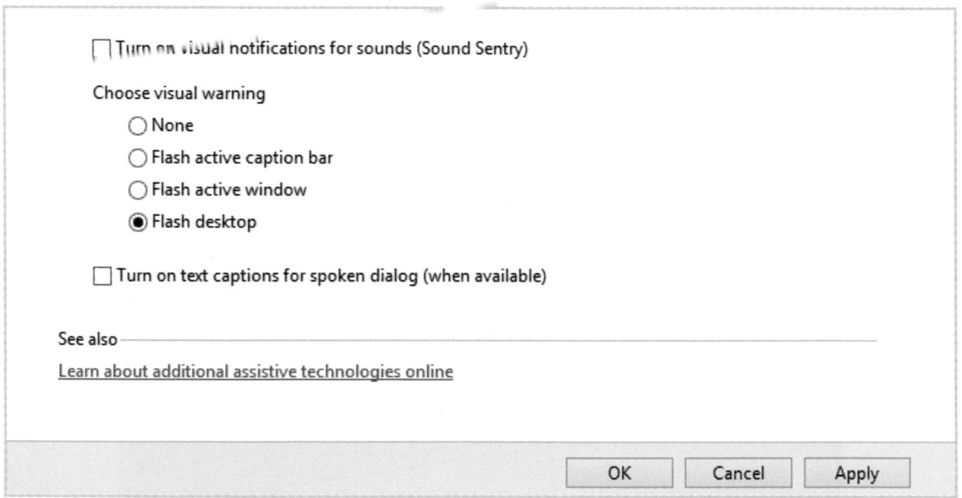

HOT TIP: Some settings that are easy to start with include setting up visual cues when sounds are played, adjusting the settings for the mouse or keyboard, and adjusting settings for touch screens and tablets.

ALERT: Sometimes it is difficult to figure out how to turn off a feature (like Magnifier, Narrator and so on) once you've enabled it. Read this chapter in its entirety before you engage any of the features, just to be safe.

Explore PC Settings options

You can enable simple Ease of Access settings from the PC Settings hub. From the Settings charm, click Change PC Settings. Note the options for Ease of Access.

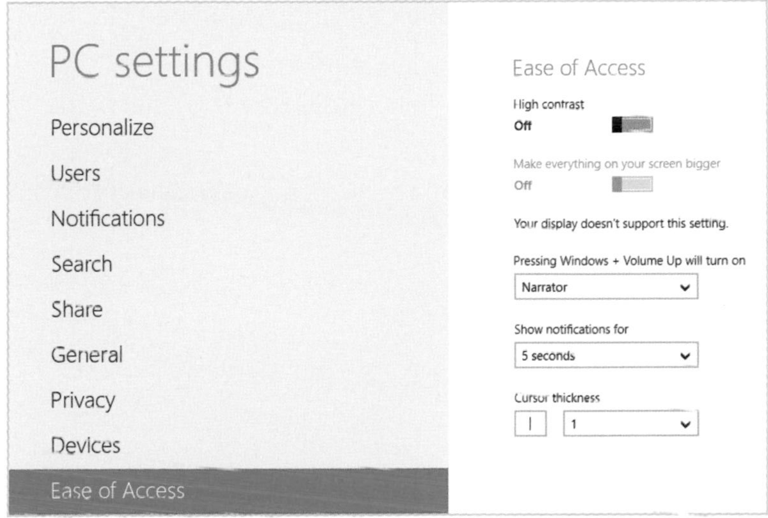

- **High contrast** – When this is enabled, the background becomes black, and the text and dialog boxes become white.

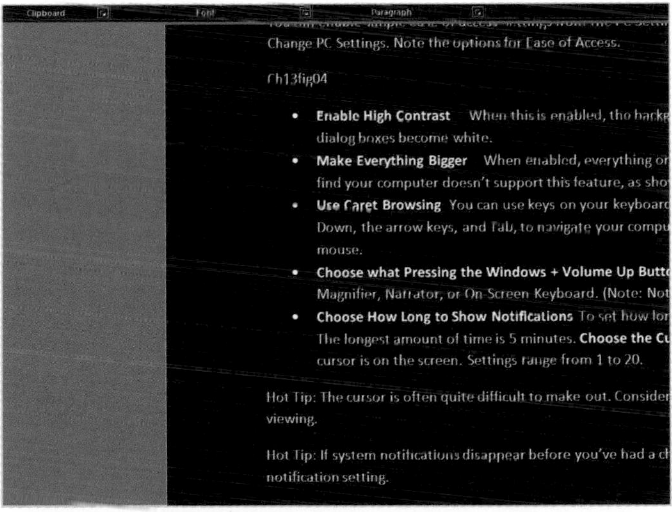

- **Make everything bigger** – When enabled, everything on the screen appears larger. You might find your computer doesn't support this feature, as shown here.
- **Caret browsing** – You can use keys on your keyboard, specifically Home, End, Page Up, Page Down, the arrow keys and Tab, to navigate your computer instead of using a keyboard and a mouse.
- **Pressing Windows + Volume Up** – Choices include Nothing, Magnifier, Narrator or On-Screen Keyboard.
- **Show notifications for** – To set how long notifications remain on the screen. The longest amount of time is 5 minutes.
- **Cursor thickness** – To set how thick the cursor is on the screen. Settings range from 1 to 20.

HOT TIP: The cursor is often quite difficult to make out. Consider changing the thickness to 10 for easier viewing.

HOT TIP: If system notifications disappear before you've had a chance to read them, lengthen the notification setting.

Use Narrator

Narrator reads information to you. It doesn't read most content though; it is best used to let you know what is happening on your computer. It will announce you've opened a word processing program for instance, and read the name of the file, but it won't read the text in the document. It will announce that you've navigated to a web page and read the URL, but it won't read what is on the web page.

1. Type Narrator at the Start screen.
2. Click Narrator in the results.
3. Narrator starts. Press the space bar or use the appropriate touch technique as prompted to access the main Narrator screen.

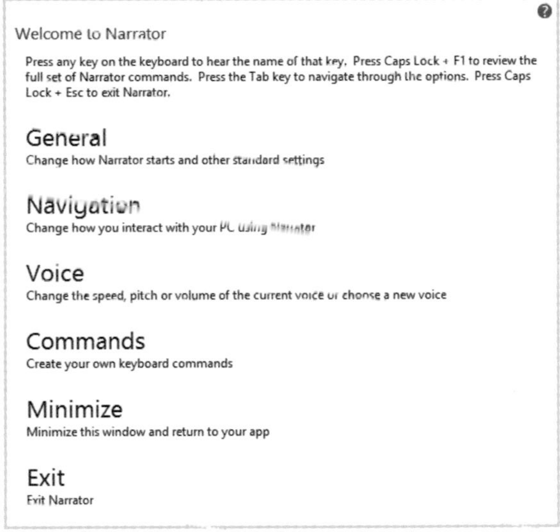

4. Read everything offered. Then, explore Narrator by opening and closing various windows.
5. To exit Narrator, at this screen click Exit and then click Yes to confirm.

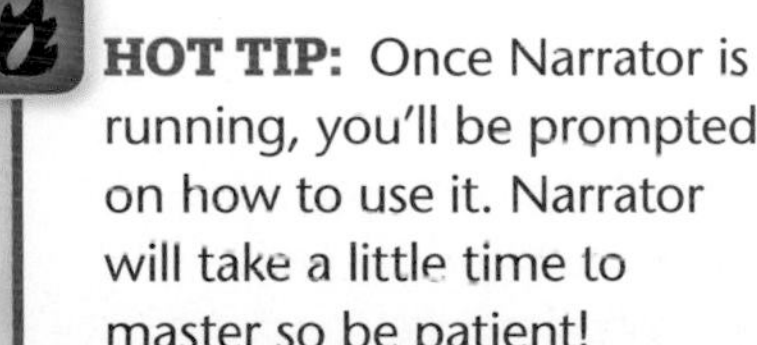

HOT TIP: Once Narrator is running, you'll be prompted on how to use it. Narrator will take a little time to master so be patient!

ALERT: If you start Narrator and want to stop it, return to the Narrator window and click Exit. Click Yes to confirm.

Use the Magnifier

The Magnifier is an Ease of Access option that lets you magnify parts of the screen by positioning the cursor in the area you want to magnify. There are a few options once Magnifier is running, and those can be selected in the small Magnifier window that appears.

1. At the Start screen, type Magnifier.
2. Click Magnifier in the results.
3. Most likely, you will see a magnification area at the top of your screen that enlarges the area where your cursor is currently positioned.
4. Click and drag downward on that magnification area. Note the box that appears and what is magnified.

5. Click the magnifying glass to display the dialog box.
6. Click the Settings icon (the round cog) to review other options.

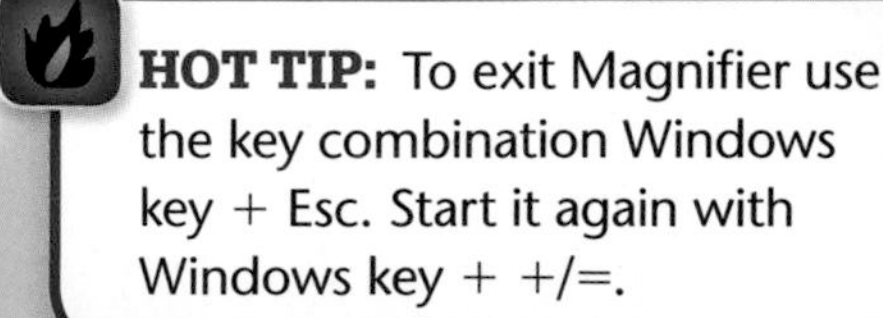

HOT TIP: To exit Magnifier use the key combination Windows key + Esc. Start it again with Windows key + +/=.

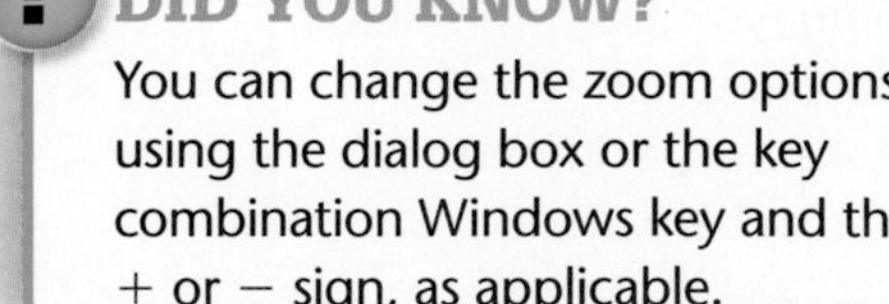

DID YOU KNOW?

You can change the zoom options using the dialog box or the key combination Windows key and the + or – sign, as applicable.

Set up Windows Speech Recognition

Windows Speech Recognition lets you speak commands to perform tasks. This is quite helpful if you have trouble using a mouse to click small areas of the screen, such as those required to close windows. Almost everything you can do with a keyboard and mouse can be done with only your voice. To set up Speech Recognition, search for it at the Start screen and work through the setup process. You will be required to (or should) do the following:

- **Configure a Microphone** – To set up and test your microphone.

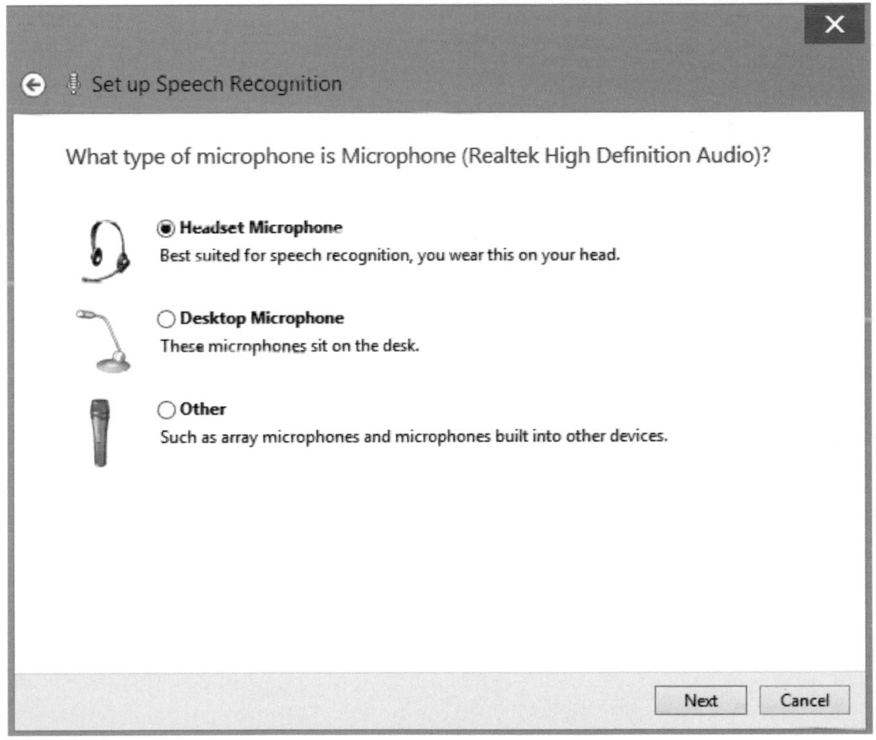

- **Enable document review** – To allow Speech Recognition to review the documents and email already on your computer. If you allow it, Windows can use your existing work to learn words and phrases you use often.
- **Choose how to activate and deactivate the program** – Learn two commands, 'Start Listening' and 'Stop Listening', and tell the program how to use them.
- **Print the Speech Reference Card** – To print the Speech Reference Card to keep a quick reference of commands available.
- **Opt to run Speech Recognition at startup** – To configure the Speech Recognition program to open every time you use your computer (or not to).
- **Work though the tutorial** – To work through the available tutorial. The tutorial teaches you how to use Speech Recognition.

HOT TIP: Take the time to work through the entire tutorial. It is very long but your efforts will pay off in the long run because the program will work more effectively.

DID YOU KNOW?

Speech Recognition is not an intrusive program like Narrator or Magnifier. You engage it when you need it, otherwise it is inactive.

14 Manage, protect and troubleshoot your laptop

Introduction

Laptops and tablet computers come with some unique challenges when it comes to managing and securing them. Some of the available options in Windows 8, like selecting a power plan, are more important to configure on a laptop than on a desktop computer. You want to do everything you can to lengthen battery life. Backing up regularly is important too, because your mobile device can go missing much more easily than a computer that isn't mobile. And sometimes with a small, mobile device, it's impossible to add more internal memory to improve performance, whereas desktop counterparts almost always include an easy way to do so. Of course, you would not use a desktop computer on an aeroplane, so Airplane mode is certainly unique to mobile devices as well.

There are steps to take that are useful to every computer user no matter the device, such as watching out for viruses, enabling a firewall, installing hardware and software, and so on. And of course, when any user has computer problems, just about everyone will migrate to the same solutions: using Help and Support, applying a System Restore point, and even restoring the computer when things go really wrong.

Set a password protected screen saver

One of the easiest ways to protect your laptop is to apply a password protected screen saver. You can configure a screen saver to engage after as little as one minute of inactivity. You can also configure your computer to display the logon screen when you are ready to access the computer again for even more protection. Should someone gain physical access to your computer, without a password they won't be able to gain internal access without the proper credentials.

1. At the Start screen, type Change Screen Saver and click Settings; click Change screen saver in the results.
2. Select a screen saver, choose how long to wait, and place a check in On resume, display logon screen.
3. Click OK.

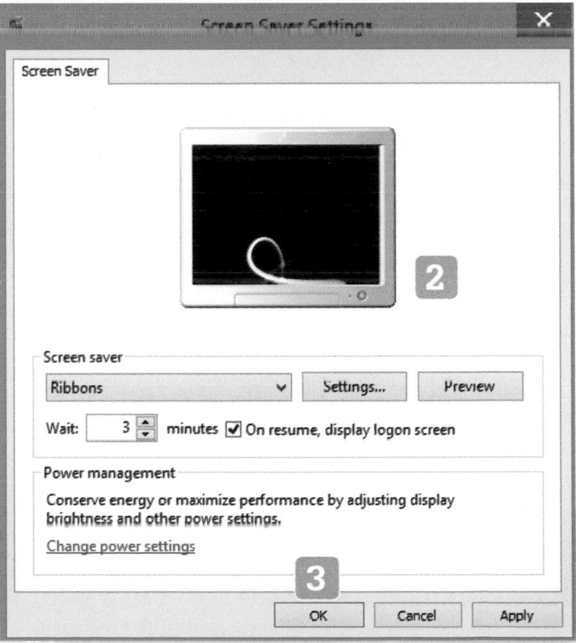

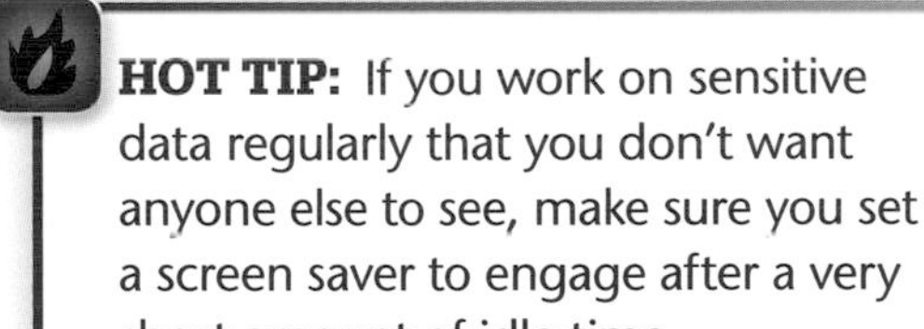

HOT TIP: If you work on sensitive data regularly that you don't want anyone else to see, make sure you set a screen saver to engage after a very short amount of idle time.

ALERT: The Bubble screen saver is see-through. Even when it's engaged you can still see what's on the screen. Select something else if you're looking for privacy.

ALERT: Even with a password protected screen saver enabled, be careful never to leave your laptop unattended. Someone might steal it.

Choose the proper power plan

All Windows 8 computers are set to use a specific power plan. This means that after a predetermined period of time, the display will dim and the hard drive will sleep. (There are two groups of settings: one for when the device is plugged in and one when it is running on batteries.) In addition, some power plans restrict some resources more than others to lengthen battery life. If you aren't happy with your computer's performance or you feel your battery is being drained too quickly, you can change this behaviour.

1. From the Start screen, type Power.
2. Click Settings, and click Power Options.
3. Next to the selected plan (or any other), click Change plan settings.
4. Use the drop-down lists to make changes as desired.
5. Click Save changes.

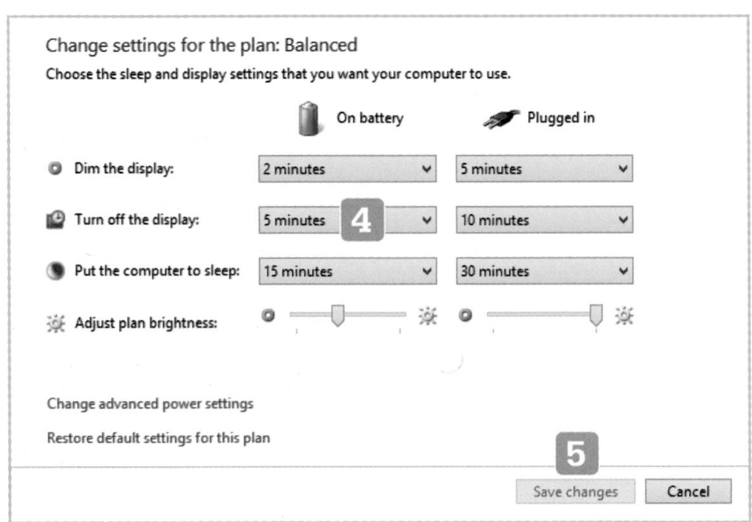

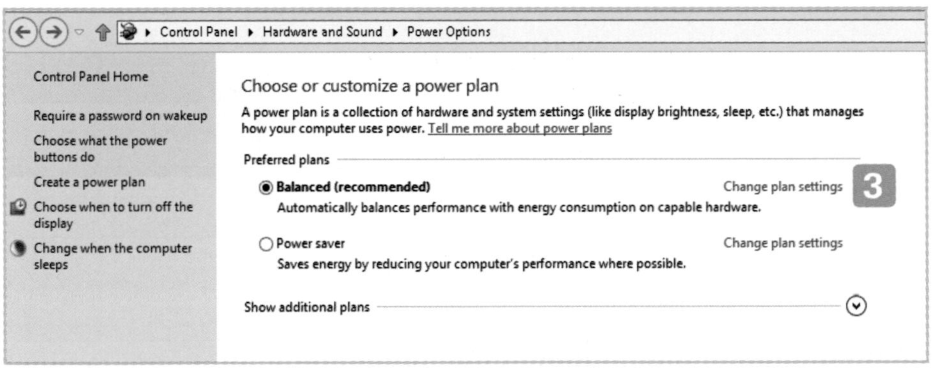

HOT TIP: One simple way to get longer battery life while still maintaining a workable laptop is to choose the Power Saver plan, lower the brightness and keep the other default settings.

DID YOU KNOW?
You can restore any power plan's defaults by clicking Restore default settings for this plan.

Use ReadyBoost

Laptops and tablets come with a specific amount of built-in 'memory'. The more memory a computer has, the better it will perform. If you want to add more memory to a small, mobile computer, you may not be able to. It may be physically impossible. In this case you can use ReadyBoost instead. ReadyBoost is a similar technology and will also improve computer performance. ReadyBoost can be used with any computer that has a USB port or smart card reader.

1. Insert a USB flash drive, thumb drive or memory card into an available slot on the outside of your laptop or tablet.
2. When prompted in the upper right corner, click to view your options.
3. Choose Speed up my system, Windows ReadyBoost.
4. Choose to dedicate the device to ReadyBoost and click OK (not shown).

ALERT: USB keys must be at least USB 2.0 and meet other requirements, but don't worry about that, you'll be told if the hardware isn't up to par.

ALERT: Some small tablet computers do not have the hardware required to support ReadyBoost.

Enable File History

File History saves copies of your files regularly so you can get them back if they're lost or damaged. While most of the security features in Windows 8 are enabled by default (such as the Firewall and Windows Defender), File History is not; you must manually enable it. You'll need a large capacity external drive for File History for it to be effective, so it's best to run backups when you have your laptop at home or at work.

1. Connect an external drive or make sure a network drive is available.
2. From the Start screen, type File History.
3. Click Settings, and then click File History.
4. In the File History window, click Turn on.
5. Wait while File History copies your files for the first time. You can always return here and click Run Now, if you want to.

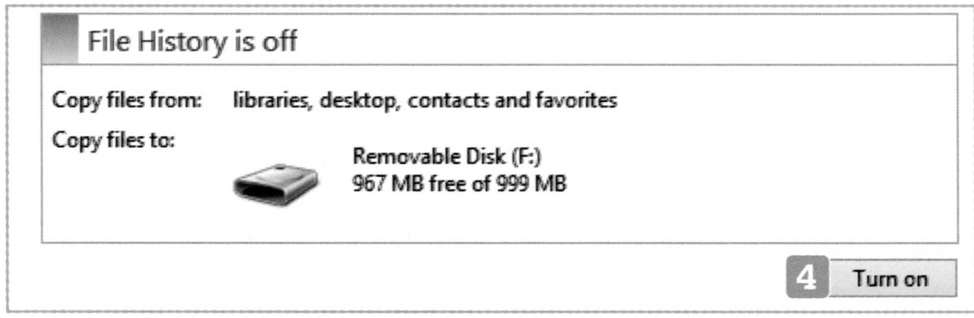

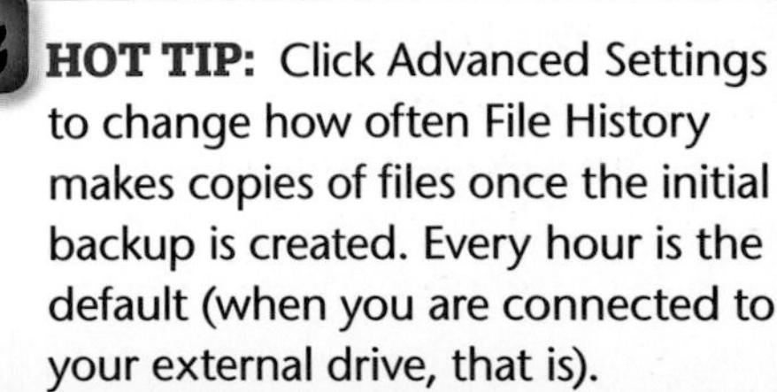

HOT TIP: Click Advanced Settings to change how often File History makes copies of files once the initial backup is created. Every hour is the default (when you are connected to your external drive, that is).

ALERT: If you ever need to restore files using File History, open the File History window and click Restore personal files.

Install hardware

Although you probably won't carry around a printer when you travel with your laptop, you may want to access a printer while at home or work. Printers are hardware and must be installed. Likewise, you must install other hardware such as digital cameras, USB drives, external monitors, external hard drives, card readers and so on.

1. Connect the device to a wall outlet if applicable.
2. Connect the device to your laptop using the applicable cable.
3. Insert the CD for the device if you have it (and if your device offers a CD drive).
4. Wait while the hardware installs.
5. If applicable, work through any set up processes.
6. From the Start screen, type Devices, then Settings. Click Devices in the results.
7. Verify the device was installed.

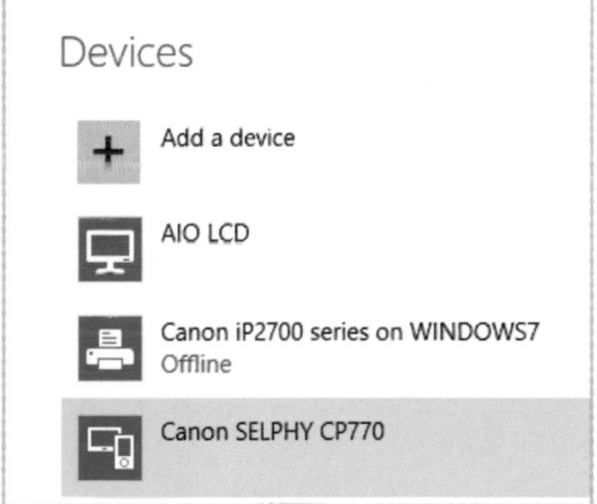

HOT TIP: If you have a small screen on your laptop, when at your desk, connect to a larger external monitor.

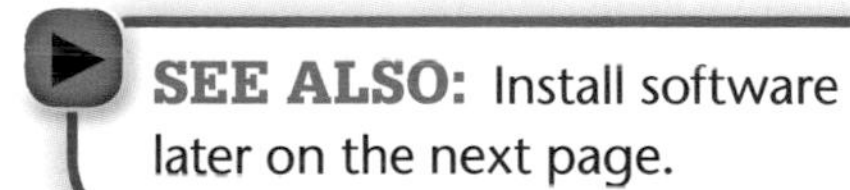

SEE ALSO: Install software later on the next page.

DID YOU KNOW?
Most of the time all you have to do is connect the new hardware and wait for it to be installed automatically.

ALERT: Read the directions that come with each new device you acquire. If there are specific instructions for installation, follow those directions, not the generic directions offered here.

Install software

As with installing hardware, software installation almost always goes smoothly. Just make sure you get your software from a reliable source, like Amazon, Microsoft's website, Apple's website (think iTunes, not software for Macs only) or a retail store.

1. Download the installation file from the internet and skip to Step 4, or, insert the CD or DVD in the appropriate drive and proceed to Step 2.

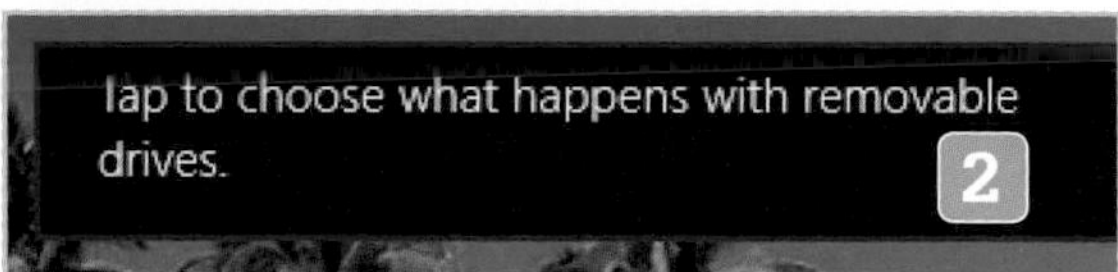

2. Click the prompt that appears in the top right corner to see your options.
3. If you are not prompted or you miss the prompt:
   - Open the Computer window. (You can type Computer at the Start screen.)
   - Double-click the CD or DVD drive.
4. Double-click the application file or do whatever else is necessary to start the installation.
5. Work through the installation wizard.

ALERT: If you have a tablet that runs Windows 8 RT, you'll have to get any software you want from the app Store, available on the Start screen. You can't install traditional applications.

Adobe screenshot reprinted with permission from Adobe Systems Incorporated.

HOT TIP: If you download software from the internet, copy the installation files to a CD or DVD for safe keeping and write the product ID or key on it.

ALERT: To install software you must locate the application file or the executable file. Often this is named Setup, Install or something similar. If you receive a message that the file you are trying to open can't be opened, you've chosen the wrong file.

Use the Action Center

Windows 8 tries hard to take care of your device and your data, and it doesn't matter if you use a laptop, tablet or desktop computer. Action Center will inform you if you don't have the proper security settings configured or if Windows Update or the firewall is disabled, among other things. You can resolve these issues easily.

1. From the desktop, on the taskbar, locate the Action Center flag.
2. Right-click the flag icon and then click Open Action Center.
3. If there's anything in red, click the down arrow (if necessary) to see the problem and resolve it.
4. Click the button that offers the resolution suggestion to view the resolution option and resolve it.

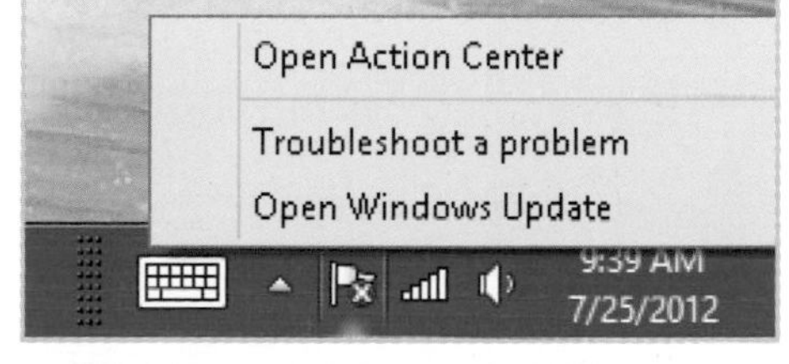

5. If there's anything in yellow, click the down arrow to see the problem and solution.
6. Close the Action Center when all problems have been resolved.

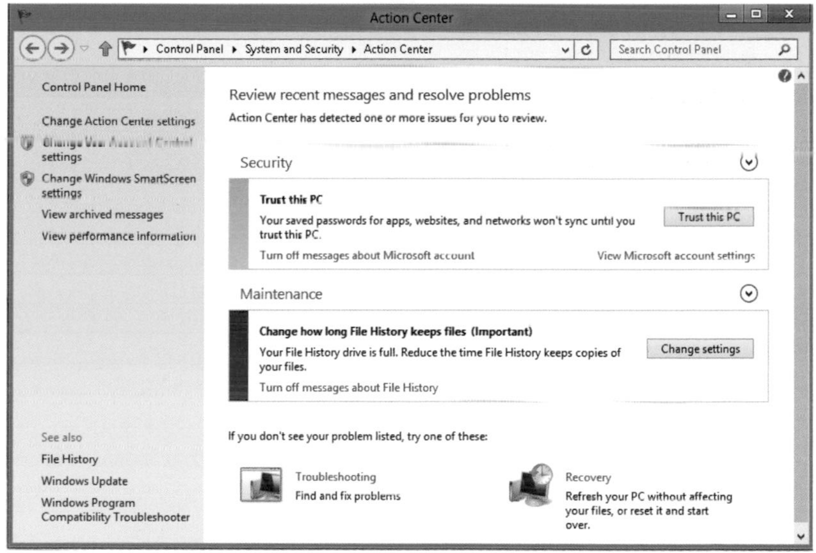

ALERT: When you see alerts, pay attention! You'll want to resolve them.

HOT TIP: If you're ever prompted after receiving an error to send information about the error to Microsoft, do so. When a solution is found, you'll be prompted by the Action Center to apply the fix.

Scan for malware with Windows Defender

You don't have to do much with Windows Defender except understand that it offers protection against some of the more common internet threats. It's enabled by default and it runs in the background. However, if you ever think your computer has been attacked by an internet threat (adware, worm, malware, etc.) you can run a manual scan here. Windows Defender may be able to get rid of it.

1. Open Windows Defender. (You can search for it from the Start screen.)
2. Verify Windows Defender is enabled and note the option to run a scan if desired.
3. Click the X in the top right corner to close the Windows Defender window.

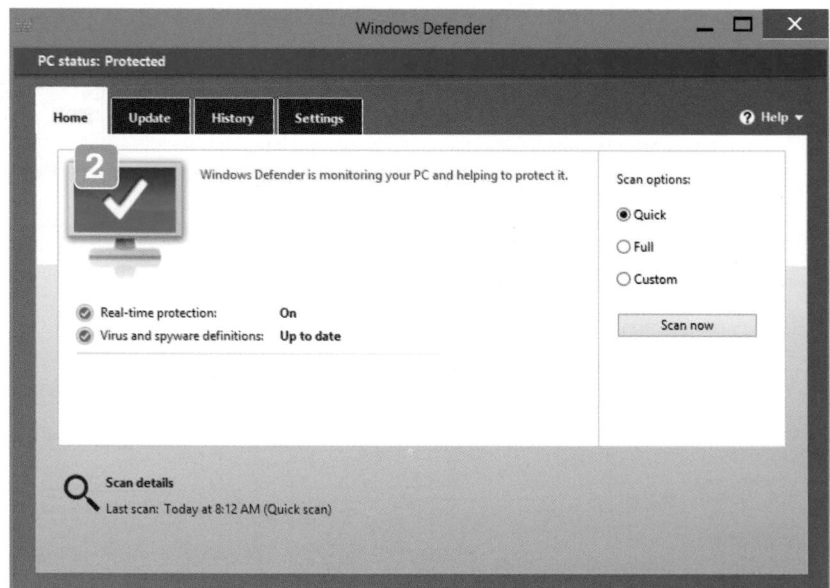

WHAT DOES THIS MEAN?

Malware: Stands for malicious software. Malware includes adware, worms, spyware, etc.

ALERT: Windows Defender and Windows Firewall will likely be disabled if you've purchased and installed a third-party anti-virus, anti-malware tool. Do not enable it if this is the case.

HOT TIP: Click each tab available from Windows Defender to explore all of the options.

Enable the Firewall

Windows Firewall is a software program that checks the data that comes in from the internet (or a local network) and then decides whether it's good data or bad. If it deems the data harmless, it will allow it to come though the firewall, if not, it's blocked.

1. Open Windows Firewall. (Type Firewall at the Start screen and click Settings to find it.)
2. Verify the firewall is on. If not, select Turn Windows Firewall on or off, enable it, and click OK.
3. Review the other settings.

ALERT: You have to have a firewall (either Windows Firewall or a third-party firewall) to keep hackers from getting access to your computer and to help prevent it from sending out malicious code if it is ever attacked by a virus or worm.

DID YOU KNOW?
The first time you use a program that is blocked by Windows Firewall by default, you'll be prompted to 'unblock' the program. This is a safety feature to protect rogue programs from gaining unwanted access to your computer.

Enable Airplane mode

During aeroplane takeoffs and landings, you are prompted to turn off all electronic devices. However, once you have the go ahead that it's OK to use 'approved electronic devices' you can turn on your laptop and use it, provided you enable Airplane mode.

1. Click Windows key + I.
2. Click the Network icon.
3. Move the slider for Airplane mode from On to Off.

HOT TIP: Another way to enable Airplane mode is to type Airplane at the Start screen, click Settings, and then click Turn airplane mode on or off.

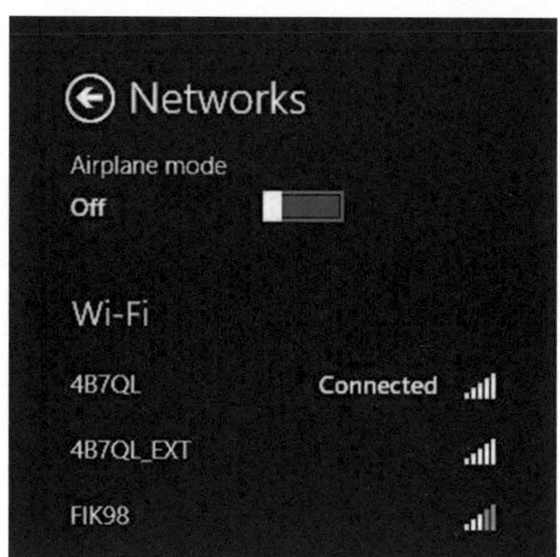

WHAT DOES THIS MEAN?

Airplane mode shuts down all network communications as well as cellular connections, theoretically so your transmissions won't interfere with the aeroplane's transmissions.

Use Help and Support

If you encounter a problem you can't resolve, you can use the available Help and Support wizards to assist you in finding a solution. These wizards walk you through the required processes to find a solution.

1. At the Start screen type Help.
2. Click Settings; click Find and fix problems.

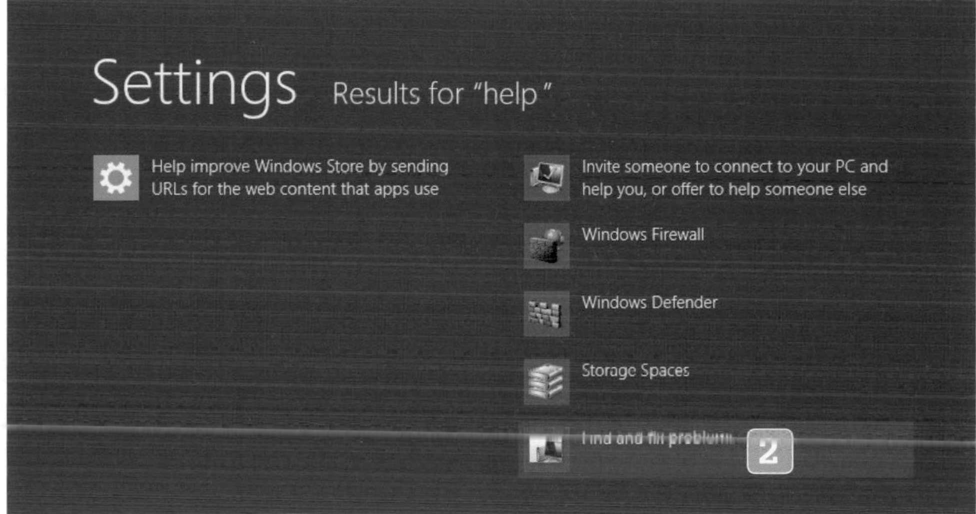

3. Use the options to find what you need help with.

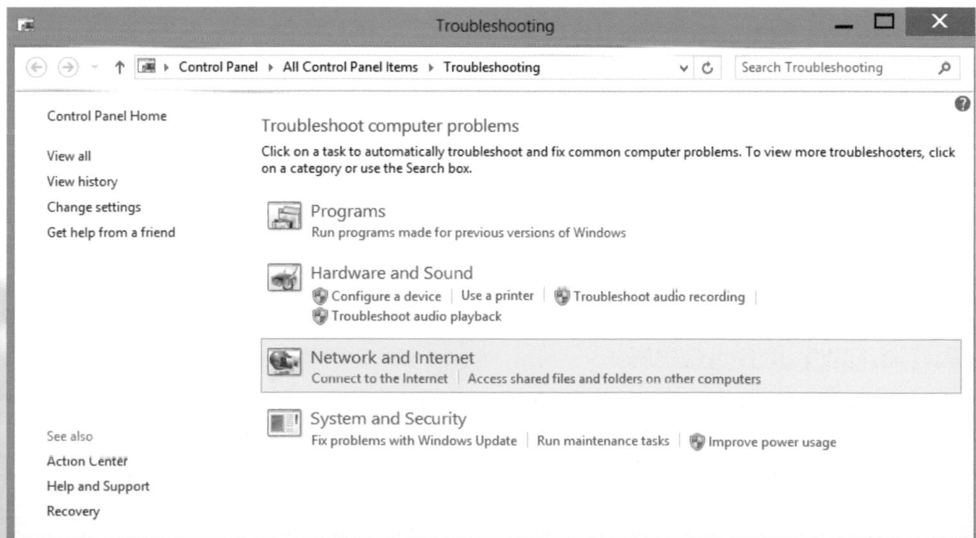

4 Work through the wizard.

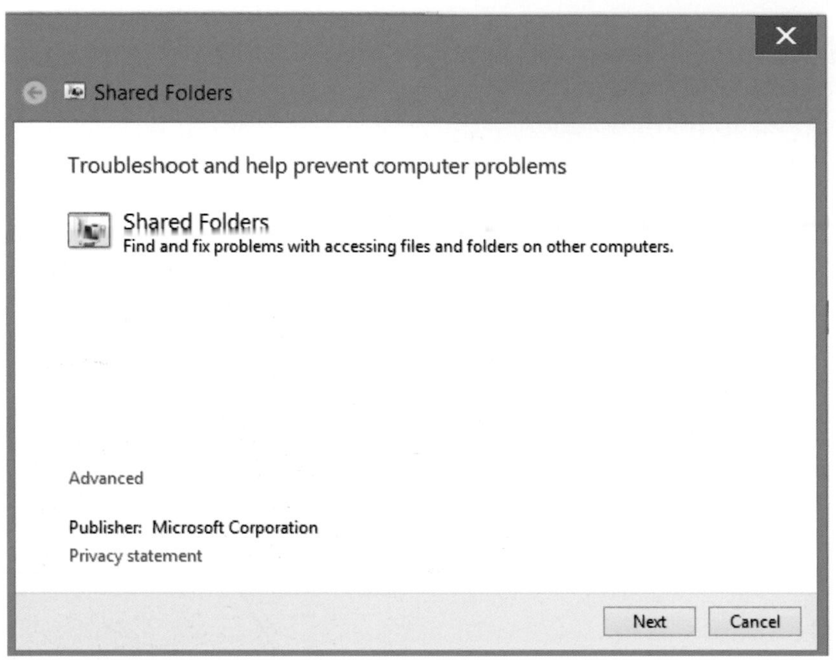

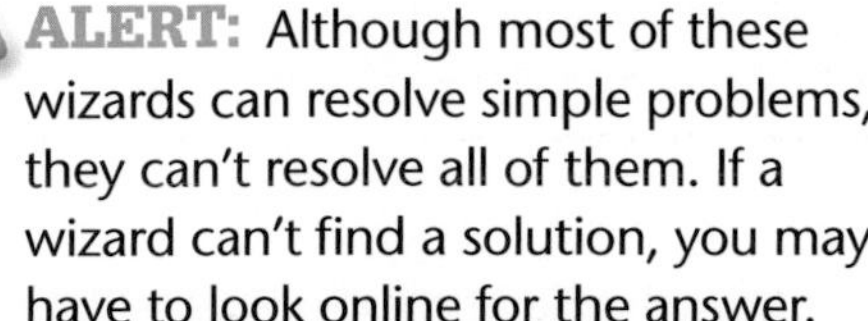

ALERT: Although most of these wizards can resolve simple problems, they can't resolve all of them. If a wizard can't find a solution, you may have to look online for the answer.

HOT TIP: Before you troubleshoot any hardware, turn off the device, turn it back on, and disconnect and reconnect it to your laptop. If it's internal hardware, restart your computer.

Use System Restore

System Restore regularly creates and saves restore points that contain information about your laptop that Windows uses to work properly. If your laptop starts acting up, you can use System Restore to restore it to a time when the laptop was working properly. Before you start, connect your laptop to an electrical outlet.

1. At the Start screen, type System Restore.
2. Click Settings, and then click Create a restore point.
3. Click System Restore.
4. Click Next to accept and apply the recommended restore point.
5. Click Finish.
6. Wait patiently while the process completes.

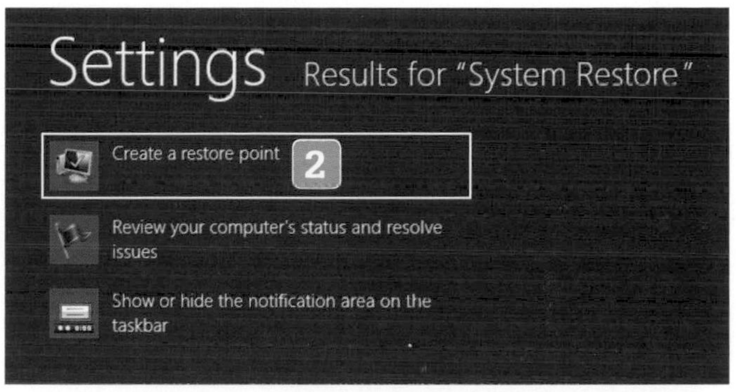

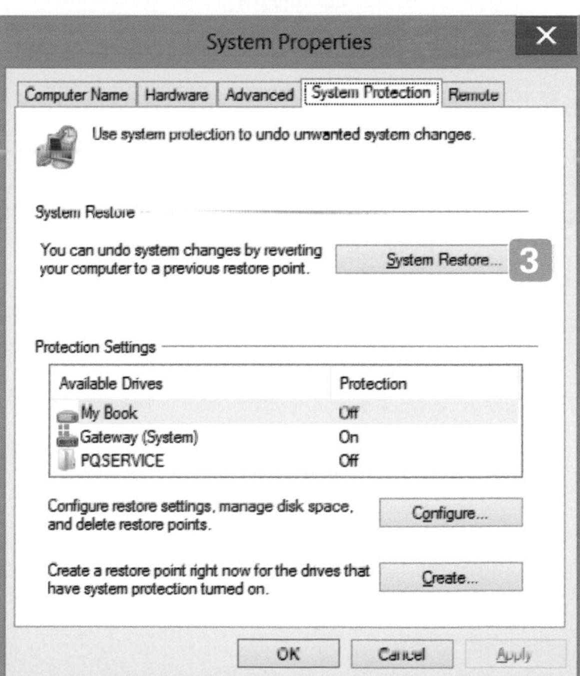

DID YOU KNOW?

System Restore works only with its own system files, so running System Restore will not affect any of your personal data. Your pictures, email, documents, music, etc. will not be deleted or changed.

ALERT: If running System Restore on a laptop or tablet, make sure it's plugged in. System Restore should never be interrupted.

WHAT DOES THIS MEAN?

Restore point: A snapshot of a computer's previous state that can be applied in place of the current state, to make an unstable computer stable again.

Refresh your laptop

If your laptop isn't running well and you've already tried the various troubleshooting options including System Restore, you may need to refresh it. When you do, all third-party programs you've installed from discs or websites are removed and your computer settings are returned to their defaults. This resolves almost all problems most users will encounter. Apps from the Windows Store will remain as will your photos, music, videos and other personal files, so you won't have to start from scratch once the refresh is complete.

1. Access the Settings charm.
2. Click Change PC settings.
3. Click the General tab.
4. Scroll to locate Refresh your PC without affecting your files.
5. Click Get started.
6. Read the information offered, click Next, and work through the refresh process.

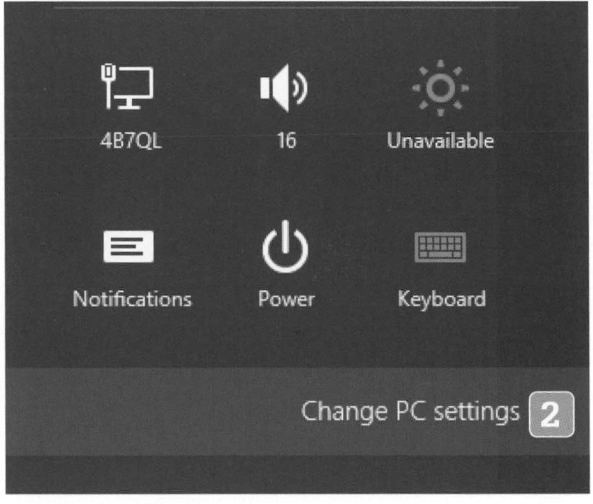

Refresh your PC without affecting your files

If your PC isn't running well, you can refresh it without losing your photos, music, videos, and other personal files.

5 Get started

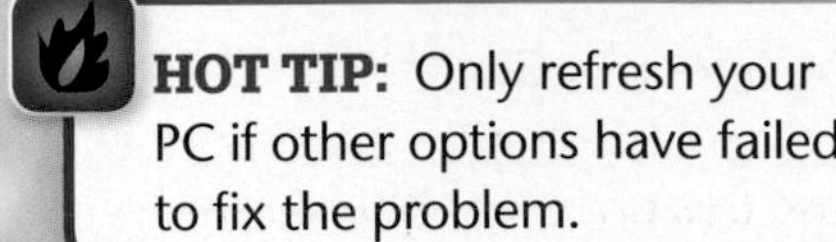

HOT TIP: Only refresh your PC if other options have failed to fix the problem.

ALERT: Before you refresh your PC, locate the product codes you'll need to reinstall third-party programs.

Reset your laptop

If refreshing your PC doesn't resolve your existing problems, you'll have to reset your PC and start over. When you do, everything will be deleted, including all of your apps, applications, settings and personal files. You'll need to back up these files before continuing here. This is a drastic step, so be sure this is what you want to do before you do it!

1. Access the Settings charm.
2. Click Change PC settings.
3. Click the General tab.
4. Scroll to locate Remove everything and reinstall Windows.
5. Click Get started.

HOT TIP: Reset your laptop before you sell it or give it away.

Remove everything and reinstall Windows

If you want to recycle your PC or start over completely, you can reset it to its factory settings.

5 Get started

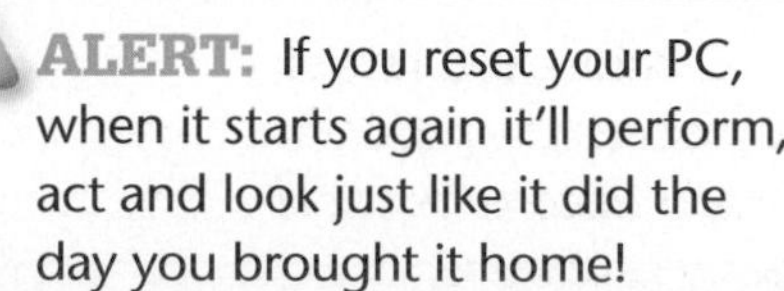

ALERT: If you reset your PC, when it starts again it'll perform, act and look just like it did the day you brought it home!

HOT TIP: The option under Remove everything and reinstall Windows is Advanced Startup. Choose this option to boot from a USB or DVD, change Windows start settings, restore from a system image and more.

15 Tips for Over 50s Tablet users

Introduction

If you have a tablet that offers a touch-only screen and does not come with any other hardware, you can purchase and connect a Bluetooth keyboard or keyboard dock if your tablet supports it. You can use this keyboard as you would any other. Likewise, you can attach a Bluetooth mouse. These devices come with instructions for 'pairing' them, which generally consists of telling Windows 8 to search for the device and typing the pairing code offered. If your tablet supports it you can opt to connect a keyboard and mouse by connecting them to available USB ports instead. This type of hardware may or may not be helpful to you though, especially if they are bulky and difficult to carry around, or if your hands are too big or too painful to use a keyboard and mouse effectively. Another option is a stylus. You can use this to tap, double tap, tap and hold, and even swipe and flick on the screen.

So, if you have a tablet and you prefer to rely on touch to navigate it, you'll want to simplify the device as best you can (such as using a four-digit PIN instead of a long, complex password at log on). You also need to know the available touch techniques, such as a tap and double tap, and a long tap and hold. There is a lot more to uncover than this though; read on to learn more.

Understand the limitations of Windows RT

Tablet computers come installed with either a full version of Windows 8 like you see on laptop computers or something called Windows RT. You can determine which operating system you have installed from Control Panel, under System and Security, System, as shown here. If you see Windows 8 RT, you'll want to read this section.

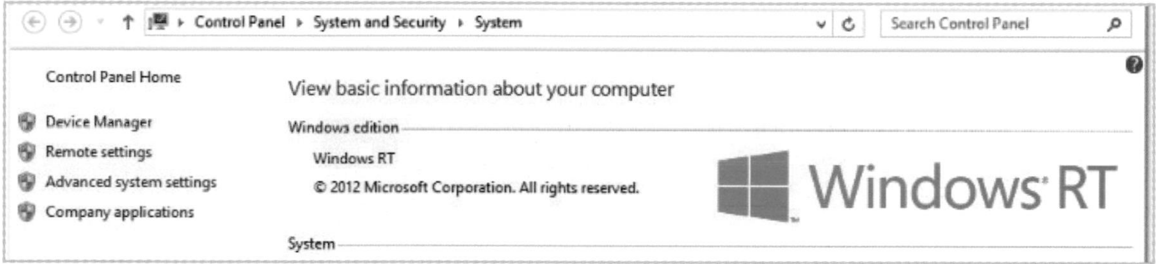

Windows RT differs from the full version of Windows 8 in many ways. To name only a few, Windows RT:

- Supports touch; offers a long battery life and great performance.
- Does not support Windows 7 or earlier desktop applications, or those you install yourself, like Photoshop, iTunes or Google Chrome.
- Comes preinstalled with the Microsoft Office 2013 Home and Student suite of applications.
- Does not include Windows Media Player, but is compatible with many media apps available in the Store, such as Netflix, Xbox Music and so on.

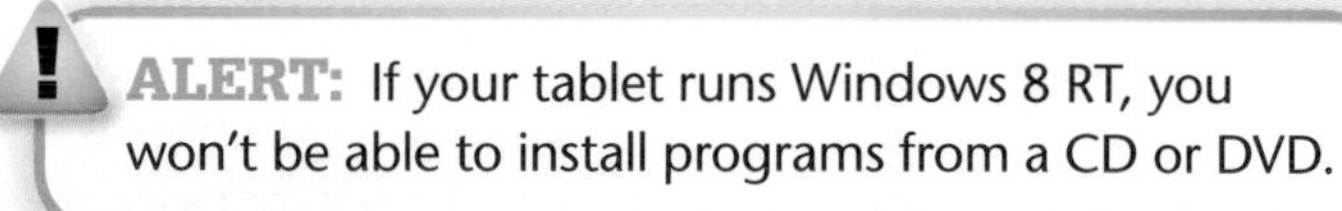

ALERT: If your tablet runs Windows 8 RT, you won't be able to install programs from a CD or DVD.

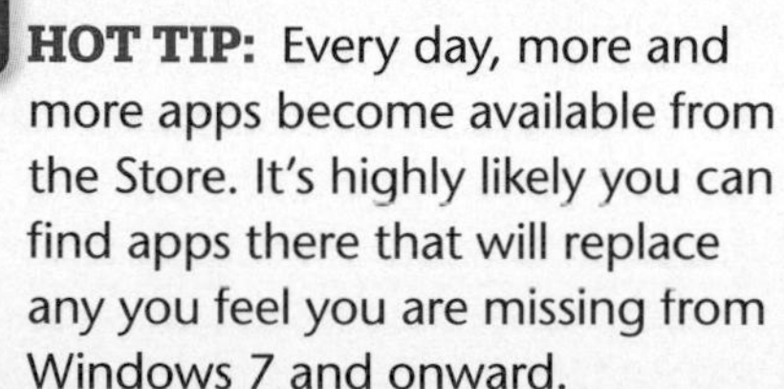

HOT TIP: Every day, more and more apps become available from the Store. It's highly likely you can find apps there that will replace any you feel you are missing from Windows 7 and onward.

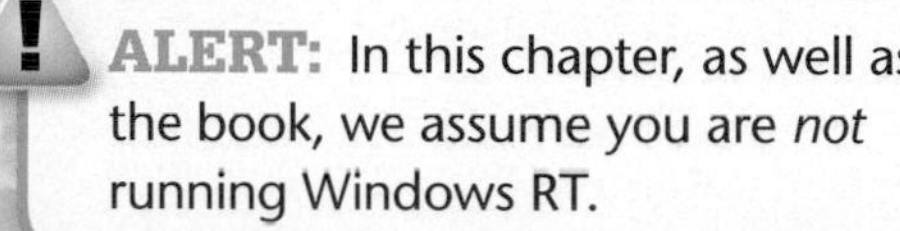

ALERT: In this chapter, as well as the book, we assume you are *not* running Windows RT.

Flick, swipe and pinch

There are three more touch techniques to explore: flick, swipe, and pinch. Flick and swipe are basically the same movement, but it's best to include both terms here. These techniques were explained in a short tutorial when you first set up your tablet, but you may have forgotten them.

1. Open any app. Try Maps or News for simplicity's sake. Position a finger at the top of the screen or the bottom, and swipe or flick slowly upward or downward as applicable. The charms will appear.

2. Tap to open several additional apps. Use Windows key + D to access the desktop. Then, position your left thumb in the middle of the far left side of the screen and flick inward. The last used app will appear.

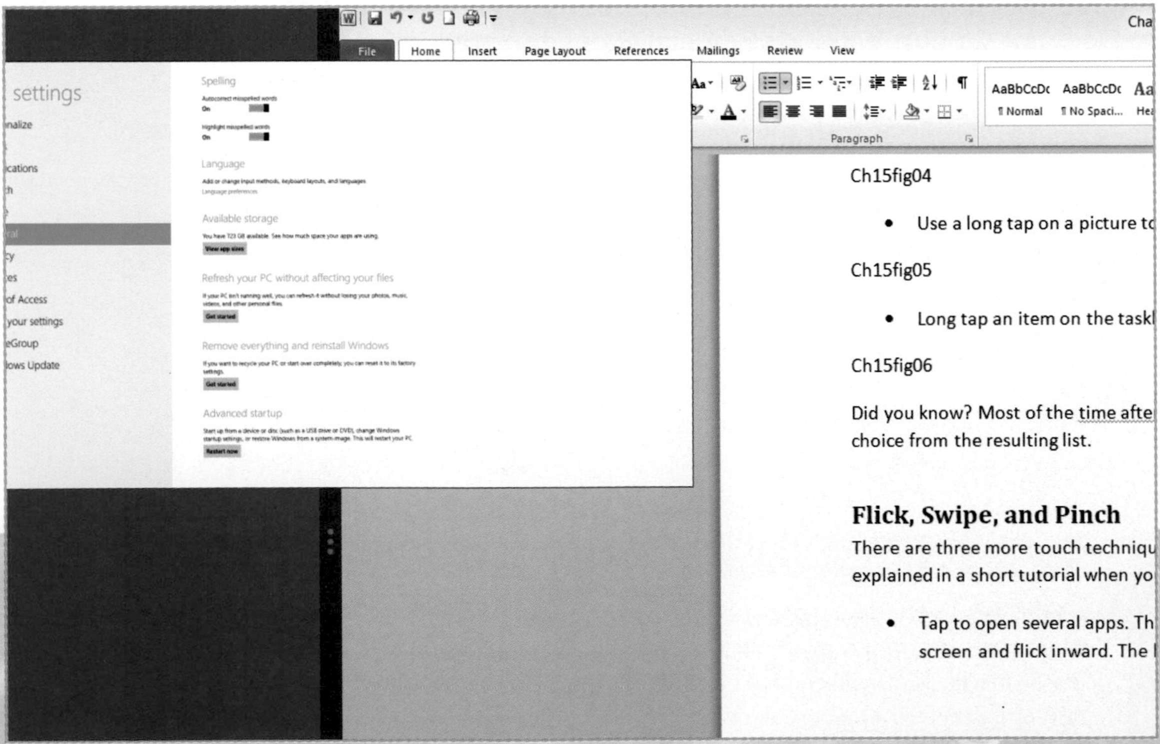

3 Position a finger or thumb in the middle of the right side of the screen and flick inward to access the charms.

4 Open Maps and find your current location. Use a pinching motion with your thumb and forefinger, pinch in and out to zoom.

5 On the Start screen, pinch inward to make the tiles very small.

6 Some third-party apps allow for rotation of certain elements. To use the rotation option, use two fingers and move them in a circle. Very few apps support this feature right now.

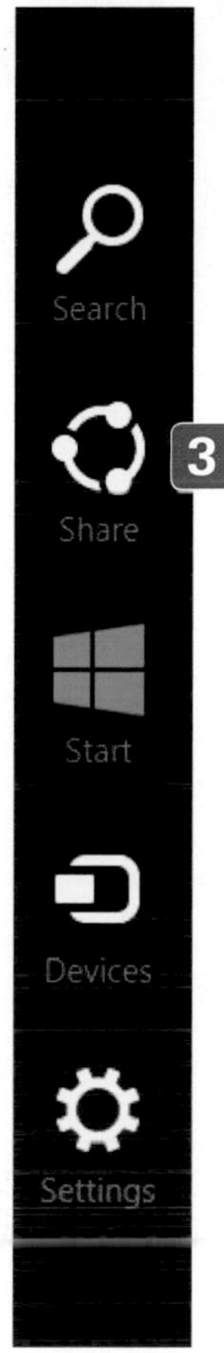

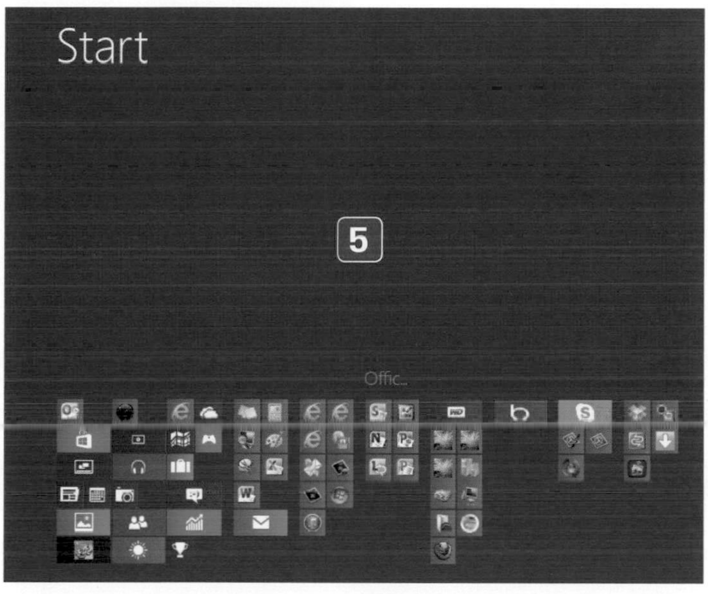

DID YOU KNOW?
You can close an app by dragging (swiping) slowly from the top of the app to the bottom of it, and dragging it off of the screen.

HOT TIP: Sometimes on web pages that offer a slide show of photos, you can swipe to move from one to the next.

HOT TIP: From anywhere, flick inward from the right side of the screen and tap Start to get to the Start screen.

DID YOU KNOW?
You can zoom in and out on almost anything! Try it on the Start screen. While there, tap and drag downward on any group of apps. Note the new option that appears to name the group of tiles.

Use tap and double tap

Two more touch techniques are tap and double tap. If you're used to using a mouse, a single tap is like a left mouse click. A double tap is like a double left mouse click. Here are a few things to try if you would like to experiment with these techniques.

1. From the Start screen, tap any tile to open its related app.
2. From the desktop, double tap the Recycle Bin to open it.
3. Use a single tap to type a key on the onscreen keyboard.
4. From File Explorer, double tap to open any folder.
5. While in a folder, tap once to select an item. Then, tap once on the Home tab to view editing options such as Cut, Copy, Paste, Move and so on. Tap any command once to engage it.

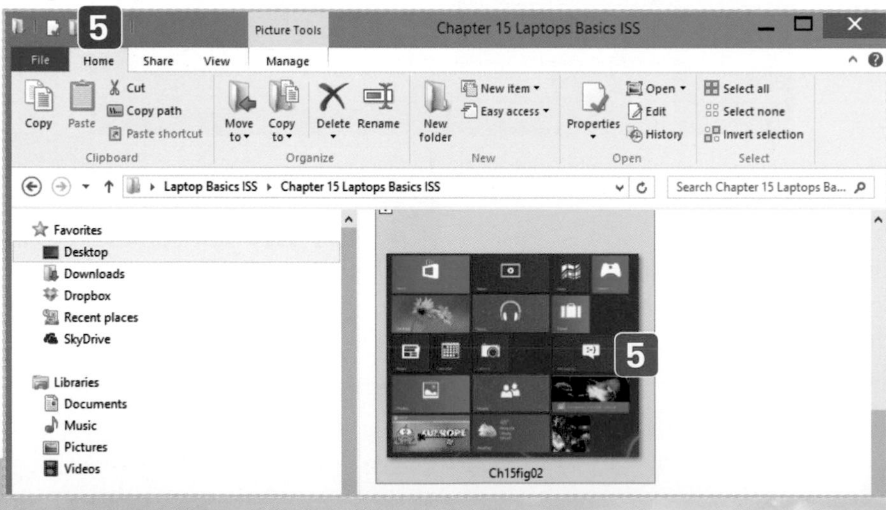

? DID YOU KNOW? When an item is selected, a check mark appears by it.

HOT TIP: Purchase a 'pen' or stylus for your touch device. You can use it instead of your finger to tap the screen.

Use a long tap

A long tap is generally equivalent to a right-click on a traditional mouse. You will use a long tap to view contextual menus or access app toolbars, for the most part.

1. Use a long tap on an empty area of the desktop to access personalisation options, among other things.
2. Use a long tap on a picture to rotate it, among other things.
3. Long tap an item on the taskbar to see its related jump list.

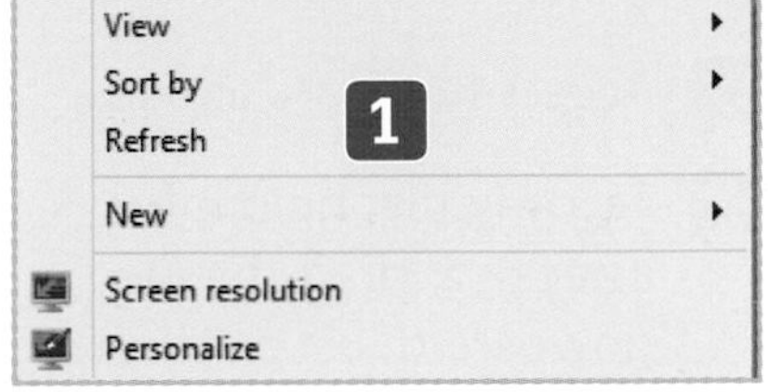

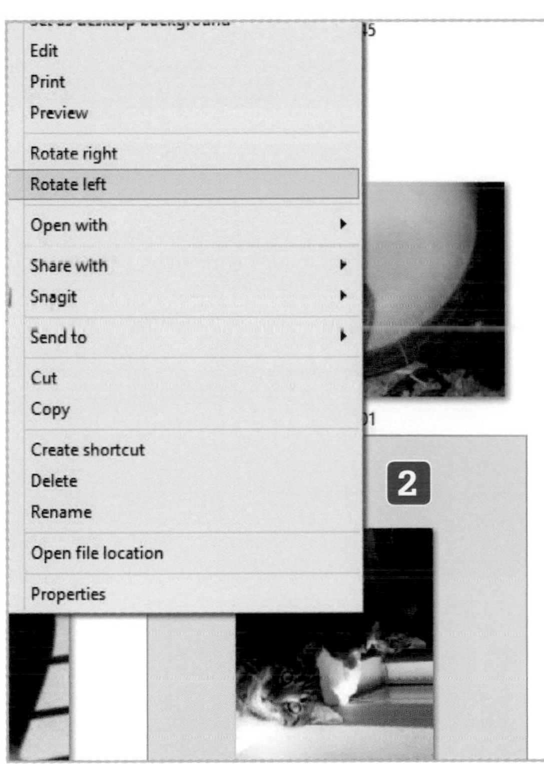

DID YOU KNOW?

When you successfully perform a long tap, a square or check mark generally appears on the screen.

DID YOU KNOW?

Most of the time after performing a long tap you then perform a single tap to make a choice from the resulting list.

Use tap, hold and drag

You can tap, hold and drag to move a tile to a new location on the Start screen. You can tap, hold and drag downward to select an item too. Practise these two techniques now.

1. Access the Start screen.
2. Tap any tile, hold it for a second, drag the tile downward just a little, and then drag it to a new location on the Start screen.
3. Drop it there.
4. Tap any tile, hold it for a second, and drag it downward just a little until a check mark appears.
5. Let go. Note the options that appear.
6. Repeat Step 4 to deselect an item. The check mark will disappear.

HOT TIP: To reposition a window on the desktop, tap and drag from its title bar.

DID YOU KNOW?
You can select multiple items on the Start screen, but when you do, some of the options may disappear, like Larger or Smaller.

DID YOU KNOW?
If you select multiple tiles on the Start screen a new option, Clear selection, appears.

Pin the onscreen keyboard to the Start screen

The desktop's taskbar offers an icon for the onscreen keyboard. You can use it to type instead of using a physical keyboard. If you need a keyboard often, you can pin this virtual keyboard to the Start screen for easier access.

1. At the Start screen, swipe in from the right to access the charms, tap Settings and tap Keyboard.
2. Tap Touch keyboard and handwriting panel.

3. Use the keyboard to tap out OSK.

4 Right-click On-Screen keyboard and then tap Pin to Start.

5 Tap to access the Start screen, locate the tile for the onscreen keyboard at the far right of the screen, and drag it to the desired position.

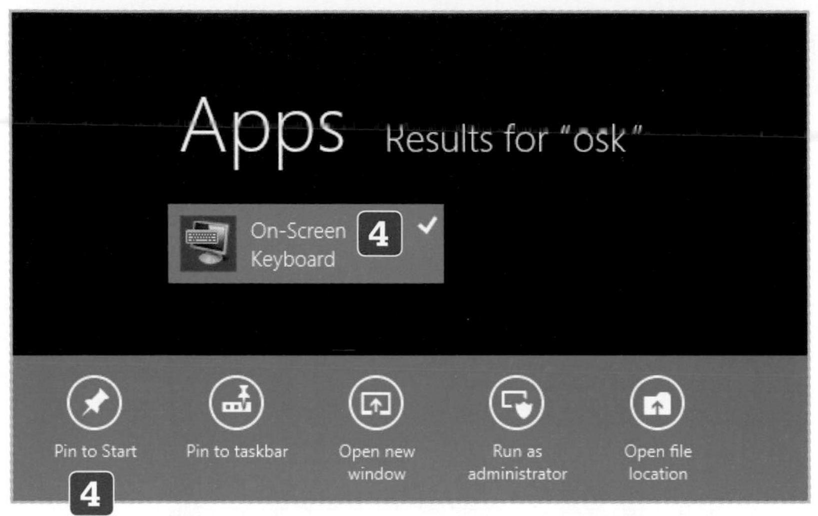

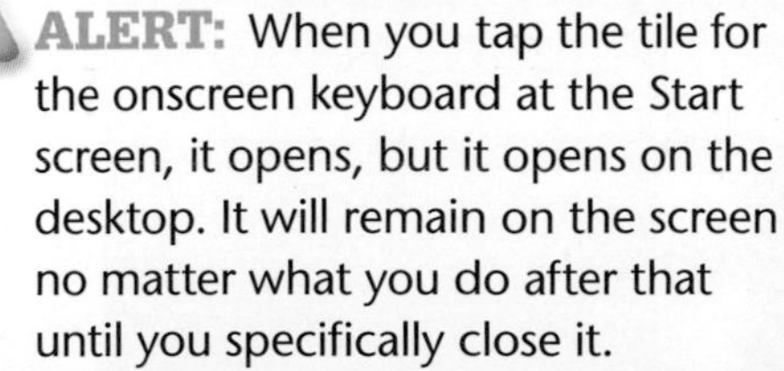

ALERT: When you tap the tile for the onscreen keyboard at the Start screen, it opens, but it opens on the desktop. It will remain on the screen no matter what you do after that until you specifically close it.

HOT TIP: You can use the onscreen keyboard to type at the Start screen.

Type at the Start screen

If you don't have a keyboard, typing at the Start screen after logging in can be a bit trying. Here are a few tips to help you get started.

- Flick inward, tap Settings, tap Keyboard, and then tap Touch keyboard and handwriting panel (the second option). A keyboard will appear on the Start screen.

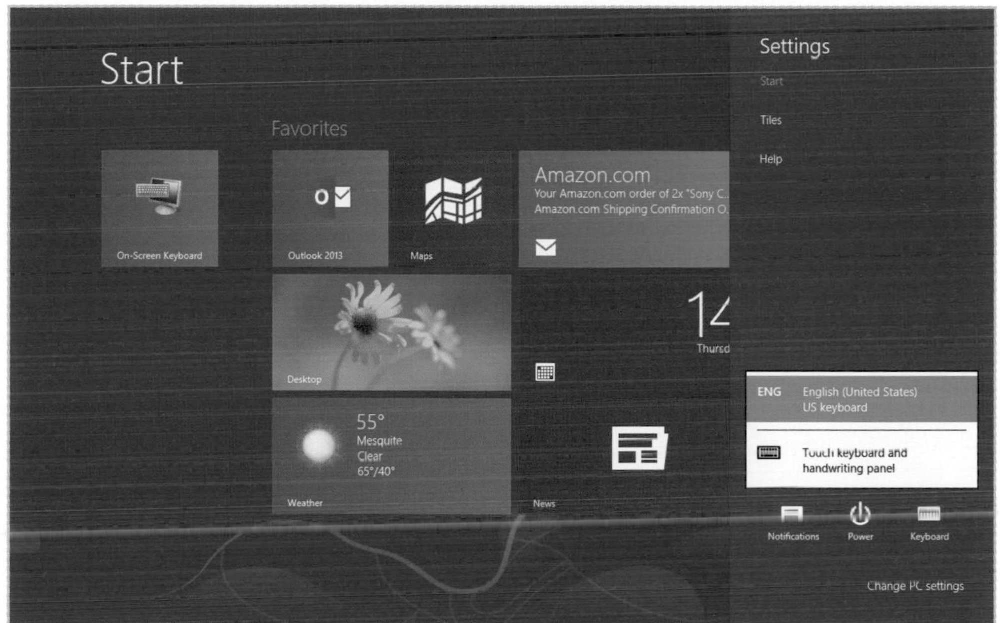

- If you created a tile for the onscreen keyboard on the Start screen, tap it, then tap the Windows key on your device to return to the Start screen.
- Access the Search charm and type OSK. From the results, tap On-Screen Keyboard. Tap the Windows key to return to the Start screen.
- Right-click, tap All Apps, tap On-Screen Keyboard, and then tap the Windows key.

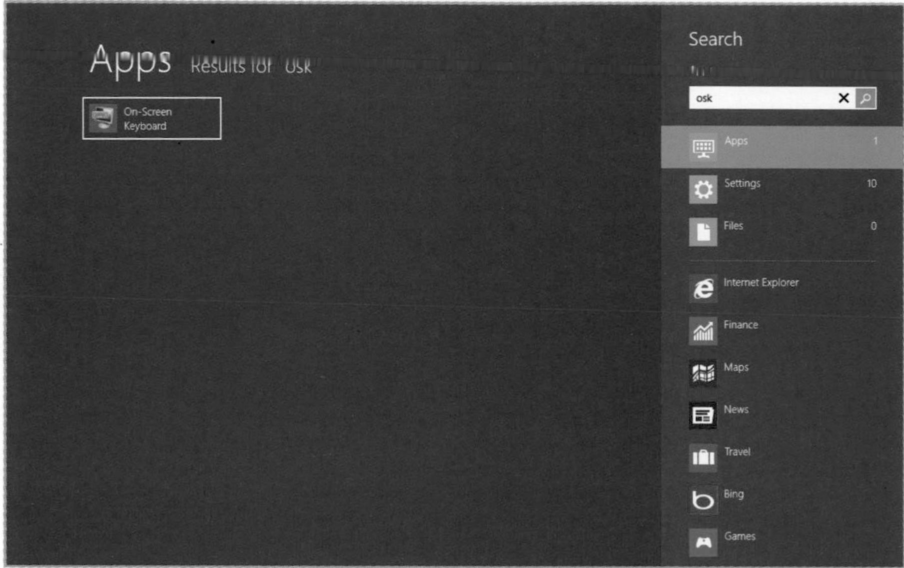

HOT TIP: Look for additional ways to type at the Start screen as time passes. There will be additional ways!

Change Pen and Touch settings

If you don't like the way some of the default settings for touch work, you can change the settings.

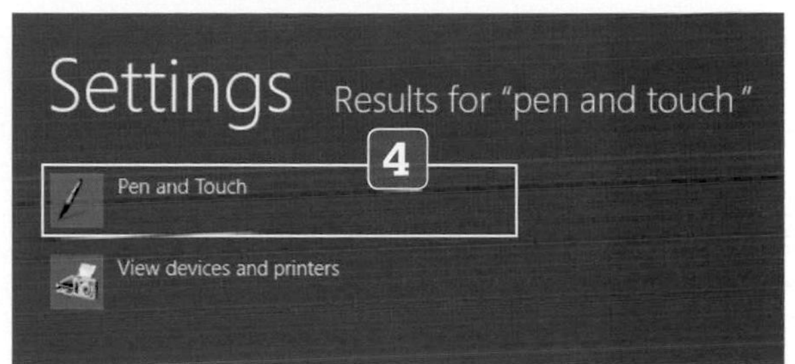

1. From the Start screen, flick in from the right side to access the charms.
2. Tap Settings, Keyboard, and then Touch, Keyboard and Handwriting Panel.
3. Type Pen and Touch.
4. Tap Settings, and tap Pen and Touch.
5. In the Pen and Touch window, select either Double-tap or Press and hold, and tap Settings.
6. Configure the settings as desired, and tap OK.
7. Tap OK to close the Pen and Touch dialog box.

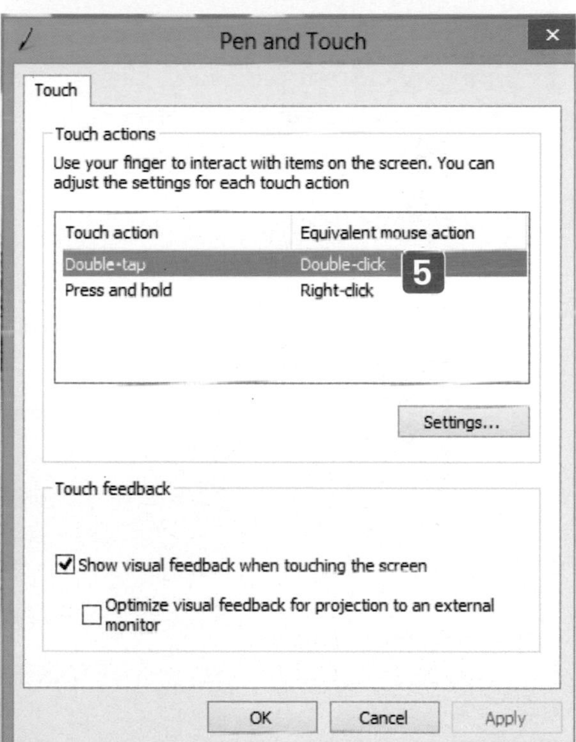

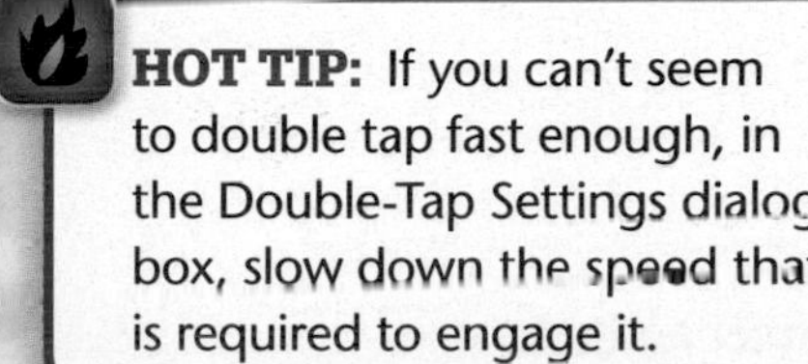

HOT TIP: If you can't seem to double tap fast enough, in the Double-Tap Settings dialog box, slow down the speed that is required to engage it.

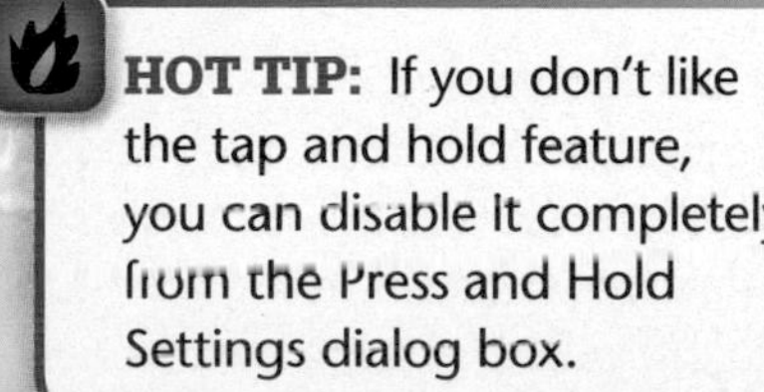

HOT TIP: If you don't like the tap and hold feature, you can disable it completely from the Press and Hold Settings dialog box.

Configure a PIN

It's difficult to type a long and complicated password at the Start screen, especially when you're tapping it out. Switch to a PIN for better ease of use.

1. At the Start screen, access the charms, tap Search and type PIN.
2. On the right side of the screen, click Settings.
3. Tap Create or change PIN.
4. Tap Create a PIN.
5. Type your current password, click OK, and then enter the desired PIN two times.
6. Tap Finish.

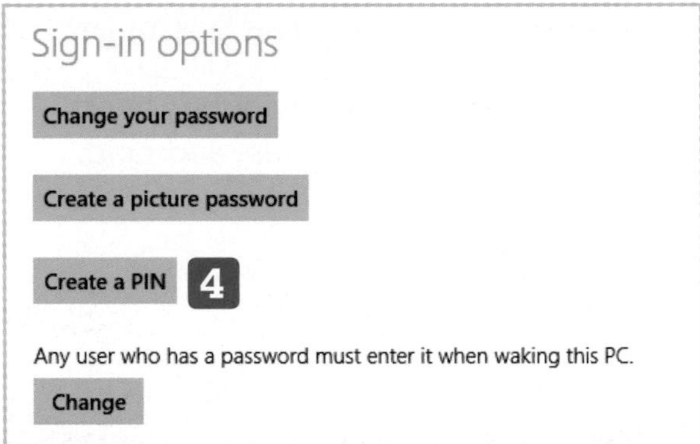

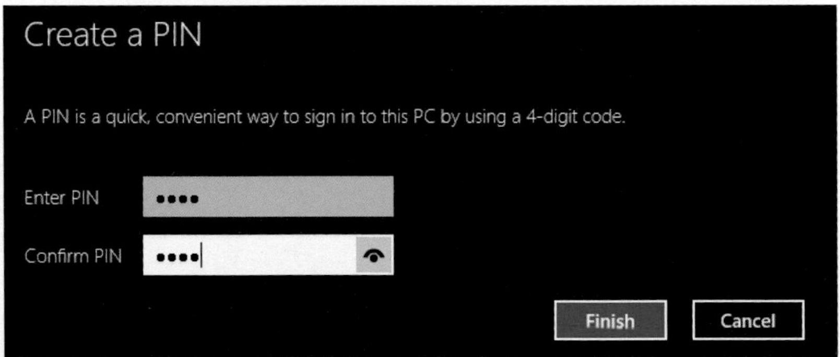

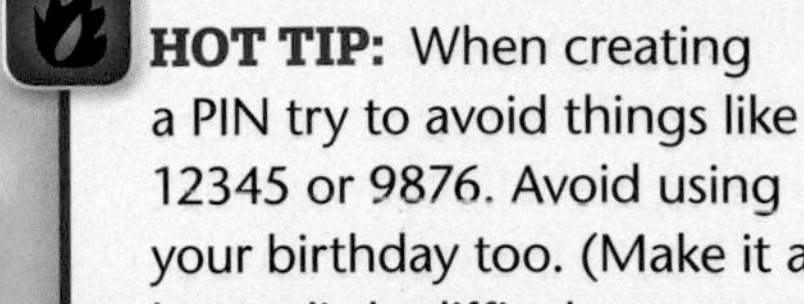

HOT TIP: When creating a PIN try to avoid things like 12345 or 9876. Avoid using your birthday too. (Make it at least a little difficult to guess!)

HOT TIP: You create a PIN in PC Settings. You can use this same interface to configure many of the personalisation tasks you'll find in this chapter and others.

Lengthen battery life

There are lots of ways to enhance battery life. You can lower the screen brightness, turn off Bluetooth, and more.

1 In the PC settings hub, tap Wireless. Turn off Bluetooth if you don't need it.

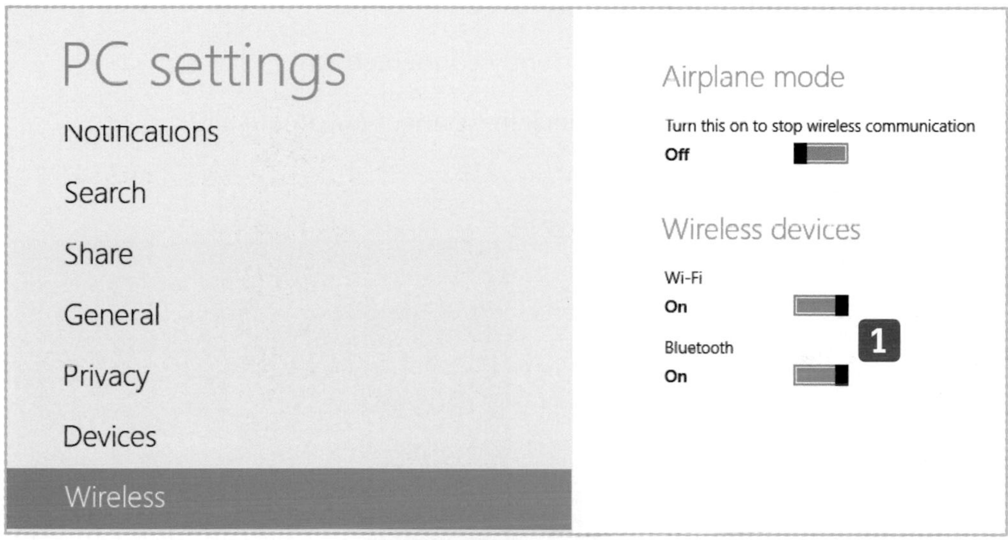

2 From the Settings charm, move the slider for Brightness down.

3 From the Settings charm, tap Power, and tap Sleep to put your tablet to sleep anytime.

4 Visit the manufacturer's website to learn more.

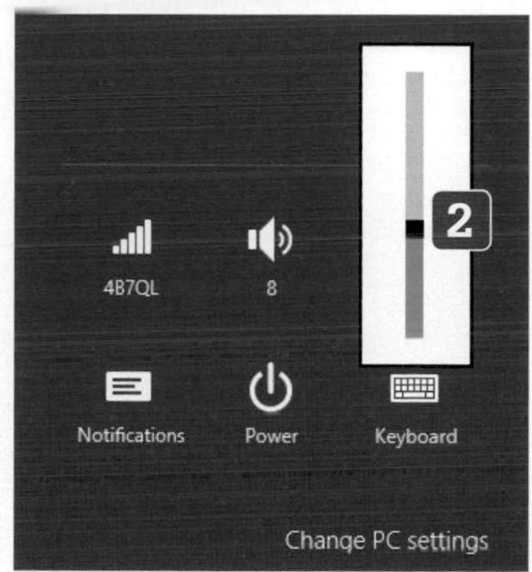

DID YOU KNOW?
It is possible to access advanced power settings from the Power Options window. You may be able to enhance battery performance there.

ALERT: Your tablet is always seeking out available wi-fi networks. If you know you don't need to be connected, you can disable wi-fi to extend your battery life.

Remember wi-fi networks

When you connect to a new wi-fi network, you are prompted to remember it (or not). It's best to remember all wi-fi networks so you'll be automatically connected the next time you are near it.

1. From the Settings charm, tap the Networks icon.
2. Select the Wi-Fi network you are currently connected to.
3. If it isn't already selected, place a check in Connect automatically.
4. Repeat as necessary.

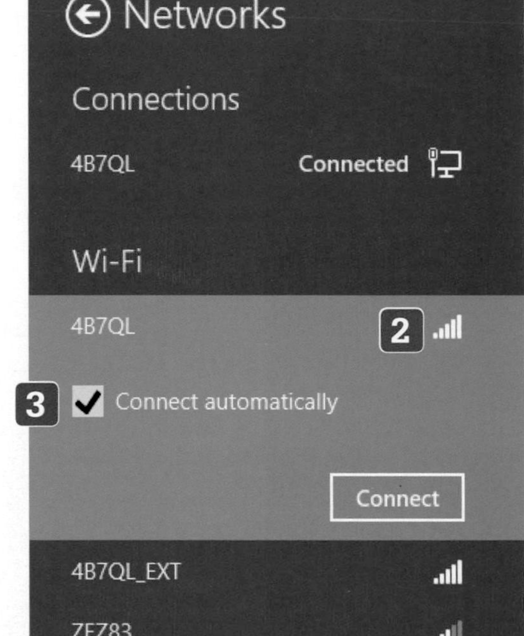

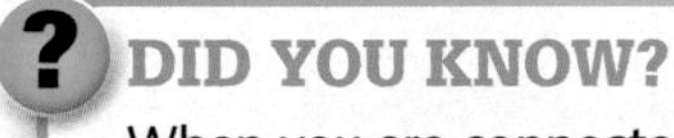

DID YOU KNOW?
When you are connected to wi-fi, nothing is counted against any metered data plan you may subscribe to.

HOT TIP: You want to be connected to wi-fi as often as possible, so that you'll have access to the internet as often as possible!

DID YOU KNOW?
You can also forget a network. To see this option (and others), long tap the network to forget.

Know when you're on wi-fi and when on a metered data plan

It's OK to watch movies on Netflix, videos on YouTube, and other large online data files when you are connected to a wi-fi network. But if you do this while connected to a cellular data network, one with a data limit, you'll use up your weekly or monthly data quota very quickly. It's important to be able to tell what kind of network you're connected to.

1. From the Settings charm, tap the Networks icon.
2. Select the network you are currently connected to.
3. Note if it is a wireless network you recognise, such as the one at your home.
4. If it is not a wireless network but is instead a metered data plan you subscribe to, be very careful about how much data you use.

HOT TIP: The only way you'll have always-available internet is to purchase a cellular data device and/or plan. Read on to learn how.

DID YOU KNOW?

Even if your device isn't supported by default by a cellular data provider, you can purchase an external USB device to connect with (provided your tablet offers this kind of port).

Consider a cellular data plan

Out of the box, your laptop or tablet can only connect to the internet when it is connected to a wi-fi network. That may be your home network, a public network, or a network where you are employed. When you don't have access to a wi-fi network, you can't connect to the internet, unless you have signed up for and pay for some sort of data plan from a third party. There are many things to consider before doing this.

1. Know what to ask before committing to a plan. Specifically understand how much data you are allowed to use each month and where coverage is guaranteed.
2. Consider a cellular provider. If you already have a cell phone plan, ask them about plans. There may be a bundled package for a discounted price.
3. Consider an ISP. If you already have a broadband, DSL or cable TV connection at home through an ISP, ask them if they offer data plans for mobile devices.
4. Consider a satellite provider only if you can't obtain a cellular or ISP plan.
5. Obtain the proper settings from any provider for logging on, and then thoroughly test the connection. If you aren't pleased you may be able to cancel the plan in a specific window of time.

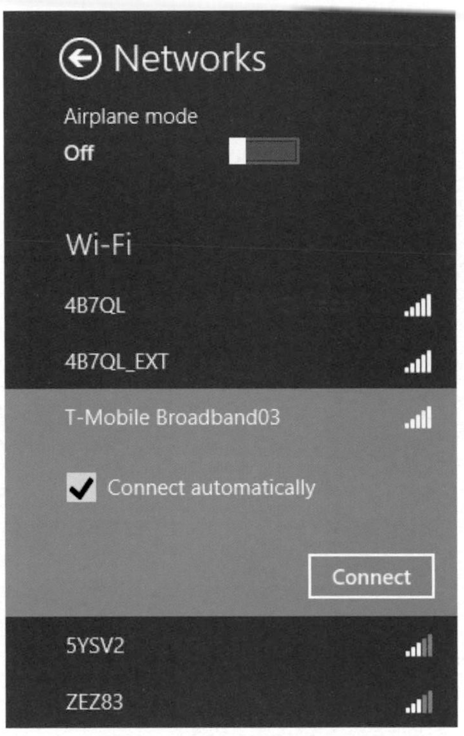

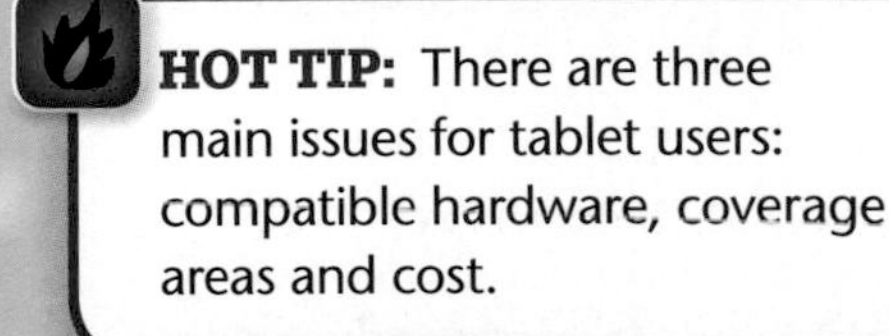

HOT TIP: There are three main issues for tablet users: compatible hardware, coverage areas and cost.

DID YOU KNOW?
If your tablet has a USB port and runs Windows 8, you should be able to obtain always-on internet service.

Look for touch friendly apps

There are a lot of touch friendly apps at the app store. You can find out about an app from its Details page. There are a few really popular touch apps though, and we've listed them here. You can find the most popular apps from the Store by searching; here we've searched for Top Free from the Spotlight category.

- Skype – For participating in video calls.
- Netflix – For watching Netflix media.
- Microsoft Solitaire collection – For playing variations of Solitaire.
- Adobe Reader Touch – For working with Adobe documents.
- Kindle – For reading Kindle books.

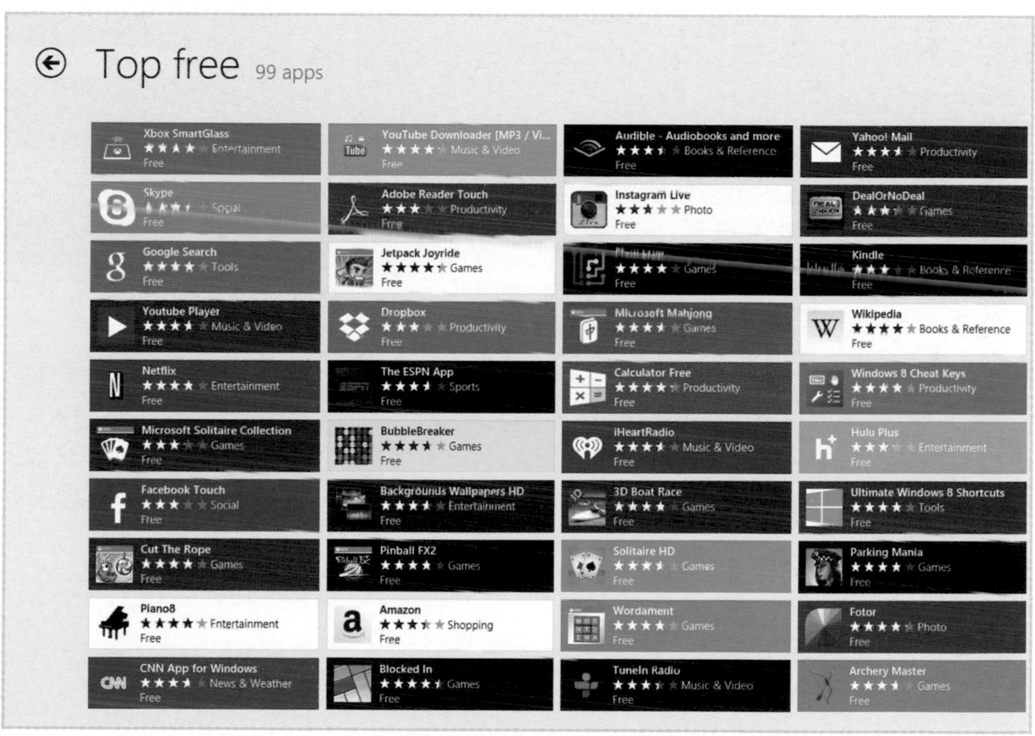

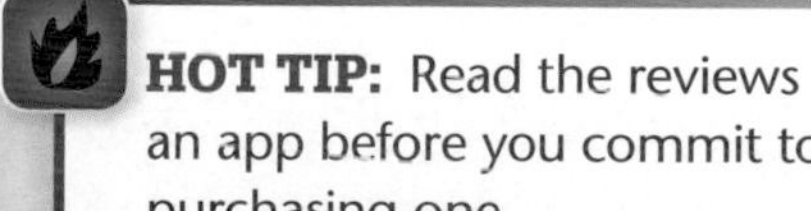

HOT TIP: Read the reviews of an app before you commit to purchasing one.

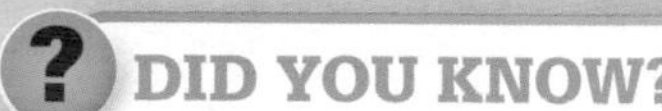

DID YOU KNOW?

You can search the Store from the Search charm (Windows key + C).

Enable Bluetooth and pair a device

As you learned in the introduction, Bluetooth is a technology that enables you to connect wireless keyboards and mice (among other things). If you own one of these devices you must enable Bluetooth in Windows 8 and then pair the device.

1. Turn on the device.
2. At the Start screen, type Bluetooth; tap Settings.
3. In the results tap Add Bluetooth device.

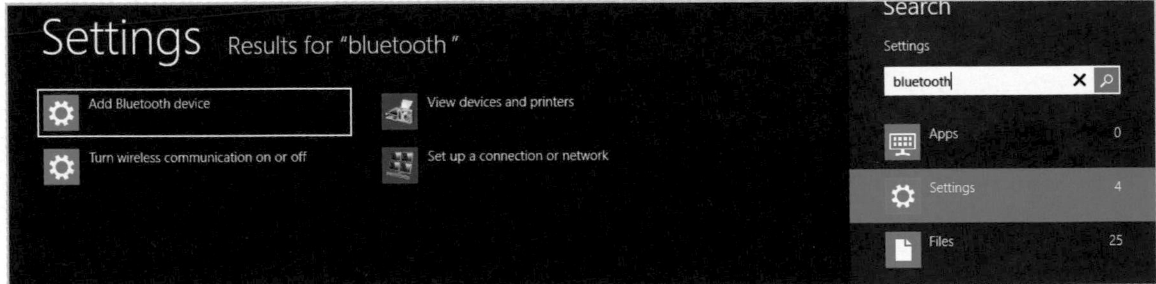

4. Wait while your tablet searches for the device.
5. When prompted, type the pairing code as instructed.

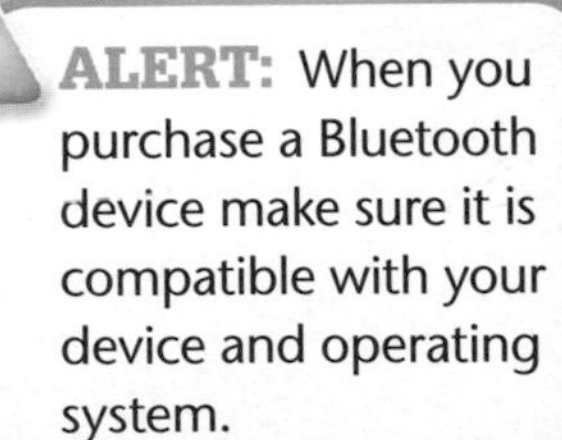

ALERT: When you purchase a Bluetooth device make sure it is compatible with your device and operating system.

DID YOU KNOW?
If you can't connect a Bluetooth device, it may be that sharing is turned off on your Windows 8 tablet, the device you want to connect is turned off or the battery needs charging, or you may need to manually pair the device using the manufacturer's instructions.

Top 10 Laptop & Tablet Problems Solved

Problem 1: I can't install programs like iTunes

Tablet computers come installed with either a full version of Windows 8 like you see on laptop computers or something called Windows RT. You can determine which operating system you have installed from Control Panel, under System and Security, System, as shown here. If you see Windows 8 RT, you'll want to read this section.

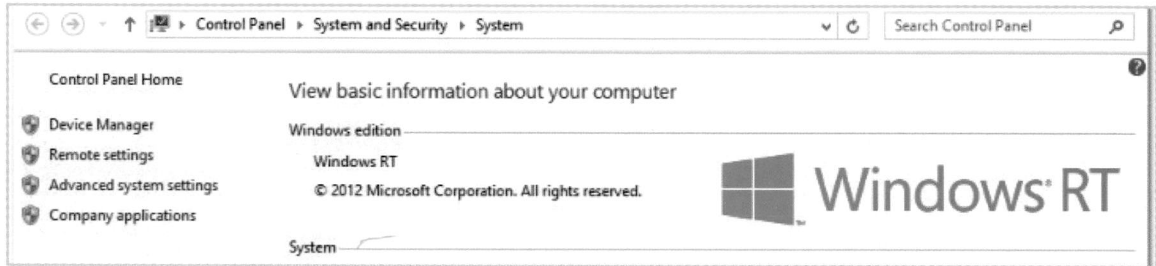

Windows RT differs from the full version of Windows 8 in many ways. To name only a few, Windows RT:

- Supports touch; offers a long battery life and great performance.
- Does not support Windows 7 or earlier desktop applications, or those you install yourself, like Photoshop, iTunes or Google Chrome.
- Comes preinstalled with the Microsoft Office 2013 Home and Student suite of applications.
- Does not include Windows Media Player, but is compatible with many media apps available in the Store, such as Netflix, Xbox Music and so on.

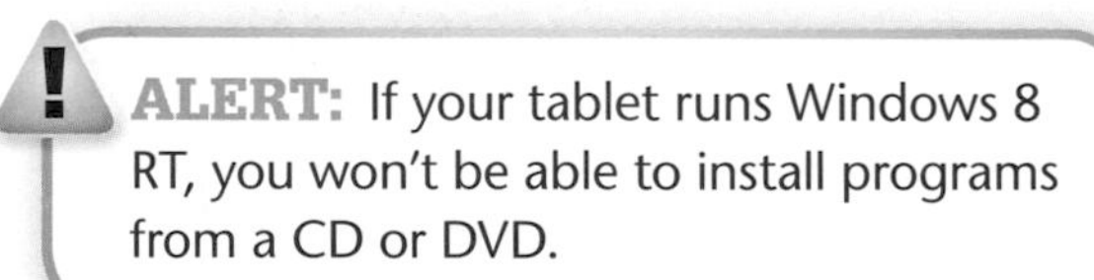

ALERT: If your tablet runs Windows 8 RT, you won't be able to install programs from a CD or DVD.

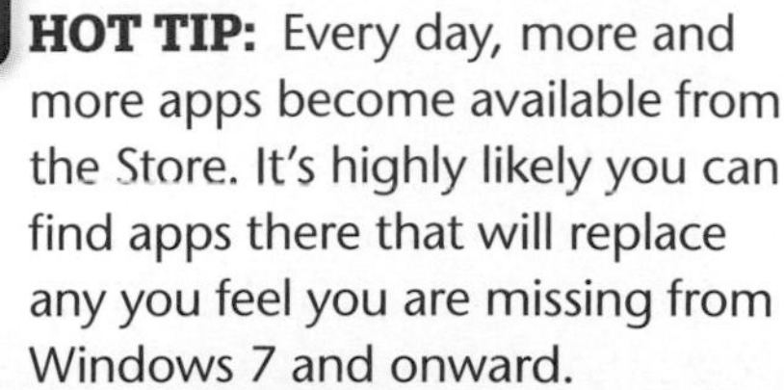

HOT TIP: Every day, more and more apps become available from the Store. It's highly likely you can find apps there that will replace any you feel you are missing from Windows 7 and onward.

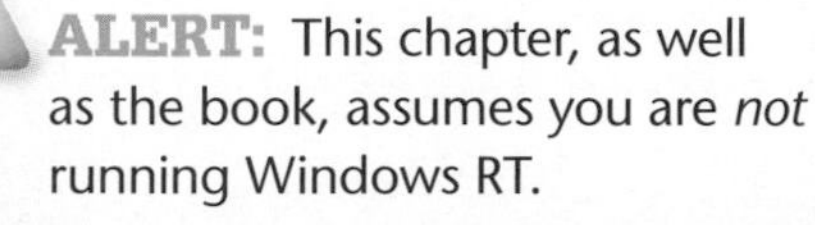

ALERT: This chapter, as well as the book, assumes you are *not* running Windows RT.

Problem 2: What happened to the desktop?

If you've ever used a computer, you've worked at the desktop, the traditional computing environment. Your Windows 8 laptop or tablet also offers a desktop – which you access from the Desktop tile. You may be more comfortable here and prefer not to use the Start screen at all; that is OK with us!

1. Use any method to access the Start screen if you aren't already on it. (You can tap the Windows key on a keyboard.)
2. From the Start screen, click or tap Desktop.
3. Note the Desktop features:

   A The Recycle Bin.

   B The Taskbar (with icons for open files and programs).

   C The Internet Explorer icon (the program is open here).

   D The File Explorer icon (we've opened File Explorer here).

   E The Notification area.

   F Various items stored on the desktop itself.

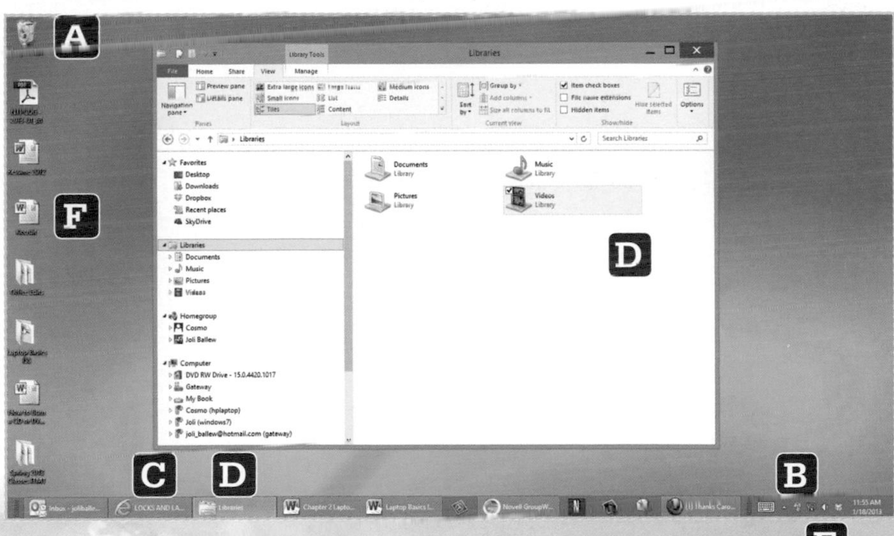

? DID YOU KNOW?
You can use the keyboard icon in the Notification area to access an onscreen keyboard.

! ALERT: The Start button is no longer available on the taskbar, at least not when this book was published. If you'd like to access something a bit like it, press the Windows key + X key combination.

Problem 3: My Start screen is cluttered with tiles I'll never use

You remove an unwanted tile from the Start screen by selecting it and then choosing Unpin from Start. If you like, you can select multiple tiles to remove at once.

1. Right-click or tap, hold and drag downward on any tile you'd like to remove.
2. Repeat as desired to select additional tiles.
3. Click or tap Unpin from Start.

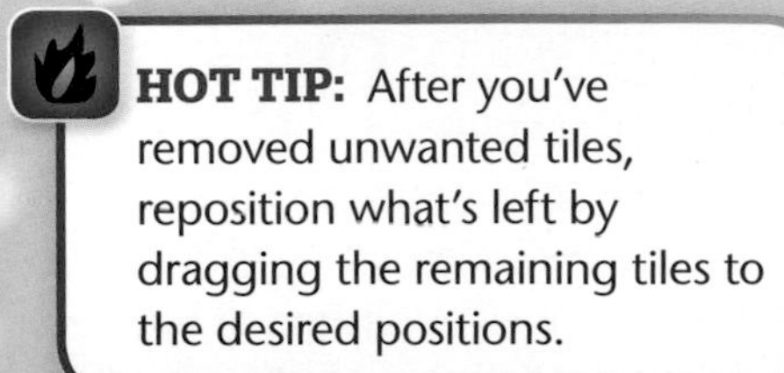

HOT TIP: After you've removed unwanted tiles, reposition what's left by dragging the remaining tiles to the desired positions.

DID YOU KNOW?
When you remove a tile from the Start screen you don't uninstall it. You can always access it (and even add it back) from the All Apps screen.

Problem 4: I need to back up my most recent data quickly

One way to back up your data is to copy it to an external drive. You can copy data to a DVD drive, a USB drive, a network drive or a larger external backup drive (among others). You copy the folder to the external drive the same way you'd copy a folder to another area of your hard drive – you use the Copy command from the Home tab of any File Explorer window.

1. Using File Explorer, select the data to copy.
2. From the Home tab, click Copy to.
3. Click Choose Location.
4. Click Copy.

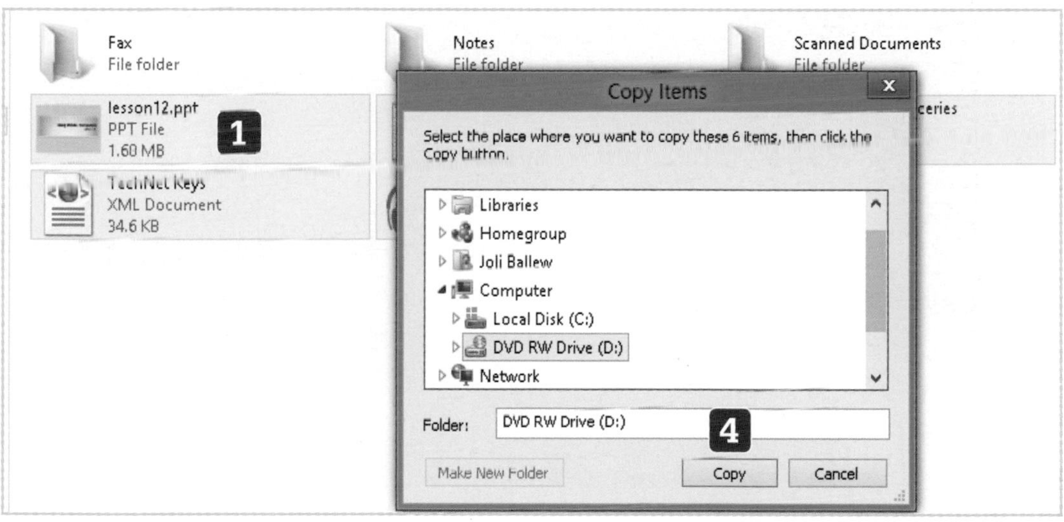

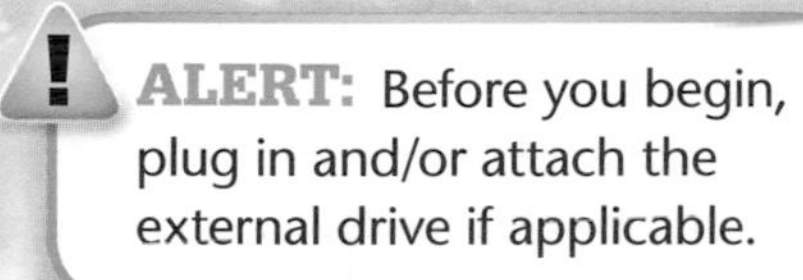

ALERT: Before you begin, plug in and/or attach the external drive if applicable.

Problem 5: Since there isn't a Start button, how do I find my favourite programs quickly?

If there is a desktop app you use often, and you don't want to have to access the Start screen to find it each time you need it, you can pin a shortcut to the taskbar for easy access.

1. Locate the app's tile on the Start screen or the All Apps screen.
2. Right-click the tile.
3. Click Pin to taskbar. (This will change to Unpin from Start after you click it.)

4. Return to the desktop to see the item on the taskbar.

DID YOU KNOW?
You can also pin any desktop app's tile to the Start screen if it isn't already there.

HOT TIP: Click the icon on the taskbar to open the related desktop app.

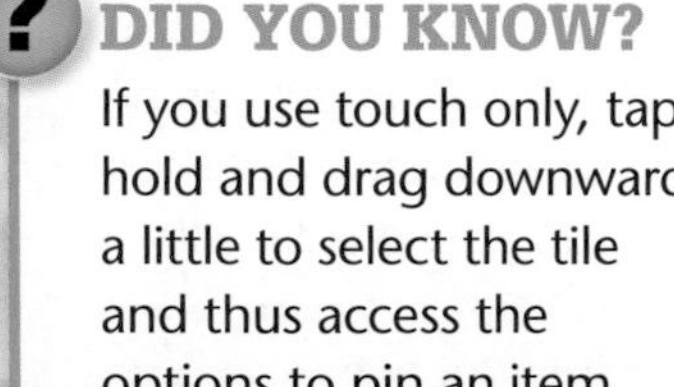

DID YOU KNOW?
If you use touch only, tap, hold and drag downward a little to select the tile and thus access the options to pin an item.

Problem 6: I know I am within range of a network but I can't see it

In order for your laptop to be able to discover available networks and join them (and ultimately share data with computers on that network), Network Discovery must be enabled. Verify that this is the case before continuing.

1. From the Start screen type Network. Click Network in the results.
2. If you see the prompt here that states 'Network discovery is turned off', click it.
3. Click Turn on network discovery and file sharing.

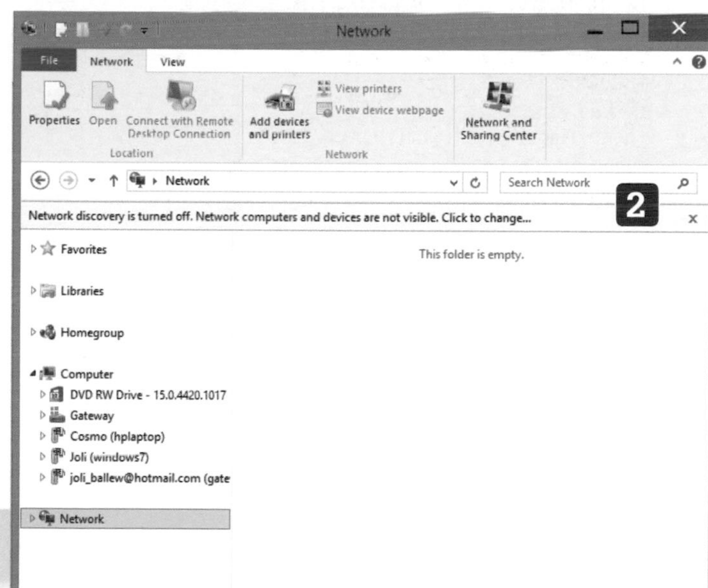

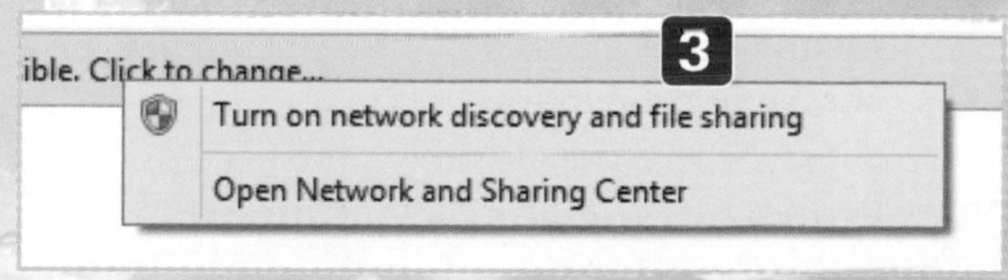

ALERT: If at any time you are prompted about the type of network you want to create or join, choose Private or Home or Work (as applicable) and opt to share data (versus not sharing it).

DID YOU KNOW?
Airplane mode should remain disabled until you are actually on an aeroplane. Enabling Airplane mode will disrupt network functionality.

Problem 7: My eyesight is poor and I can't make out the small print on web pages

The Magnifier is an Ease of Access option that lets you magnify parts of the screen by positioning the cursor in the area you want to magnify. There are a few options once Magnifier is running, and those can be selected in the small Magnifier window that appears.

1. At the Start screen, type Magnifier.
2. Click Magnifier in the results.
3. Most likely, you will see a magnification area at the top of your screen that enlarges the area where your cursor is currently positioned.
4. Click and drag downward on that magnification area. Note the box that appears and what is magnified.
5. Click the magnifying glass to display the dialog box.
6. Click the Settings icon (the round cog) to review other options.

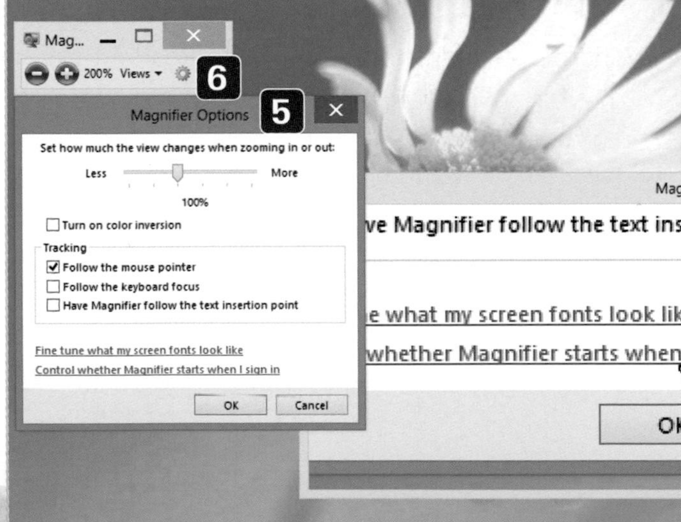

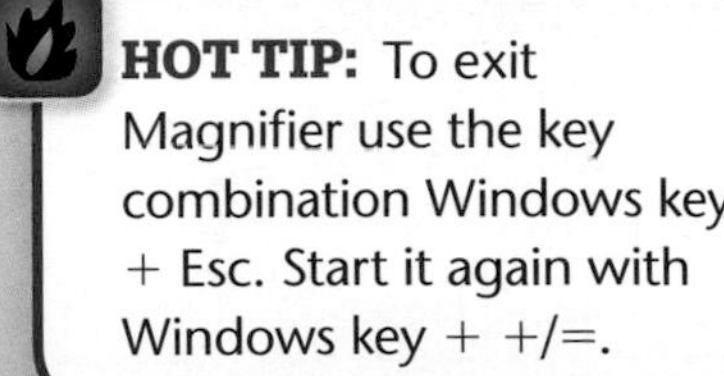

HOT TIP: To exit Magnifier use the key combination Windows key + Esc. Start it again with Windows key + +/=.

DID YOU KNOW?

You can change the zoom options using the dialog box or the key combination Windows key and the + or − sign, as applicable.

Problem 8: My laptop needs a performance boost but I can't add more RAM

Laptops and tablets come with a specific amount of built-in 'memory'. The more memory a computer has, the better it will perform. If you want to add more memory to a small, mobile computer, you may not be able to. It may be physically impossible. In this case you can use ReadyBoost instead. ReadyBoost is a similar technology and will also improve computer performance. ReadyBoost can be used with any computer that has a USB port or smart card reader.

1. Insert a USB flash drive, thumb drive or memory card into an available slot on the outside of your laptop or tablet.
2. When prompted in the upper right corner, click to view your options.
3. Choose Speed up my system, Windows ReadyBoost.
4. Choose to dedicate the device to ReadyBoost and click OK (not shown).

Removable Disk (F:)

Choose what to do with removable drives.

Speed up my system
Windows ReadyBoost

Configure this drive for backup
File History

Open folder to view files
Windows Explorer

Take no action

ALERT: USB keys must be at least USB 2.0 and meet other requirements, but don't worry about that, you'll be told if the hardware isn't up to par.

ALERT: Some small tablet computers do not have the hardware required to support ReadyBoost.

Problem 9: I need help but I don't know where to look for answers

If you encounter a problem you can't resolve, you can use the available Help and Support wizards to assist you in finding a solution. These wizards walk you through the required processes to find a solution.

1. At the Start screen type Help.
2. Click Settings; click Find and fix problems.

3. Use the options to find what you need help with.

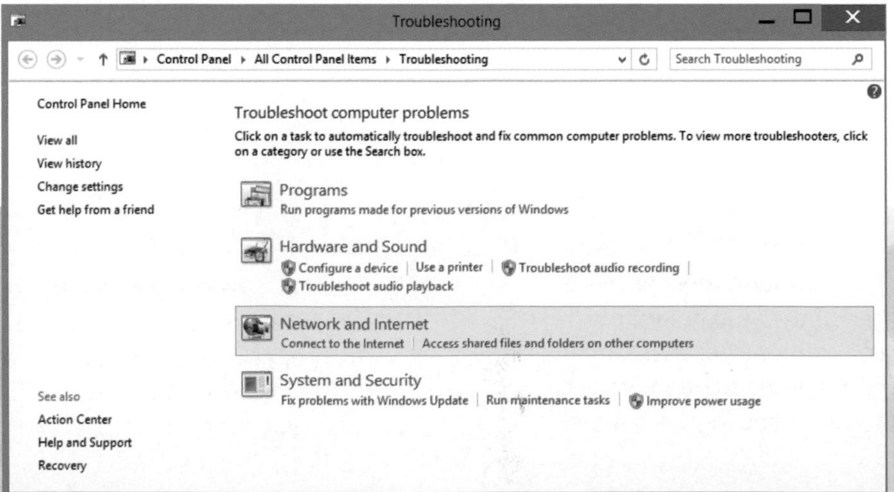

4 Work through the wizard.

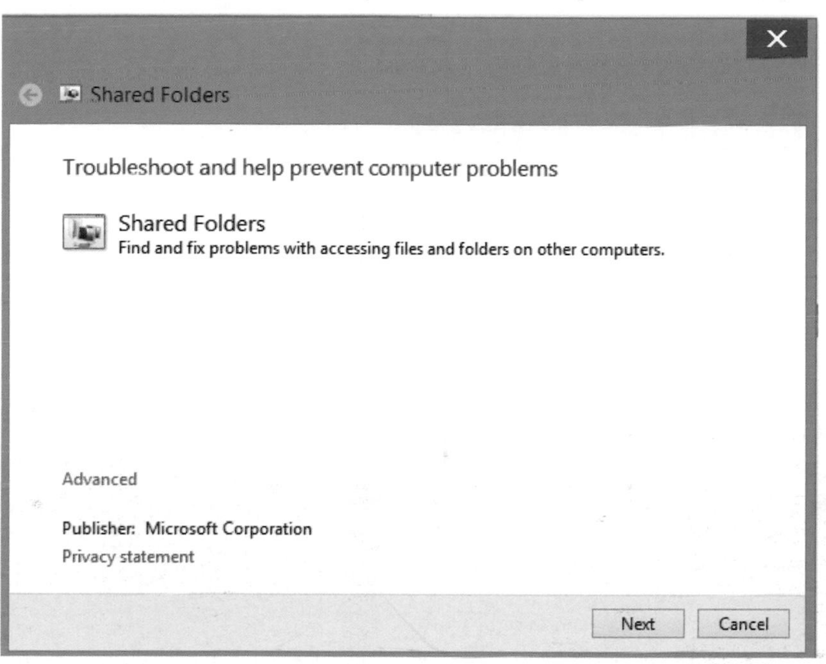

ALERT: Although most of these wizards can resolve simple problems, they can't resolve all of them. If a wizard can't find a solution, you may have to look online for the answer.

HOT TIP: Before you troubleshoot any hardware, turn off the device, turn it back on, and disconnect and reconnect it to your laptop. If it's internal hardware, restart your computer.

Problem 10: My laptop seemed fine yesterday but today it's acting strangely

System Restore regularly creates and saves restore points that contain information about your laptop that Windows uses to work properly. If your laptop starts acting up, you can use System Restore to restore it to a time when the laptop was working properly. Before you start, connect your laptop to an electrical outlet.

1. At the Start screen, type System Restore.
2. Click Settings, and then click Create a restore point.
3. Click System Restore.
4. Click Next to accept and apply the recommended restore point.
5. Click Finish.
6. Wait patiently while the process completes.

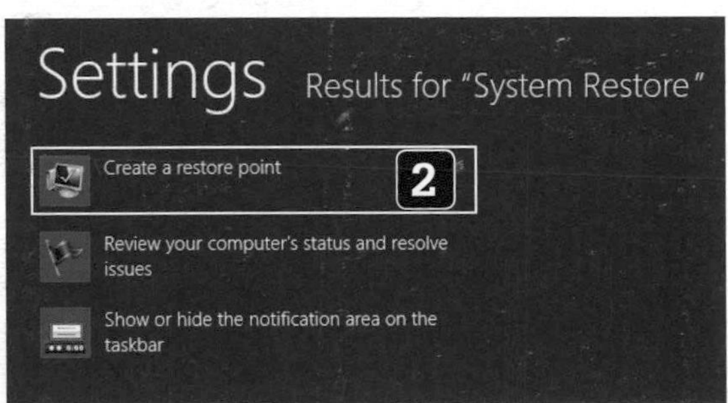

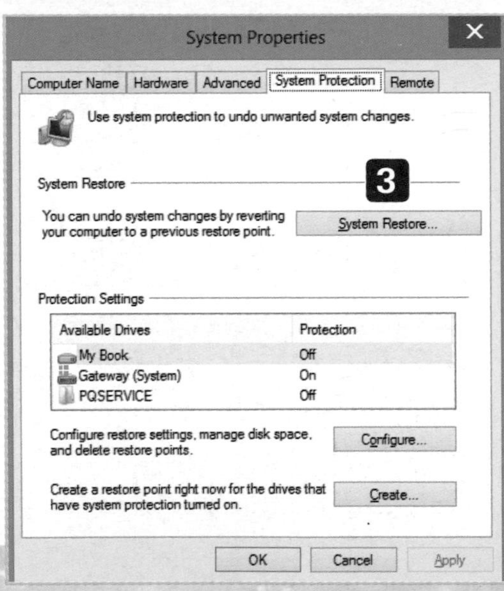

? DID YOU KNOW?

System Restore works only with its own system files, so running System Restore will not affect any of your personal data. Your pictures, email, documents, music, etc. will not be deleted or changed.

! ALERT: If System Restore doesn't resolve the problem, run a scan with Windows Defender.

WHAT DOES THIS MEAN?

Restore point: A snapshot of a computer's previous state that can be applied in place of the current state, to make an unstable computer stable again.